D1713663

Racial Profiling

They Stopped Me Because I'm
_____!

Racial Profiling

They Stopped Me Because I'm
_____ *!*

Michael L. Birzer

CRC Press
Taylor & Francis Group
Boca Raton London New York

CRC Press is an imprint of the
Taylor & Francis Group, an **informa** business

CRC Press
Taylor & Francis Group
6000 Broken Sound Parkway NW, Suite 300
Boca Raton, FL 33487-2742

Printed in the United States of America on acid-free paper
Version Date: 20120719

International Standard Book Number: 978-1-4398-7225-3 (Hardback)

Library of Congress Cataloging-in-Publication Data

Birzer, Michael L., 1960-
    Racial profiling : they stopped me because I'm-- / Michael L. Birzer.
      p. cm.
    Includes bibliographical references and index.
    ISBN 978-1-4398-7225-3
    1. Racial profiling in law enforcement. I. Title.

HV7936.R3B57 2013
363.2'3089--dc23
                                                   2012026416

Visit the Taylor & Francis Web site at
http://www.taylorandfrancis.com

and the CRC Press Web site at
http://www.crcpress.com

I dedicate this book to my loving wife, Gwynne,
and my precious son, Michael Jr.

Contents

Preface

Recently, in Atlanta, Georgia, Tyler, a 42-year-old African American male was driving to the airport. As he eased his vehicle toward an intersection, he suddenly made a left turn from a far right lane. That's illegal under Georgia traffic law. Tyler's driving caught the attention of two nearby police officers who, within a matter of seconds, stopped him. Tyler rolled his window down and waited for the officers to make contact with him.

This is a summary of Tyler's encounter with Atlanta law enforcement authorities from what's been reported in the news, and from his Facebook page (www.facebook.com/thetylerperry) where he wrote at length about his run-in with the police.

After the officers made contact with Tyler, he attempted to explain to them that he made the turn to ensure he wasn't being followed. One officer asked, "Why do you think someone would be following you?" But before he was able to answer, the second officer started banging on the passenger side window. The window was tinted and at first Tyler did not know who was doing the banging. Tyler was directed to roll his window down. He complied and rolled the passenger side window down and he discovered that it was another police officer who immediately asked, "What is wrong with you?" Both officers began launching questions at Tyler about why he thought he was being followed.

The officer on the driver's side reached into the car and started pulling on the switch that turns the car on and off. He directed Tyler to (as Tyler writes on his Facebook page), "put your foot on the brake, put your foot on the brake!" Tyler later said he was confused as to what the officer was doing, or what he thought he was doing. "It looked like he was trying to pull the switch out of the dashboard. I finally realized that he thought that switch was the key, so I told him that it wasn't the key he was grabbing."

Tyler reached down into the cup holder to get the key, not realizing that the key had a black leather strap on it. As he grabbed the key, he saw that both officers tensed up. Tyler dropped the key and suddenly thought back to the advice his mother had given him when he was a young boy. He wrote, "My mother would always say to me, if you get stopped by the police, especially if they are white policemen, you say, 'yes sir' and 'no sir,' and if they want to take you in, you go with them. Don't resist, you hear me? Don't make any quick moves, don't run, you just go."

Tyler reported that the officer on the driver's side continued to badger him with questions about why he thought he was being followed. Tyler wrote on his Facebook page that he finally said, "I think you guys need to just write the ticket and do whatever you need to do." According to Tyler, the officers were hostile, and he was confused. He said it was happening so fast he could easily see how this situation could get out of hand. Tyler said that he didn't feel safe at all. According to Tyler, one officer said, "We may not let you go. You think you're being followed, what's wrong with you?" Tyler said that at this point he wanted to get out of his vehicle because he wanted a passerby to see what was occurring.

A second police cruiser pulled up to the scene of the stop. This police officer happened to be Black. Tyler writes on his Facebook page, "'He [the Black police officer] took one look at me and had that Oh No look on his face." He immediately took both officers to the back of my car and spoke to them in a hushed tone. After that, one of the officers stayed near his car while one came back, very apologetic."

They probably did not know it at the time, but the police officers stopped Tyler Perry. Mr. Perry is a successful actor, director, screen and playwright, producer, author, and songwriter. In 2011, he was said to be the highest paid man in the entertainment business, earning reportedly over $130 million that year. Tyler claimed he was racially profiled. The Atlanta police department's Office of Professional Standards is looking into the racial profiling allegation.

You might be questioning the validity of Mr. Perry's allegation of racial profiling. After all, he did commit a traffic violation in full view of the police. Furthermore, you may question the possibility that the officers did not know who they were stopping at the time. It is also reasonable to question the notion that if you are rich, famous, or powerful, or a combination of them all then you shouldn't be stopped and you should get a pass. That is not the intent of sharing Tyler's story.

It really should not matter who you are when you are stopped by the police. We expect the police to treat every citizen they encounter, especially when stopping a motorist for a minor violation of the traffic code, with the utmost professionalism and fairness. This is regardless of social standing, class, position, race, religion, ethnicity, and the like. For many citizens, being stopped by the police for a traffic violation is the only contact they will ever have with the police. Thus, the manner in which the police conduct themselves can leave lasting impressions on citizens.

What is salient from Tyler Perry's encounter with the police is how he said the police treated him. He said the officers were hostile and that he could see how the situation could have gotten out of control in a hurry.

In this book, you will hear many stories that are similar to Mr. Perry's. He is speaking about something that many African Americans and other racial minorities know. Racial minority's history with the police, generation after generation, has been far from congenial. This is particularly the case with African Americans. The stains of slavery, Jim Crow, racism, and discrimination very much still impact racial minorities' experiences with the police and the larger criminal justice system. It is a sobering fact that the police were once used to enforce and sustain discriminatory and racist practices. This has to be fully recognized in any honest discussion of the intersection of race and the criminal justice system, including racial profiling.

Mr. Perry points out that he was taught by his mother at a young age, if stopped by the police, you do as they tell you, you don't run; if they want to take you in, you go with them. Don't resist. You see, Mr. Perry's mother was born in the segregated rural south. She saw injustice in its finest hour. As Mr. Perry writes on his Facebook page, "She had known of many colored men at the time who were lynched and never heard from again." Mrs. Perry passed this caveat and wisdom down to her son which, reading between the lines, really means, they really want to, but don't give them a reason to. I heard this very same theme from scores of racial minority citizens who I interviewed for this book. Many talked about being taught at a young age what to do if stopped by the police. It was just a part of growing up.

Fortunately, America has progressed considerably beyond the unjust segregation laws of the past and blatant in your face racism. Despite our seeming progression, it cannot be denied that for each injustice that is incurred today, anywhere by a racial minority citizen at the hands of the police, invokes collective memories of what they have been taught. These injustices are also a reminder that bias and disparate practices are still present. For every Rodney King beating at the hands of the police, for every Abner Louima torture at the hands of the police, for every Black citizen in the town of Tulia, Texas who was falsely arrested by a corrupt drug law enforcement officer, or for every motorist who was racially profiled by the New Jersey State Police, it significantly impacts the current discourse centering on racial profiling.

In the pages ahead, you will learn about racial profiling. You will learn not by reading data in the form of police stop statistics or sophisticated statistical prediction models, but you will learn from the citizens who have experienced it. Their voices will be illuminated. Their stories, which have been carefully collected and analyzed, are compelling. I present racial profiling from their worldview. I construct how they interpret and give meaning to their experiences with what they firmly believe to be racial profiling by police authorities.

Many of their stories share a similar salient reinforcement of Tyler Perry's encounter with the police. You will learn, as noted previously, they, too, have been taught from a young age, if they should have an encounter with the police do not give them a reason to make the situation worse. Police are to be respected but eyed with suspicion, and kept at arm's length.

Direction of the Book

The book consists of eight chapters. In a strange way, the book is like a road that divides into many different directions. Over the course of almost two years, talking with more than 100 racial minority citizens about racial profiling brought about the realization that it was necessary to take several directions in the book. In order to effectively tell their stories, many different discussions had to be included. It was particularly challenging to know how much to include in the discussion, for example, on providing historical context and how that is relevant today. In the end, the writer never really knows if too much or too little was said. I trust that you will find it just about right. Let me share a little bit more on the various directions the book takes.

First, it is necessary to look at what racial profiling is and how formal legal codes and public policy generally define it. In this same vein, a discussion is waged on how researchers often take racial minority citizens' direct experiences for granted in racial profiling studies as we attempt to carry out objective and bias-free research. Citizen experiences with what they believe to be racial profiling can be a very powerful informative form of data, especially if the data is carefully collected through use of sound interview and focus group practices, and the data is subjected to rigorous and balanced analysis. The results of such research, as I hope you will discover in the pages ahead, are very rich descriptions of how racial minority citizens experience racial profiling and, perhaps more importantly, how they interpret and give meaning to those experiences.

This book is not simply anecdotal accounts of racial profiling. It goes further by taking narratives, significant statements, and themes and subjecting them to a thorough analysis using a qualitative research approach called *phenomenology*. You will learn something about this method as you read the book. If you are new to reading research, you will be enlightened.

The material presented in this book is presented in the most comprehensive manner because it is anticipated that most readers will not be familiar with *phenomenology* and, for some, qualitative research methods. The book introduces qualitative research methods and how they are simply other ways to study racial profiling, just like those researchers who prefer to study the phenomenon using statistics or quantitative analysis. Neither approach is superior or inferior, but they both produce important insight and understanding of racial profiling, while doing so from different lenses. In the end, the research questions should drive the research method and the kind of data to be collected. The best way to answer the questions regarding citizens' experiences with racial profiling is to use a qualitative research method with a phenomenological approach.

As I began interviewing citizens for the book, it became very clear that history is very relevant to perceptions of racial profiling today. With this in mind, an entire chapter (Chapter 2) is devoted to putting racial profiling into historical context. As you read Chapter 2, some of you may ask what these past injustices have to do with racial profiling today. When this happens, bear down and continue to read on because it will be clear at the end of the chapter. I am thoroughly convinced after spending nearly two years interviewing racial minority citizens across the State of Kansas that past injustices at the hands of police and the larger criminal system are very much relevant to the discourse on racial profiling.

The book also devotes some pages to discussing the various methods of data collection. It addresses the advantages for police agencies to collect racial profiling data in some form. Furthermore, there is a poignant discussion on how data collection (police stop data) is sometimes limited in its ability to identify racial profiling or bias-based policing practices. It is not necessarily that it can't identify racial profiling, but in some cases it is limited. However, police agencies are still encouraged to collect said data.

One of the more troublesome problems in the investigation of racial profiling is the nature of the pretextual stop. In short, a pretextual stop is where a police officer stops an individual for a traffic violation (in most cases a minor traffic violation), in order to investigate the driver for another unrelated reason. Throughout the book, the pretextual stop is discussed because it is the very core of racial profiling. I argue in Chapter 3 that the U.S. Supreme Court has not made it any easier to address suspected racially biased police practices. In fact, it may have exacerbated the problem.

While racial profiling is an unacceptable police practice, the 1996 Supreme Court decision in *Whren v. United States* allows the police to stop motorists and search their vehicles if police reasonably believe or probable cause exists that the occupants are trafficking illegal drugs or weapons. Chapter 3 opens discussion about the seemingly paradoxical nature of the *Whren* decision. On the one hand, the decision grants police the authority to stop motorists based merely on a pretext; a pretext that in some cases the police may need in order to perform essential law enforcement duties and keep communities safe.

The meat of this book is the discussion of how minority citizens experience racial profiling, and how they ascribe and give meaning to these experiences. This is largely presented in Chapter 5.

There is also brief discussion of data analysis, and how it established that I got it right. Put another way, the methods of determining the validity of the data and results are trustworthy. The common themes and meaning units grounded in the data made it possible to construct a unifying structure of racial profiling. The unifying structure is simply a statement that describes how racial minority citizens experienced racial profiling in terms of conditions, situations, and context.

The book concludes with implications of what it all means. This involves a candid discussion of what the findings of the research mean for the police, racial minority citizens, and future racial profiling research. The reader will appreciate the much-applied nature of the discussion of implications. For example, you will find a section that addresses citizens who may read the book. They are reminded to know their rights. They are informed of accepted police protocol during a traffic encounter. They are encouraged to learn reporting venues in the event they are racially profiled. It is anticipated that this will make citizens more informed as to what they can do in the event they feel they have been racially profiled by the police. There is also a brief discussion on what a citizen should do if stopped by the police. This section offers some very practical advice. All of this advice is offered because of lessons learned during the interviews.

Audience

I wrote this book for a wide range of readers. First, undergraduate and graduate students studying race and the criminal justice system will find the book useful. For example, it would be ideal for use in courses centering on racial profiling, race and justice, and critical issues, as well as policing seminars. Because of the book's discussion of, and use of, qualitative research, specifically using a phenomenological approach, it could also potentially be used as a supplemental book in qualitative research methods courses as a way to illuminate how phenomenology can be used to produce meaningful and practical results.

My second intent for the book is that it may be read by citizens who simply want to learn more about racial profiling and how racial minority citizens experience and give meaning to it. Citizens should also find the advice presented in Chapter 8 on what they can do regarding racial profiling useful.

Finally, I would invite rank and file police officers to read the book. They may discover something that they did not previously know about racial minorities' perceptions they had and how they did their job. It is always a good thing to learn about the very citizens that they are entrusted to protect and serve, especially those citizens who have historically not had the best experiences with the police.

Tone of the Book

This book is not anti-police in any way, shape, or form. It is not an extreme left or right view in the political sense. The book simply reports how racial minority citizens experience and give meaning to what they believe to be racial profiling while driving in their automobiles. The book is a candid and to-the-point account of racial profiling from the racial minority citizenry.

The book may be a difficult read for some, possibly in the sense that you may question some of the narratives presented in the book as simply being mere complaints about the police from overly sensitive citizens. However, remember, unless you have experienced something that you deeply feel is an injustice simply because of your race, one may question how you can honestly disagree with someone's perceptions and experiences.

Other content of the book may pose the same difficulties for some readers. One such area may be the discussion of past injustices inflicted on racial minorities by representatives of the criminal justice system. Why not open Pandora's Box? The content is relevant to the contemporary discussion of racial profiling and the intersection of race and the criminal justice system.

Enjoy the Venture

Whether you are a student taking a course on racial profiling, critical issues in the criminal justice system, a policing seminar, or a citizen wanting to learn more about the racial profiling phenomenon, or perhaps a police officer who desires to enhance his or her ability to serve racial minority communities better, I sincerely hope the book fulfills your needs. I now invite you to turn the pages ahead, keep an open mind, and enjoy the learning experience.

Michael L. Birzer
Wichita, Kansas

Acknowledgments

This book was largely inspired by a qualitative research study on racial profiling that I was commissioned to do by the Governor's Task Force on Racial Profiling in Kansas (Task Force). If not for their support of the research, the book would not have been possible. There were many people working on the Task Force at the time when much of the early data was collected, and I can't possible name them all here. However, I am especially indebted to Danielle Dempsey-Swopes and Dr. Mildred Edwards who both served on the Task Force. Danielle is the past Executive Director of the Kansas African American Affairs Commission, and Dr. Edwards is the current Executive Director. Thank you both for ensuring that the resources were always available to carry out the study.

I am indebted to all of the citizens across the state of Kansas for giving me the opportunity to chat about racial profiling. I learned much from you. Thank you all for helping me to understand.

A special thank you to my dear friend and colleague Professor Paul Cromwell. He was always interested in hearing about the research and the book while we consumed gallons of coffee at our local hangout in Wichita, Kansas—Starbucks.

A special thank you is due to Carolyn Spence of CRC Press who was more than patient with me during this book project. The entire CRC Press team, which includes Jay Margolis, David Fausel, and Sophie Kirkwood, deserves special thanks, too.

Finally, to the people in my life who have had to put up with me the past few years while I completed the research and book, my wife Gwynne, and our son Michael Jr. Words cannot express how I feel about you both. Thank you for the continued support and patience with me. I love you both very much.

About the Author

Michael L. Birzer is the Director of the School of Community Affairs and Professor of Criminal Justice at Wichita State University. He was recently named a Leadership Fellow at his university. Professor Birzer's research interests include the intersection of race and the criminal justice system, police behavior and policy, and criminal justice training and education strategies. He is the author or co-author of eight books in such areas as policing, private security, and criminology. He earned both bachelor's and master's degrees from Wichita State University and a doctorate from Oklahoma State University. Prior to academia, he served more than 18 years with the Sedgwick County Sheriff's Department in Wichita where he worked in a wide variety of patrol, investigative, supervisory, and management positions. In his spare time, he enjoys spending time with his wife, Gwynne, and son, Michael Jr.

Stylin' n' Profilin'

1

"Racial profiling is wrong and we will end it in America."

President George W. Bush, address to a joint session of congress, February 27, 2001

Introduction

Richard's Story

Early one September morning, Richard, a Black male business owner in his 60s and a lifelong resident of Wichita, Kansas, was steering his newer model Mercedes-Benz toward the train station in Newton, Kansas. His 88-year-old mother and his sister had an early Amtrak to catch. Newton is a small Kansas community with a population of just over 18,000 citizens. Newton is home to the Amtrak rail, which serves a good portion of Kansas. Despite the 3:00 a.m. time, the interior of the Mercedes was full of conversation. Richard's mother, sister, and brother-in-law, all African Americans, were passengers in the car.

Richard first saw the police car as he was turning onto the main street to drive the few remaining blocks to the train station. Richard recalls, "We made eye contact with each other as I turned the corner." It wasn't long that Richard noticed that the police car had turned around and was now following him. He remained aware of the following police car as he continued to travel toward the train station. Richard said, "I really didn't think too much about it at first but the longer he followed the more I thought that he was looking for a reason to stop me." After Richard pulled into the train station, parked, and began to off load his mother's and sister's luggage from the trunk, he noticed the police car pulled into a parking lot across the street and seemed to be watching him. Even though he had done nothing wrong, Richard worried that he may be stopped.

After seeing his mother and sister off safely, Richard, along with his brother-in-law, climbed back into the Mercedes to make the 30-minute drive back home to Wichita. As he pulled the car back onto the road, he noticed the police car pulled out of the parking lot and was again following him. *What is going on?* he wondered. Richard recalls paying close attention to his driving as not to provoke the officer. Richard's fear was soon realized. Suddenly he saw the illumination of red flashing lights in his rearview mirror. Richard immediately eased the Mercedes to the far right of the street and stopped. A few seconds later, two police officers were at his windows, one on the passenger's side and one on the driver's side.

"Can I see your driver's license?" the officer at the driver's window said.

"Why am I being stopped, Officer?" Richard said.

"You are being stopped because you ran that stop sign back there," the officer said.

"How am I going to run a stop sign when I knew you were following me?" Richard said.

"Do you have any drugs or weapons on you?" the officer said.

Richard was outraged at the officer's question and yelled, "No I don't have any drugs or weapons on me!"

Richard wondered aloud if the officer asked all motorists if they have drugs or weapons on them. Richard said one of the officers replied, "That's a routine question, we ask everyone that."

The officer shined his flashlight illuminating the interior of the Mercedes. Richard said the officers then went back to the police car. A few minutes passed and Richard noticed two more police cars pulled up. The officers met behind Richard's Mercedes. He could hear them talking. *What's going on!* Richard thought. Richard was detained for what he said was about 45 minutes. He received a ticket for running the stop sign, and without further explanation was released. Richard told me, "I firmly believe I was stopped for being a Black man and driving an expensive car at 3:00 a.m." As an African American male, Richard was well aware that driving an expensive car was enough to arouse police suspicion. He said, "This is well known in the African American community." Richard said, "I know they made up the stop sign charge to have a reason to stop me hoping they would find something illegal. They realized after they stopped me that they made a mistake and stopped a law-abiding citizen."

The stop bothered Richard tremendously. The next day, Richard drove back to Newton and filed a complaint with the chief of police. To Richard's surprise, the chief furnished him with a copy of the police radio transmission of the stop. What Richard heard in the transmission confirmed his belief that he had been racially profiled. As Richard listened to the taped police transmission, he hears one officer say to another, "I have a drug dealer that's just entered town." Another officer is heard saying, "Is that the one with deep tinted windows?" The radio transmission continues with an officer saying, "We have to stop that car." Richard told me his windows had only factory tint and were legal. He said the chief of police inspected the windows the day after the stop and concluded they were legal. According to Richard, the officers in question were not disciplined and he ultimately ended up paying the traffic ticket.

David's Story

Many miles to the northeast of Newton, Kansas, another citizen believed he was profiled because of his ethnicity. It all began one late Saturday afternoon in April when David, a 54-year-old Hispanic male who holds a Ph.D. and works in the educational field began the 250-mile drive from Manhattan, Kansas to his home in western Kansas. David recalled that it was a beautiful spring afternoon in northeast Kansas as he drove out of Manhattan. He was exhausted after spending the day sitting in class at Kansas State University where at the time he was studying for a doctorate. In the passenger seat of his 1997 Chevy van sat his 17-year-old son who he brought along for the company. David was lost in conversation with his son when without warning he was alerted to red lights flashing in his rearview mirror. David recalls that the location must have been about 10 or 20 miles west of Manhattan on Interstate 70 highway. He remembers thinking to himself *What have I done?* He pulled over to the shoulder of the highway and, seconds later, a Kansas State Trooper appeared at the driver's side window.

"Can I see your license and proof of insurance?" the trooper said.

"Why am I being stopped?" David said.

"You were going 10 miles over the speed limit," the trooper said.

"I don't know if I was speeding. I was having a conversation with my son," David said.

David gave the trooper his driver's license and proof of insurance. David said what happened next caught him completely off-guard. The trooper asked him and his son to get out of the van. They complied at once with the trooper's request. David remembers that the trooper had his hand on his sidearm and was very unfriendly in his tone of voice. The trooper directed them to stand on the shoulder of the highway. David recalled that the trooper walked around the van glancing through the windows and then said, "Do you mind if I search your van?" David, still not sure what was going on, complied with the trooper's request and said, "You're welcome to search, but you're not going to find anything." The trooper asked David to open the rear and side doors and then began to search through the van. David said the trooper never told him what he was searching for. David recalled that the trooper was not very friendly and didn't seem interested in anything he (David) had to say. After about 20 minutes, the trooper gave him a speeding ticket and said, "You are free to go." David recalled:

The whole thing was very demeaning because he had his hand on his gun, he was walking up to me, and you know this man was making me feel guilty. He made us get out, he checked the van, and he investigated everything. I mean we were sitting by the highway and all that, and he reviewed us for everything even though we didn't do anything. All we were doing around 4:00 o'clock in the afternoon—we were coming back from Manhattan after a daylong class. I told him I was just coming back from class at K State, but he did not seem too interested in hearing what I had to say. He just kept his hand on his gun as he searched through the van. He really made us feel like we were guilty of something. It was very demeaning for me. It made me very angry.

David is convinced that he was profiled because he is Hispanic. He said the trooper probably thought he would find drugs or guns.

Purpose of the Book

This book is about racial profiling or, as many now call it, biased-based policing. The overarching purpose of this book is to describe how racial minority citizens experience racial profiling, and how they interpret and give meaning to it. The book constructs a unifying structure of how racial minorities themselves experience racial profiling. Put another way, the data reported in this book sorts through and analyzes the commonalities of racial minorities experience with racial profiling, and describes how they ascribe meaning to their experiences.

Racial profiling represents one of the most pressing issues of our time. American Presidents have spoken about it and denounced it. Police authorities are trained not to engage in it. Laws have been passed criminalizing it, and reported cases have been the subject of endless hours of media stories. In spite of the considerable attention centering on racial profiling, a great many racial minority citizens still say it happens frequently in their communities, while police authorities emphatically deny that they do it. When Black and White Americans are surveyed about the prevalence of racial profiling, they both believe it is a widespread phenomenon in the United States (Police Executive Research Forum, 2001). Profiling based solely on one's race cannot be tolerated. Authorities who engage in racial profiling must be held accountable.

The Cambridge Incident

Racial profiling is a polarizing issue. Phrases such as driving while Black or Brown, shopping while Black or Brown, and walking or bicycling while Black or Brown are embedded into any discussion of racial profiling. In order to provide a starting framework for understanding the complex nature of racial profiling, let us briefly examine a case that occurred on July 16, 2009 involving the Cambridge, Massachusetts Police Department and Harvard University Professor Henry Louis Gates, Jr., a prominent African American professor.

Professor Gates was returning from a weeklong travel abroad in China to his home, located in an upscale, predominately White neighborhood, a few blocks away from the Harvard University campus. When he arrived home, he discovered that the front door of his residence was jammed. His efforts to open the door were unsuccessful. Professor Gates summoned the help of his driver, also a Black man, to assist in forcibly opening the door. An alert neighbor, seeing the two men force the door open, thought that they might be breaking into the house. The neighbor called the Cambridge Police Department and reported what she saw. The police dispatcher put the call out to responding police officers as a possible breaking and entering in progress.

A few moments later, police Sgt. James Crowley, an 11-year veteran of the police department, who is White, arrived on the scene. Sgt. Crowley reported seeing an unidentified Black male (later identified as Professor Gates) in the residence. Sgt. Crowley requested identification from Professor Gates. That's when a verbal confrontation of sorts ensued between Sgt. Crowley and Professor Gates, and accounts of what happened next differ slightly, but subsequently, Professor Gates was arrested for exhibiting loud and tumultuous behavior. The charge was later dropped. The arrest has prompted some legal observers to raise doubts about the legality of the arrest (Ogletree, 2010).

Professor Gates alleged that the incident centered on him being a Black man in America. The police maintained that they were just doing their job. The President of the United States, Barack Obama, quickly weighed in on the incident when he publicly criticized the police for the way they handled the matter. President Barack Obama accused the police of "acting stupidly" in arresting Professor Gates when there was adequate proof that he was in his own home (Cooper, 2009). President Obama fell short of accusing the police of racial profiling. Union officials for the Cambridge Police were outraged by the President's comments and questioned his seemingly quick condemnation of the police (Ford & Schapiro, 2009). The President later said that he regretted his comments and hoped that the incident would serve as a teachable moment. President Obama invited both Sgt. Crowley and Professor Gates to the White House to have a beer and talk about the incident in what has become known as the "beer summit" (Cooper & Goodnough, 2009).

The Cambridge incident received a voluminous amount of national and international media coverage. Perhaps a positive outcome did in fact blossom from this incident. If anything, the incident stimulated dialogue about something that many would rather not discuss, the issue of race, which continues to challenge our nation. Moreover, this incident represents a vivid reminder of the complex nature of racial profiling. Here we have a prominent African

American scholar employed by Harvard University allege that he experienced at the hands of the police what so many Black men say they experience
every single day in America.

According to Sgt. Crowley's official police report, Professor Gates accused
him of being a racist police officer. Sgt. Crowley reported that Professor
Gates went on a verbal tirade demanding to know what he (Sgt. Crowley)
was doing. Sgt. Crowley said he attempted to inform Professor Gates several
times that he (Crowley) was investigating the report of a break-in in progress
at the residence.

Professor Gates' explanation of the incident differs from Sgt. Crowley's.
The professor reports that he in fact produced his driver's license and Harvard
identification, both of which have his photograph. Professor Gates says he
asked for the name and badge number of the officer several times and Sgt.
Crowley did not give it to him. Professor Gates said he followed the officer
as he left his house onto his front porch, and that is when he was handcuffed
and arrested. Sgt. Crowley's writes in his police report,

> As I began walking through the foyer toward the front door, I could hear Gates
> calling my name. I again told Gates that I would speak with him outside. My
> reason for wanting to leave the residence was that Gates was yelling very loud
> and the acoustics of the kitchen and foyer were making it difficult for me to
> transmit pertinent information to ECC or other responding units. His reply
> was "Ya, I'll speak with your mama outside."
>
> As I descended the stairs to the sidewalk, Gates continued to yell at me,
> accusing me of racial bias and continued to tell me that I had not heard the last
> of him. Due to the tumultuous manner Gates had exhibited in his residence
> as well as his continued tumultuous behavior outside the residence, in view
> of the public, I warned Gates that he was becoming disorderly. Gates ignored
> my warning and continued to yell, which drew the attention of both the police
> officers and citizens, who appeared surprised and alarmed by Gates' outburst.
> For a second time I warned Gates to calm down while I withdrew my depart-
> mental issued handcuffs from their carrying case. Gates again ignored my
> warning and continued to yell at me. It was at this time that I informed Gates
> that he was under arrest. (Sgt. Crowley's Police Incident Report, 2009, p. 2)

A blue ribbon committee commissioned to study the incident recently
released its report titled, Missed Opportunities, Shared Responsibilities:
Final Report of the Cambridge Review Committee. The committee believes
that the incident was sparked by misunderstandings and failed communications between both Professor Gates and Sgt. Crowley, and that the incident
was avoidable. They reported that each man felt a certain degree of fear of the
other. Sergeant Crowley was responding to a 911 call of a breaking and entering in progress, a potentially dangerous situation. His training and 11 years
of police experience gave him reason to be cautious. The review committee's

report goes onto say that Professor Gates was also wary of the police. He did not recognize Sergeant Crowley's concerns or why the sergeant wanted him to step outside his own home (Cambridge Review Committee, 2010).

Let us look at this incident from Professor Gates' worldview. For just a moment, place yourself in Professor Gates' shoes. How would you react? Would you question the police officer if you were in your home and had done nothing wrong? Would you challenge the police officer? How do you think Professor Gates should have reacted? If your race is White, it is highly likely that you would argue that Professor Gates should have complied without questioning the police officer. On the other hand, if you are a Black citizen, you may be more likely to question Sgt. Crowley's actions. This bold statement is qualified by relying on a vast amount of empirical literature showing that Black citizens view the police less favorably when compared with Whites (Birzer, 2008; Brown, Benedict, & Wilkinson, 2006; Garcia & Cao, 2005; Weitzer, & Tuch, 2004), and with more suspicion (Parker, Onyekwuluje, & Murty, 1995; Tyler, 2002; Weitzer & Tuch, 2002).

Racial minority citizens, especially Black citizens, know all too well of the longstanding fractured and contentious relationship with police authorities. There is a great deal of historical context that must be taken into account when any constructive analysis such as this takes place. It is much more complex than concluding that if the professor would have only cooperated with Sgt. Crowley or that Sgt. Crowley was only doing his job. To many in the African American community, the reality is, "If the players are a Black person and a policeman, the policeman will receive the benefit of the doubt" (Nelson, 2000, p. 20).

Given what we know about the Cambridge incident, it is not the best case to critique in terms of racial profiling for two primary reasons. First, Sgt. Crowley was responding to a 911 call of a possible breaking and entering in progress. It is not conceivable that he selected to respond to this call because of the involvement of a Black citizen. In fact, the dispatchers initial broadcast did not indicate that there was a Black citizen involved in the incident (Ogletree, 2010). Second, Sgt. Crowley had a duty to assess the situation as quickly as possible. Experts on police operations agree that it is proper police protocol to ask for identification, get control of the situation, and then establish what is occurring or has occurred. This would seem to transcend race. It is imperative that the first officer responding on the scene "quickly obtain as much information as possible and broadcast this information to other units responding to the call" (Birzer & Roberson, 2008, p. 65).

The Cambridge case presents an important question: After Sgt. Crowley arrived on the scene and discovered that there was a Black citizen involved, did this invoke stereotypes, prejudices, or biases? If so, did they influence Sgt. Crowley's decision to arrest Professor Gates?

This Cambridge incident, perhaps more appropriately, illuminates the stark complexities of police relations with racial minority communities in America. It is, however, a good example of the perception of racial profiling, and perhaps more importantly, the sharp divide that continues to exist between Black citizens and police authorities. The perception of racial profiling and treating racial minority citizens disparately are by no stretch of imagination new. The literature documents this going back many years. This is especially the case for the African American community. As the Cambridge Review Committee's report points out, the salience of this incident is that there were indeed misunderstandings on the part of both Professor Gates and Sgt. Crowley.

It is troubling that we are 12 years into the 21st century and these perceptions still exist. It is equally perplexing that dialogue on race and police relations with racial minority communities, for the most part, only take place subsequent to an incident (like the Cambridge incident) that draws such heavy media attention. Ideally, constructive dialogue that captures the intersection of race at both the micro and macro levels in society, as well as in policing and the larger criminal justice system, should be ongoing. Police authorities must engage the context of why many racial minority communities approach them (the police) with considerable mistrust and suspicion. Of corollary importance, the general citizenry must be willing to see an incident from the police worldview, from their standard operating procedure, and must be willing to learn why they do the things they do in a prescribed and fairly uniform manner.

Scope of the Problem

It is no secret that police relations with many racial minority communities are not the best. Because of this fractured relationship, it is no surprise that there is a perception among some racial minority citizens that the police engage in racial profiling. In fact, for many years anecdotal reports have revealed that many racial minority citizens believe that the police routinely stop and search them simply because of the color of their skin (Birzer & Smith-Mahdi, 2006; Tomaskovic-Devey, Mason, & Zingraff, 2004; Harris, 2002). In many cases, reports of racial profiling by racial minority citizens were not taken seriously and were therefore subsequently dismissed. Perhaps *they* were overly sensitive, maybe *it* was an extremely rare incident, or perhaps *they* were in the wrong place at the wrong time.

Recent national opinion polls have found that a large number of American citizens feel racial profiling is prevalent in our society. For example, a 2004 Gallup poll of citizens found a substantial proportion of Americans believe racial profiling is widespread. Fifty-three percent of those polled think the practice of stopping motorists because of their race or ethnicity is widespread (Carlson, 2004). In another analysis of public opinions of racial profiling, it was revealed that 90 percent of Blacks who were polled thought that profiling was widespread, followed by 83 percent of Hispanics, and 70 percent of Whites (Weitzer & Tuch, 2005).

Several studies have found that racial minority citizens are subjected to traffic stops and searches at disproportional rates. Antonovics and Knight (2004) reviewed vehicle search data from the Boston Police Department and found that more than 43 percent of all searches were of Black motorists even though they represented only 33 percent of the cars that were stopped by the police. One other study in Ohio found that Black citizens were twice as likely to be stopped by the police than non-Blacks (Harris, 1999). In San Diego, Black and Hispanic drivers were found to be overrepresented in vehicle stops (Cordner, Williams, & Velasco, 2002).

Studies in Maryland found that 70 percent of the drivers stopped on Interstate 95 were African Americans, while according to an American Civil Liberties Union survey, only 17.5 percent of the traffic and speeders on that road were Black (Cole, 1999). Similarly, studies in New Jersey found that the state police routinely stopped a disproportionate amount of Black drivers. For example, the *State v. Pedro Soto* (1996) case involved consolidated motions to suppress evidence under the equal protection and due process clauses of the Fourteenth Amendment. Seventeen defendants of African ancestry claimed that their arrests on the New Jersey Turnpike between 1988 and 1991 were the result of discriminatory enforcement of the traffic laws by the New Jersey State Police.

In the New Jersey case, researchers employed a windshield survey. This entailed stationing observers by the side of the road in randomly selected periods of 75 minutes from 8:00 a.m. to 8:00 p.m. with the objective to count the number of cars and the race of the occupants. It was determined by the windshield survey that out of 40,000 New Jersey turnpike drivers observed, 13.5 percent were Black motorists. A violator survey was also employed. The violator survey was conducted over 10 sessions in 4 days between Exits 1 and 3 on the New Jersey Turnpike. Researchers traveled with the cruise control calibrated and set at 55 miles per hour (5 miles per hour over the legal speed limit). They observed and recorded the number of vehicles that passed them, the number of vehicles they passed, the race of the driver, and whether the driver was speeding. Fifteen percent of the violators were Black; however, they made up more than 46 percent of the drivers stopped by the New Jersey State Police, a disparity of more than three to one. The Court found the defendants to have established a prima facie case of selective enforcement. The Court's finding resulted in suppression of all contraband and evidence seized.

In *Fuchilla v. Layman* (1988), the Court found that in the New Jersey State Police agency, profiling drivers based on the color of their skin was tolerated and in some ways encouraged at the highest levels of the state police. Profiling by the New Jersey State Police prompted an investigation by the U.S. Department of Justice and led to a consent decree being issued by the government to the State of New Jersey. The consent decree was for a period of 5 years.

In its complaint, the U.S. Government alleged that New Jersey State Police troopers engaged in a pattern of conduct that deprives persons of rights, privileges, or immunities secured or protected by the Constitution and laws of the United States, including the Fourteenth Amendment and the Omnibus Crime Control and Safe Streets Act. Furthermore, it was alleged that this pattern or practice of conduct had been made possible by the failure of the State Police to adopt and implement proper management practices and procedures. The New Jersey State Police were accused of tolerating this conduct.

The United States further alleged that New Jersey State Police policy, training, supervision, and complaint procedures allowed for a high degree of discretion to individual troopers in conducting motor vehicle stops and did little to prevent individual troopers from improperly using race to target racial minority drivers and passengers. However, the government also recognized that the majority of state troopers had performed their jobs in a lawful manner (*U.S. v. State of New Jersey, and the New Jersey Department of Public Safety*, 1999).

Consent Decree, New Jersey State Police

1. **Policy Requirements**: State troopers may not rely to any degree on the race or national or ethnic origin of motorists in selecting vehicles for traffic stops and in deciding upon the scope and substance of post-stop actions, except where state troopers are on the look-out for a specific suspect who has been identified in part by his or her race or national or ethnic origin. The State Police shall continue to require that troopers make a request for consent to search only when they possess reasonable suspicion that a search will reveal evidence of a crime, and all consent searches must be based on the driver or passenger giving written consent prior to the initiation of the search.
2. **Traffic Stop Documentation**: State troopers engaged in patrol activities will document the race, ethnic origin, and gender of all motor vehicle drivers who are the subject of a traffic stop, and also will record information about the reason for each stop and any post-stop action that is taken (including the issuance of a ticket or warning, asking the vehicle occupants to exit the vehicle and frisking them, consensual and non-consensual vehicle searches, uses of force, and arrests).
3. **Supervisory Review of Individual Traffic Stops**: Supervisors regularly will review trooper reports concerning post-stop enforcement actions and procedures, and patrol car video tapes of traffic stops, to ensure that troopers are employing appropriate practices and procedures. Where concerns arise, supervisors may require that the

trooper be counseled, receive additional training, or that some other non-disciplinary action be taken. Supervisors also can refer specific incidents for further investigation, where appropriate.

4. **Supervisory Review of Patterns of Conduct**: The State will develop and implement an early warning system, called the "Management Awareness Program," that uses computerized information on traffic stops, misconduct investigations, and other matters to assist State Police supervisors to identify and modify potentially problematic behavior. At least quarterly, State Police supervisors will conduct reviews and analyses of computerized data and other information, including data on traffic stops and post-stop actions by race and ethnicity. These reviews and analyses, as appropriate, may result in supervisors implementing changes in traffic enforcement criteria, training, and practices, implementing non-disciplinary interventions for particular troopers (such as supervisory counseling or additional training), and/or requiring further assessment or investigation.

5. **Misconduct Allegations**: The State Police will make complaint forms and informational materials available at a variety of locations, will institute a 24-hour toll-free telephone hotline, and will publicize the State Police toll-free number at all State-operated rest stops located on limited access highways. The State also will institute procedures for ensuring that the State Police is notified of criminal cases and civil lawsuits alleging trooper misconduct. Allegations of discriminatory traffic stops, improper post-stop actions, and other significant misconduct allegations will be investigated by the Professional Standards Bureau inside the State Police or by the State Attorney General's Office. All investigations will be properly documented. Where a misconduct allegation is substantiated concerning prohibited discrimination or certain other serious misconduct, discipline shall be imposed. Where a misconduct allegation is not substantiated, the State Police will consider whether non-disciplinary supervisory steps are appropriate.

6. **Training**: The State Police will continue to implement measures to improve training for recruits and incumbent troopers. The training will address such matters as supervisory issues, communication skills, cultural diversity, and the nondiscrimination requirements of the Decree. The State Police also will take steps to continue to improve its trooper coach program for new troopers. The Independent Monitor selected by the parties will evaluate all training currently provided by the State Police regarding traffic stops, and will make recommendations for improvements.

7. **Auditing by the New Jersey Attorney General's Office**: The State Attorney General's Office will have special responsibility for ensuring implementation of the Decree. The Office will conduct various audits of State Police performance, which will include contacting samples of persons who were the subject of a State Police traffic stop

to evaluate whether the stops were appropriately conducted and documented. The Office also will audit State Police implementation of the Management Awareness Program, and procedures used for receiving, investigating, and resolving misconduct allegations.

8. **State Police Public Reports:** The State Police will issue semiannual public reports containing aggregate statistics on certain law enforcement activities, including traffic stop statistics.

9. **Independent Monitor:** An Independent Monitor, who will be an agent of the court, will be selected by the United States and the State of New Jersey to monitor and report on the State's implementation of the Decree. The responsibilities of the Monitor will include evaluating samples of trooper incident reports, supervisory reviews of incidents, and misconduct investigations, supervisors' use of the Management Awareness Program, and the use of non-disciplinary procedures to address at-risk conduct (*U.S. v. State of New Jersey, and the New Jersey Department of Public Safety,* 1999).

In 2005, the State of New Jersey passed legislation to prohibit racial profiling and required every police officer within its borders to undergo intensive instruction on profiling and protecting citizens' rights. Moreover, the New Jersey legislature passed legislation that made racial profiling a criminal offense.

Disparate police stops have also been discovered in Florida. On a stretch of Interstate 95 in Florida, known for being a drug trafficking route, Blacks and Latinos comprised only 5 percent of drivers, but accounted for 70 percent of those stopped by members of the highway patrol. Only 9 drivers out of the 1100 stopped during the study were ticketed for a violation, let alone arrested for possession of illegal contraband (Wise, 2005).

Some studies found that racial minority communities are less likely to hold favorable attitudes toward the police because of the perception of racial profiling (Harris, 2005; Russell, 1998). One study found that 80 percent of Black citizens believed racial profiling was pervasive in their own city, and an alarming 90 percent believed racial profiling was widespread in the United States. The same study revealed 59 percent of Hispanic citizens believed racial profiling was pervasive in their city, and 77 percent believed it was widespread across the United States. Only one-third of White citizens believed racial profiling was pervasive in their city (Weitzer & Tuch, 2005). In another study that focused on Hispanics' perceptions of racial profiling, it was discovered that they were more likely than non-Hispanics to believe profiling was widespread and they had been profiled (Reitzel, Rice, & Piquero, 2004).

The Police Executive Research Forum's (2001) attempt to address racial profiling has been admirable. They asserted that it is a very complex problem

for police departments to address. Moreover, they identified the core problems centering on racial profiling at a minimum to be:

- targeting motorists for traffic stops on the basis of racial profiles;
- applying discretionary enforcement on the basis of race;
- tolerating different degrees of disorder and deviance on the basis of
  race;
- interfering with citizens' routine activities on the basis of race (e.g.,
  stopping, questioning, and searching citizens without adequate
  cause);
- assuming someone is dangerous on the basis of race;
- unduly relying on race as a part of suspect identification; and
- providing different levels of police patrol and protection on the
  basis of race, or because of unfounded racial fears (Police Executive
  Research Forum, 2001, pp. 82–83).

What further exacerbates allegations of racial profiling is that police
authorities themselves, for the most part, deny that they engage in racially
biased police tactics. This presents an irony of sorts. On the one hand, a vast
literature points out that many racial minority citizens say racial profiling
occurs frequently in their communities, while on the other hand, police
authorities themselves deny these allegations. This underpins a longstanding
problem in America. The national discourse has been a "he said/she said,"
or one side hurdles allegations of racial profiling and other injustices, and
the other side denies such allegations (Walker, 2000, p. 11). We must move
beyond this stalemate. Police authorities and citizens alike are duty bound to
roll up their sleeves and craft solutions acceptable to both sides.

Defining Racial Profiling

Although defining racial profiling is difficult, it is generally thought to be law
enforcement activities that are initiated solely based on race. In other words,
if police authorities stop motorists, and arrest and search them solely based
on their race, this would constitute racial profiling. The U.S. Department of
Justice defines racial profiling as:

> Any police-initiated action that relies on the race, ethnicity, or national origin
> rather than the behavior of an individual or information that leads the police
> to a particular individual who has been identified as being, or having been,
> engaged in criminal activity. (United States Department of Justice, 2000)

The American Civil Liberties Union simply defines racial profiling as:

> The discriminatory practice by law enforcement officials of targeting individuals for suspicion of crime based on the individual's race, ethnicity, religion or national origin. (American Civil Liberties Union, 2005)

Racial profiling does not refer to the act of a law enforcement agent pursuing a suspect in which the specific description of the suspect includes race or ethnicity in combination with other identifying factors (American Civil Liberties Union, 2005).

In the State of Kansas, where this research was carried out, racial profiling or other biased-based policing is defined as:

> The unreasonable use of race, ethnicity, national origin, gender or religion by a law enforcement officer in deciding to initiate an enforcement action. It is not racial or other biased-based policing when race, ethnicity, national origin, gender or religion is used in combination with other identifying factors as part of a specific individual description to initiate an enforcement action. (State of Kansas Attorney General's Office, 2012)

The State of Kansas specifically defines acts that constitute racial or other biased-based policing as:

1. Using race, ethnicity, national origin, gender, or religion as a general indicator or predictor of criminal activity.
2. Using the race, ethnicity, national origin, gender, or religion of a person in the course of law enforcement action unless the officer is seeking to detain, apprehend, or otherwise be on the lookout for a suspect sought in connection with a crime who has been identified or described in part by race, ethnicity, national origin, gender, or religion.
3. Using the race, ethnicity, national origin, gender, or religion of a person in the course of any reasonable action in connection with a status offense, such as, runaways, child in need of care, missing persons, and other non-criminal caretaker functions unless the person is identified or described in part by race, ethnicity, national origin, gender, or religion.
4. Using race, ethnicity, national origin, gender, or religion as motivating factors in making law enforcement decisions or actions, unless the person is identified or described in part by race, ethnicity, national origin, gender, or religion.

5. Using race, ethnicity, national origin, gender, or religion as the basis for discretionary law enforcement, that is, who they will cite, arrest, warn, search, release or which persons to treat with respect and dignity (State of Kansas Attorney General's Office, 2012).

Criminal Profiling

While racial profiling is any law enforcement activity that relies on the race, ethnicity, or national origin, rather than the behavior of the individual, criminal profiling relies on specific information about an offender that is discerned through a crime scene. Specifically, criminal profiling is the process where "police authorities use available information about a crime and crime scene to compose a psychological portrait of the unknown perpetrator of the crime" (Muller, 2000, p. 235).

Criminal profiling generally works best when there is considerable interaction between the offender and the victim (O'Hara & O'Hara, 2003). Therefore, criminal profiling may be useful in crimes committed by serial killers, arsonists, and sexual offenders, but may not be so useful in crimes such as robberies and thefts. Criminal profiling allows investigators to develop a psychological makeup of an offender based on the evidence at the crime scene. In other words, criminal profiling is a technique that infers the traits of individuals responsible for the commission of criminal acts (Turvey, 2012). With criminal profiling, the objective is to assist in narrowing down specific behavioral, psychological, and personality features possessed by suspects based on the manner in which the crime was committed (Douglas & Olshaker, 1996).

Because of the lack of uniformity among definitions of criminal profiling, it is not unusual to find definitions that encompass behavioral profiling, psychological profiling, crime scene profiling, criminal personality profiling, and offender profiling (Turvey, 2012). Nevertheless, criminal profiling is one of several tools that can be used to identify the type of individual responsible for a particular crime (Lyman, 2010). The operational methods used in criminal profiling seek to analyze information available to an investigation in order to predict characteristics of offenders, to establish whether the crime appears to be part of a series, and how to take the best advantage of any media interest in the case (Davies & Dale, 1995).

Can police authorities use race as one of several factors in developing a criminal profile of a suspect? The answer is yes. Can an investigator use race as the only factor in developing a criminal profile? The answer is no. If race is used as the sole factor in developing a criminal profile, that constitutes racial profiling. The scope and aim of criminal profiling is drastically different from racial profiling.

What's in a Name?

There is some debate over the use of the term "racial profiling" versus the term "biased-based policing," which many police organizations now use. Biased-based policing is generally defined as employing law enforcement strategies that exclude consideration of a person's race, ethnicity, creed, color, national origin, sexual orientation, disability, gender, or religion. Central to this debate is the argument that the term "biased-based policing" is a considerably more appropriate and encompassing definition when compared to racial profiling. Some argue the definition of racial profiling is so restrictive that it does not capture the concerns of both police practice and citizens (Police Executive Research Forum, 2001).

Racial profiling is often defined as any law enforcement activities that are initiated solely based on the race of the individual. What is problematic here is the use of the word "solely." One could hardly argue that even the most racially prejudiced police officer would use only race as the sole factor in determining which motorist to stop. For example, usually there are other factors involved in a police officer's decision to stop a motorist. The officer may indeed use the race of the individual in constellation with a host of other factors in the determination to make a stop. For instance, an officer may see a racial minority motorist driving in a predominately White neighborhood. He may hone in on the appearance of the car, which has expensive rims and a customized paint job. The officer may also associate the vehicle as one, in his mind, that likely may be driven by a racial minority citizen, a symbolic racial minority vehicle of sorts. The officer may follow the vehicle until a minor violation is detected such as failing to use a turn signal, lane straddling, or some other low-level traffic infraction.

Based on these factors, the officer stops the motorist. In this scenario, the officer does not use the race of the motorist alone to make the stop, but rather uses it in constellation with other factors. It is important to note, however, that "profiling exists either when race or ethnicity is used as the sole indicator or more of several indicators that enters into a police officer's decision making calculus" (Walker, 2001, p. 64).

Racial profiling definitions that include language such as "stopping a motorist solely because of his or her race" would certainly be problematic when applied to the above facts. For example, in the scenario presented above, the officer could simply say that the motorist failed to use his turn signal, or that he observed the motorist lane straddle, when of course, the underlying motive for the stop was the race of the driver.

The biased-based policing definition appears to be a more inclusive definition. According to a position paper prepared by the National Latino Peace Officers' Association (2002), the narrowest of definitions of racial profiling limits it to vehicle stops and fails to consider other police actions where the unlawful consideration of race enters the mind of the officer. The paper goes on to support the use of biased-based policing definitions. The Police Executive Research Forum (2001) made the same recommendation.

Experience Is Powerful

As stated previously in this chapter, this book is about racial profiling. It attempts to understand this troubling phenomenon from those racial minority citizens who say they have experienced it. The objective is to give meaning to how racial minority citizens experience what they believe to be racial profiling. More specifically, the book spotlights two mutually important areas centering on racial profiling. First, it is concerned with the textural descriptions of racial minority citizen's experiences; in other words, what they experienced. Second, the book elucidates the structural description of their experiences. That is, how they experienced what was perceived as racial profiling in terms of the situations, conditions, and context.

This book represents over 18 months of field research across the State of Kansas. During these 18 months, I was the student of well over 100 racial minority citizens who believed they had been racially profiled by police authorities. In the end, I used 87 citizen accounts of perceived racial profiling for purposes of data reporting in this book.

I learned a great deal from these citizens, perhaps more so than any book on racial profiling could teach me. During my research, I carefully interviewed, listened, recorded, transcribed, and analyzed their stories. Their stories, or narratives as they are more appropriately called, were powerful and constructive. Interviews that culminate in descriptive and rich narratives have the potential to illicit the temporal, the social, and the meaning structures of the interview (Mishler, 1986).

The reader should know upfront that this book does not stop at simply reporting anecdotal accounts of perceived racial profiling. I find this problematic in other treatments of racial profiling that report just the stories without any rigorous qualitative method and analysis. This is where I go much further in the analysis. The participants' stories have been subjected to rigorous qualitative analysis using a phenomenological approach in order to uncover themes and patterns. I was curious to see where the data would take me, and what the themes and patterns would reveal.

Good interviews have a number of features that cannot be mistaken. They are cooperative and well motivated, they are eloquent and knowledgeable, they are truthful and consistent, and "they provide coherent accounts and do not continually contradict themselves" (Kvale & Brinkmann, 2009, p. 165). I made great effort in identifying interview participants who, in the researcher's judgment, have the best stories to tell about their experiences with racial profiling. As Kvale and Brinkmann (2009, p. 165) point out, "Good subjects can give long and lively descriptions of their life situation, they tell capturing stories well suited for reporting" and, as I add, for careful study and analysis.

In the end, these data reveal a great deal of information about the context in which racial minority citizens experience and give meaning to what they believe is racial profiling. Although racial profiling may encompass many forms, the focus of this work is driving while Black or Brown; that is, racial minority citizens who reported that they were stopped by police authorities while driving in their automobiles for what they allege to be racial profiling.

What was learned from these women and men who told their stories was at times heart wrenching. Often it was difficult not to become emotionally attached to them as they reflected and in many cases struggled to tell me the way it happened to them. Many sobbed as they told their stories. Simply put, I felt their pain. Use of the interview as a research instrument can be powerful, and the researcher should never take it for granted. Kvale and Brinkmann (2009, p. 17) viewed interviewing as an active process, "where interviewer and interviewee through their relationship produce knowledge." The effective interviewer can travel with his participants moving from the front stage, which is primarily the presentation of the self, to the back stage, which is saturated with rich, hidden emotions, thoughts, and experiences (Tunnel, 1998). The emotional pain and agony that was visible on the participants' faces, and the sometimes visible sobbing I witnessed as they recalled their experiences, convinced me that I was there. I had indeed journeyed from the front stage to the back stage.

Ferrell and Hamm (1998) suggest that the experiences of the field researcher are important and should not be taken lightly. They argue that a positive experiential outcome is a subjective understanding that researcher and participant come to share. I sought solace in these words as I embarked on my journey to understand and give meaning to racial profiling as experienced by these participants. At the conclusion of my research, I understood Ferrell and Hamm's thesis. I had uncovered through interviews and focus groups, a subjective understanding with the participants. A criminological *verstehen* of sorts, which I conclude can only be gained through active involvement with participants in this study, and by active involvement as a listener, describer, and interpreter of their experiences. Criminological *verstehen* denotes a method that bridges the old dualisms of researcher and research situation, researcher and subjects of research, by utilizing the researcher's own experiences of the subjects. It implies a degree of subjective understanding between researcher and research subjects, an engaged methodological process such that the researcher and research subjects come to share (Ferrell and Hamm, 1998, p. 13).

Within the confines of the interview, I attempted to construct what the participants experienced during their perceived racial profiling. Criminal justice can benefit tremendously by recognizing that experience matters, both the experience of the researcher and the participant. Of course, this entails acknowledging that in order to fully understand phenomena we will have to evolve from the positivistic or quantitative hegemony that currently guides the majority of racial profiling research. I propose in this book that qualitative methods that are robust in design and rigor will increasingly assist researchers and police authorities in more fully understanding the complexities of racial profiling.

Discussion Questions

1. Do you think that the "Cambridge case" discussed in this chapter is racial profiling? Why or why not?
2. Why do you think there is such a strong divide in the opinions of racial minority citizens and White citizens regarding the existence of racial profiling in our society?
3. Describe the differences between racial profiling and criminal profiling.
4. Discuss what is central to the debate in regards to using the term biased-based policing versus racial profiling.
5. In regards to qualitative research interviews, how does the author use the terms *front stage* and *back stage*?

References

American Civil Liberties Union. (2005). Racial profiling: Definition. Retrieved from http://www.aclu.org.

Antonovics, K.L., & Knight, B.G. (2004). *A new look at racial profiling: Evidence from the Boston Police Department*. Cambridge, MA: National Bureau of Economic Research.

Barlow, D.E., & Barlow, M.H. (2002). Racial profiling: A survey of African American police officers. *Police Quarterly, 5*, 334–358.

Birzer, M.L. (2008). What makes a good police officer? Phenomenological reflections from the African-American community. *Police Practice and Research, 9*, 1–14.

Birzer, M.L., & Roberson, C. (2008). *Police operations: Theory meets practice*. Boston: Allyn and Bacon.

Birzer, M.L., & Smith-Mahdi, J. (2006). The phenomenology of discrimination experienced among African-Americans. *Journal of Black Studies, 10*(2), 22–37.

Brown, B., Benedict W.R., & Wilkinson, W.V. (2006). Public perception of the police in Mexico: A case study. *Policing: An International Journal of Police Strategies & Management, 29*(1), 159–175.

Carlson, D.K. (2004). Racial profiling seen as pervasive, unjust. *Gallup*. Retrieved from http://www.gallup.com/poll/12406/racial-profiling-seen-pervasive-unjust.aspx.

Cambridge Review Committee (2010). Missed opportunities, missed shared responsibilities: Final report of the Cambridge review committee. Retrieved from http://policelegal.com/2010/06/30/final-report-of-the-cambridge-review-committee/.

Cole, D. (1999). *No equal justice: Race and class in the American criminal justice system.* New York: The New Press.

Cooper, H. (2009, July 22). Obama criticizes arrest of Harvard Professor. *The New York Times.* Retrieved from http://www.nytimes.com.

Cooper, J., & Goodnough, A. (2009, July 30). Over beers, no apologies, but plans to have lunch. *The New York Times.* Retrieved from http://www.nytimes.com.

Cordner, G., Williams, B., & Velasco, A. (2002). *Vehicle stops in San Diego: Executive report.* Retrieved from San Diego CA Police Department website: http://www.sandiego.gov/police/pdf/stoprpt.pdf.

Crowley, J. (2009). Police incident report. Retrieved from www.thesmokinggun.com/file/henry_lou.

Davies, A., & Dale, A. (1995). Locating the serial rapist: Special interest series, paper 3. London: Home Office Research Group.

Douglas, J. E., & Olshaker, M. (1996). *Mind hunter.* New York: Pocket Books.

Ferrell, J., & Hamm, M.S. (1998). True confessions, crime deviance and field research. In J. Ferrell and M.S. Hamm (Eds.), *Ethnography at the edge: Crime, deviance, and field research* (pp. 2–19). Boston: Northeastern University Press.

Flores, W. (2002). Position paper, nonbiased based policing. Santa Ana, CA: National Latino Peace Officer Association.

Ford, B., & Schapiro, R. (2009, July 23). Cambridge cops demand apology from President Obama over Harvard Professor Henry Louis Gates. *New York Daily News.* Retrieved from http://articles.nydailynews.com.

Garcia, V. and Cao, L. (2005). Race and satisfaction with the police in a small city. *Journal of Criminal Justice, 33*(2), 19–199.

Jefferies, E.S., Kaminski, R.J., Holmes, S., & Hanley, D.E. (1997). The effect of a videotaped arrest on public perceptions of police use of force. *Journal of Criminal Justice, 25,* 381–395.

Kvale, S., & Brinkmann, S. (2009). *Interviewing: Learning the craft of qualitative research interviewing.* Los Angeles, CA: Sage.

Harris, D.A. (1999). The stories, the statistics, and the law: Why driving while Black matters. *Minnesota Law Review, 84,* 265–326.

Harris, D.A. (2002). *Profiles in injustice: Why racial profiling cannot work.* New York: The New Press.

Harris, D.A. (2005). *The case for preventive policing: Good cops.* New York: The New Press.

Lyman, M.D. (2010). *Criminal investigation: The art and science* (6th ed.). Thousand Oaks, CA: Prentice Hall.

Mishler, E.G. (1986). Research interviewing: Content and narrative. Cambridge, MA: Harvard University Press.

Moustakas, C. (1994). *Phenomenological research methods.* Thousand Oaks, CA: Sage.

Muller, D.A. (2000). Criminal profiling: Real science or just wishful thinking. *Homicide Studies, 4,* 234–264.

Nelson, J. (2000). *Police brutality.* New York: W.W. Norton and Company.

Ogletree, C.J. (2010). *The presumption of guilt: The arrest of Henry Louis Gates, Jr. and race, class and crime in America.* New York: Palgrave-Macmillan.

O'Hara, C.E., & O'Hara, G.L. (2003). *Fundamentals of criminal investigation* (7th ed.). Springfield, IL: Charles C Thomas.

Parker, K.D., Onyekwuluje, A.B., & Murty, K.S. (1995). African-American's attitudes toward the police: A multivariable analysis. *Journal of Black Studies, 25,* 396–409.

Police Executive Research Forum (2001). *Racial biased policing: A principled response.* Washington, DC: United States Department of Justice.

Reitzel, J.D., Rice, S.K., & Piquero, A.R. (2004). Lines and shadows: Perceptions of racial profiling and the Hispanic experience. *Journal of Criminal Justice, 32,* 607–616.

Russell, K.K. (1998). *The color of crime: Racial hoaxes, White fear, Black protectionism and police harassment and other macro aggressions.* New York: New York University Press.

State of Kansas Attorney General's Office (2012). Racial or biased-based policing policy. Accessed at: http://ag.ks.gov/home.

Tomaskovic-Devey, D., Mason, M., & Zingraff, M. (2004). Looking for the driving while Black phenomena: Conceptualizing racial bias processes and their processes and their associated distributions. *Police Quarterly, 7,* 3–29.

Tunnell, K.D. (1998). Honesty, secrecy, and deception in the sociology of crime: Confessions and reflections from the backstage. In J. Ferrell and M.S. Hamm (Eds.), *Ethnography at the edge: Crime, deviance, and field research* (pp. 206–220). Boston: Northeastern University Press.

Turvey, B.E. (2012). *Criminal profiling: An introduction to behavioral evidence analysis.* Boston: Elsevier.

Tyler, T.R. (2002). A national survey for monitoring police legitimacy. *Justice Research and Policy, 4,* 71–86.

United States Department of Justice (2000). A resource guide on data collection systems. U. S. Dept. of Justice. Retrieved from www.https://www.ncjrs.gov/pdffiles1/bja/184768.pdf

Walker, S. (2001). Searching for the denominator: Problems with police traffic stop data and an early warning system solution. *Justice Research and Policy, 3*(1), 63–95.

Weitzer, R., & Tuch, S.A. (2002). Perceptions of racial profiling: Race, class and personal experience. *Criminology 40*:435–457.

Weitzer, R., & Tuch, S.A. (2004). Race and perceptions of police misconduct. *Social Problems, 51,* 305–325.

Weitzer, R., & Tuch, S.A. (2005). Racially biased policing: Determinants of citizen perceptions. *Social Forces, 83,* 1009–1030.

Wise, T. (2005). Racial profiling and its apologists. In J.L. Victor and J. Naughton (Eds.), *Annual editions, criminal justice* (pp. 100–103). Dubuque, IA: McGraw-Hill/Dushkin.

Cases Cited

Fuchilla v. :Layman, 537 A.2d 652, 654, cert denied, 488 US 826 (1988).

State v. Pedro Soto, 324 N.J. Super. 66; 734 A.2d 350 (1996).

United States of America v. State of New Jersey and the New Jersey Department of Public Safety, Joint Application for Consent Decree. United States District Court for the District of New Jersey, No. 99-5970, December 30, 1999, pp. 1–29.

Putting Racial Profiling into Context

2

"I had the craziest thought at that moment, I began to think about all the blacks down South who were slaves and had been beaten and lynched. I felt a strange power at that moment, as if their spirits were all coming together to help me through this."

Rodney King (1945–2012) describing his thoughts during a 1991 beating by Los Angeles Police Officers
The Riot Within: My Journey from Rebellion to Redemption (2012)

Introduction

Racial minorities, particularly Black Americans, have had a long and troubling history of disparate treatment by U.S. criminal justice authorities. Some have argued that the police, the law and the courts, and the prison system have all been used as "instruments of oppression and subordination based on race," and if the nation is to complete the processes eliminating this subjugation we "must move to eliminate all vestiges of racial bias" from the criminal justice system (Moss, 1990, p. 88).

I make two overarching arguments in this chapter. The first is that many of the perceptions of racial profiling held by racial minorities, especially Black Americans, exist in part because of a long history of disparate treatment by the criminal justice system. Second, because of this disparate treatment, there is a resulting constructed view by the public of a symbolic criminal threat—the Black offender—which is reinforced by the print and electronic media images, as well as television and Hollywood movies (Pickett, Chiricos, Golden, & Gertz, 2012).

Consequently, there is a race coding of sorts that takes place which culminates in reinforced stereotyping that associates race to crime (Quillian, & Pager, 2001, 2010). The symbolic criminal figure, often a Black male, is in turn subjected to increased surveillance, profiled, policed, adjudicated, and incarcerated disproportionately. The underlying premise of my argument is that racially biased policing in law enforcement is merely a symptom of a more serious pathology that afflicts the entire criminal justice system. Moreover, it represents one of the single most pressing issues that face fundamental criminal justice policy and practice, which to date has only been addressed in a superficial manner. In other words, researchers (with the exception of the critical, postmodern theorists in criminal justice) are quick to investigate disproportionalities without paying serious attention to the possibility of systemic institutionalized discriminatory practices.

Vigilante Justice?

A more recent example to support the premise of the stereotyped and socially constructed and criminalized Black male can take you to February 26, 2012. On this date, Trayvon Martin, a 17-year-old African American male, was shot and killed while walking home from a convenience store in a gated community in Sanford, Florida. The teenager, who was wearing a hooded sweatshirt, had been watching the NBA All-Star Game and walked to a nearby store to buy iced tea and Skittles candies.

George Zimmerman, a 28-year-old neighborhood watch volunteer, was patrolling the gated community. Zimmerman spotted the Black teenager and called 911 to report him as a suspicious person. Zimmerman is heard on the 911 emergency tapes saying, "These assholes always get away." Zimmerman also illuminated the fact that the suspicious person was "Black" and "wearing a hoodie." Zimmerman left his car and began to follow the teenager on foot, ignoring the police dispatcher's advice not to do so. Shortly thereafter, a confrontation of some sort ensued between Zimmerman and the Black teen. Seconds later, the teen is shot to death. Just before the shooting, police emergency tapes recorded what may have been a racial slur muttered by Zimmerman.

The shooting of Trayvon Martin made both national and international news when the Sanford police department neither arrested Zimmerman nor confiscated his weapon. The police said that he was shielded by a controversial law in Florida (Stand Your Ground). The law allows private citizens to use deadly force if they feel threatened. President Barack Obama weighed in on the shooting saying this incident should "prompt Americans to do some soul searching." The case has resulted in mass protests across the United States demanding that justice be served. The FBI and the Justice Department are investigating the case for Civil Rights violations.

The Trayvon Martin case has sparked a renewed interest by many for an honest discussion about race in the United States. The case gained national prominence with rallies held across the country demanding that Zimmerman be arrested and charged with murder. Zimmerman and his supporters say that the shooting had nothing to do with race and that he shot Martin in self-defense. Several weeks after the shooting, Florida Governor Rick Scott appointed a special prosecutor to take over the case. On April 11, 2012, George Zimmerman was charged with second degree murder in the death of Trayvon Martin.

Many questions need to be answered in this case. What we know is that race is deeply embedded in this shooting. The way police authorities handled this case raises many questions. Would a Black male who had just shot and killed a White person be handled differently by police authorities? Would a Black man have been arrested and taken to the police station? Was a different style of justice afforded to Zimmerman that may have not been afforded to a Black man or another racial minority in a similar situation?

One must also ask why a young Black male wearing a hoodie is suspicious. What if it had been a middle-aged White man walking his dog late one night and wearing a hoodie? Would he have been deemed suspicious? What if it was a White businessperson who went out for a late evening jog? Would he have been considered suspicious? Society has constructed a symbolic criminalized figure, the Black male. The wearing of a hoodie along with the victim's race perpetuates and lends support to this stereotyped and symbolic figure. Symbolic figures will be discussed to a fuller extent in Chapter 5.

As a result of the Trayvon Martin killing, not only does the larger discussion of the intersection of race and the criminal justice system need to take place, but also a discourse on laws that seem to empower a vigilante style of justice in the United States. These laws may very well sustain intended or unintended discrimination and racism in police and criminal justice practices. The Florida "Stand Your Ground" law is also salient in the Trayvon Martin shooting. Does the Florida law along with a host of similar ones that are being proposed in other states breed a culture where individuals will strap on a gun and take the law into their own hands? Did George Zimmerman, the man at the center of the racially charged killing of an unarmed Black teen, take the law into his own hands?

Some reports suggest that Zimmerman is a cop wannabe. Over the years, he called the police dispatchers as a matter of routine. Numerous calls to police authorities showed he pursued shoplifters and errant drivers with zeal, reporting pit bulls, potholes, children playing in the street, open garage doors, and suspicious youth, especially Black youth. Ask any police officer who has worked the street for any period of time and they will most likely tell you that they have met their fair share of George Zimmermans. Zimmerman had an arrest record including battery of a law enforcement officer and domestic violence against his fiancée. How is it possible then, that Zimmerman had a legal permit to carry the firearm he used to kill Trayvon Martin?

Looking through a macro lens, social scientists agree that as a national cultural frame, racism in its various forms has harmful effects on the way Whites perceive and act toward Blacks (Wilson, 2009). In the United States today, "there is no question that the more categorical forms of racist ideology, in particular, those that assert the biogenetic inferiority of Blacks, has declined significantly, even though they still may be embedded in institutional norms and practices"(Wilson, 2009, p. 15).

Experience Matters

In order to understand fully how racial minorities give meaning to their experiences with racial profiling, it is beneficial to provide historical context to the broader issue of the intersection of race and the criminal justice system. It is also important to view this complex phenomenon through the lens of racial minority citizens, something that has not always been done. The way in which racial minorities interpret and give meaning to issues that center on racial profiling and how race intersects with criminal justice processing will likely differ from Whites because of their life experiences. Experience matters. It shapes our perceptions of views. This is one area where positivist approaches to criminal justice have come up short in providing important insight.

There seems to be a preference in criminal justice research with examining the correlations, odds ratios, and the outcomes of complex prediction models that control for so many potentially confounding effects that they often result in more questions than answers. Using quasi-experimental and cross-sectional designs, criminal justice researchers disassociate parts from the whole, examine and control variables, and ultimately uncover at a specific probability what may or may not be the way things really happen in the social world. When researchers control for specific variables (sometimes referred to as holding a variable constant), that variable cannot account for variation in the dependent variable, so in essence we are eliminating its effect from consideration. In other words, we are saying that the variable cannot account for any variation. It is like saying it doesn't matter. Some would argue that controlling for the variable of race is like saying it doesn't matter.

James (2008, p. 43) argued that often in social science research "race is presented as a demographic or control variable, implying a theoretical neutrality not supported by the substance of the argument or techniques used in the research." James further argued that this trend is readily seen in the empirical journals. According to James, "in the fall 2001 issue of the *American Sociological Review, Demography, Social Forces,* and *American Journal of Sociology,* 67 percent of the articles that mention race make use of race as a disembodied variable in a regression model" (James, 2008, p. 43). As James further pointed out, "The use of race as a control variable flattens out the meanings of racial differences and replaces it with a generic notion of difference" (p. 43).

When applying James' thesis to criminal justice research, the point hits home. The variable of race in criminal justice research is important. It is embedded in virtually every facet in the criminal justice system. Criminal justice researchers often use the variable of race and examine its effect on different outcomes, but in many cases, do not necessarily examine the embedded underpinnings of the reasons for the racial differences. This would seem to be a fatal flaw, not examining the reasons for the differences.

There is a tendency of some researchers to play down or even dismiss racial discrimination in the criminal justice system (Russell-Brown, 2009). Deemphasizing or ignoring the possibility of racial discrimination in the criminal justice system is like controlling for it, saying it does not matter. Likewise, if race were controlled, it would seem that we only see what we want to see, which in turn culminates in a jaded view of the criminal justice system. One only has to take a look at prison demographics to realize that race indeed matters in the criminal justice system, and to say it doesn't is naive. Think about this for a moment. If racist consequences accrue to institutional laws, customs, or practices, the institution is racist whether the individuals maintaining those practices have racist intentions (Jones, 1997).

A History of Disparate Treatment

As a starting point, in order to more effectively understand the complexities of racially biased policing, I will attempt to frame race and the criminal justice system from a historical context. This is important in the larger discourse if we are serious about addressing racially biased policing.

As I will discuss later in the book, my research illuminates that Black males are much more emotionally affected by racially biased policing when compared to Black females and Latinos of both genders. While they experience racial profiling much in the same manner, Black males are much more structural in their accounts. Because of Black America's troublesome history of disparate treatment and disproportionate incarceration, this is not surprising. No other racial minority group has endured the amount of systemic discrimination than Black Americans.

Color by the Numbers

Race and the criminal justice system are inextricably linked, and to ignore this fact is somewhat naïve (Mauer, 1999). More than 60 percent of the individuals in prison are racial and ethnic minorities. In the case of Black males, the data are more alarming. One out of eight Black males in their twenties is in prison or jail on any given day. While Black Americans represent between 13 and 14 percent of the general population, "they are disproportionally represented in every aspect of the criminal justice system, as victims, offenders, prisoners and arrestees" (Ogletree, Prosser, Smith, & Talley, 1995, p. 13). In just the federal prisons alone, Blacks represent almost 38 percent of inmates serving time. Similarly, over half the inmates incarcerated in our nation's jails are either Black or Hispanic (Federal Bureau of Prisons, 2012).

Racial minority youths' involvement in the U.S. juvenile justice system also reveals a disturbing pattern. In recent years, the number of racial minority youth being held in our nation's juvenile justice facilities has increased exponentially (Center on Juvenile and Criminal Justice, 2002). The violent crime index arrest rate indicator for Black juveniles is five times what it is for white juveniles, six times the rate of American Indians, and thirteen times the rate for Asian American juveniles (Puzzanchera & Adams, 2011). Black youth are more likely than any other racial or ethnic minority group to come into contact with the juvenile justice system. Some research has pointed out that the disproportionate minority involvement in the juvenile justice system is more likely found at the front end of processing; that is, they are arrested and referred to court more often than White youth (Poe-Yamagata, 2009). Other studies have found that minority youth are overrepresented at all stages of the juvenile justice process (Leiber, 2002). It should be pointed out that although the size of the disproportion will generally vary from state to state, the disproportion is an indication that something is terribly wrong.

A Legacy of Racialized Justice

A look at the intersection of race and the criminal justice system through a historical lens uncovers a pattern of the disparate treatment of racial minorities, especially for Blacks. This includes the legacy of Jim Crow Laws and other injudicious acts. From the inception of the American police, they were charged with upholding the status quo, a status quo that in some cases legally mandated inequality (Barlow & Hickman-Barlow, 2000). The following is a telling description of this legacy:

> The fact that the legal order not only countenanced but sustained slavery, segregation, and discrimination for most of our nation's history, and the fact the police were bound to uphold that order, set a pattern for police behavior and attitudes toward minority communities that has persisted until the present day. That pattern includes the idea that minorities have fewer civil rights, and the police have little responsibility for protecting them from crime within their communities. (Williams & Murphy, 1990, p. 2)

During slavery in the United States, slave catchers acting with police authority in many southern states were charged with the duties of returning runaway slaves to their masters. Every slave-owning state had active, established slave patrols, and though they had many functions within the community, their primary objective was to act as the first line of defense against a slave rebellion. Slave patrols caught runaway slaves, enforced slave codes, discouraged any large gathering of Blacks, and generally perpetuated the atmosphere of fear that kept the slaves in line (Hadden, 2001).

Slave patrols were a unique form of policing. They worked closely with the militia and were virtually given free rein to stop, search, and when necessary, beat slaves all under the protection of the legal system (Russell-Brown, 2009). It is an uncomfortable fact that police forces in the south actively pursued slaves. Slave patrols proved to be an integral step in the development of southern police organizations (Wadman & Allison, 2004). Professor Samuel Walker referred to slave patrols as "a distinctly American form of law enforcement." He went on to say that they were probably the first modern police forces in the United States (Walker, 1999, p. 22).

Slave patrols were made up of mostly poor Whites who frequently brutalized slaves caught without passes after curfew (Genovese, 1976). The influence of slave patrols in the southern states is the cornerstone to what some contend is the institutional racism mentality that continues to plague some American police departments (Wadman & Allison, 2004).

At the conclusion of the radical reconstruction (the year 1877) in the south, the criminal justice system represented one of the major instruments of White supremacy (Walker, 1980). Some police agencies in the south maintained White supremacy through their brutal and discriminatory practices toward African Americans (Barlow & Hickman-Barlow, 2000). Slavery was officially abolished in 1865, but its dark shadow would continue to impact African Americans for many years to come (Patterson, 1998). Southern Whites found ways to defy reconstruction and preserve their social order, which subsequently limited economic growth (Lynch, 1968). The humiliation and subjugation of African Americans continued through the enforcement of Jim Crow laws, economic and educational segregation, and the acceptance of lynching as a means of social control (Wadman & Allison, 2004).

If an African American found himself on the wrong side of the criminal justice system, he had a mark even going into a trial. If he did go to trial, the deck was stacked against him.

> The standards of evidence in most court trials were so low, the means of obtaining damaging testimony so dubious, the importance of constituted authority so evident, that insurrection prosecutions at law must be seen as a religious more than a normal criminal process. By such means individual slaves, and sometimes Whites affiliated with them, were made sacrifices to a sacred concept of White supremacy (Wyatt-Brown, 1982, p. 402).

Jim Crow laws (roughly 1880s through the 1960s) were passed throughout the south as a way to keep African Americans in inferior positions segregated from Whites. For example, under Jim Crow laws it was permissible in Mississippi to require African Americans to pass literacy tests in order to vote. Other states throughout the south in unison fashion passed similar Jim Crow laws that mandated separate bathrooms for African Americans, forbade interracial marriage, prohibited African Americans from eating in the same room as White customers in restaurants, forbade Black barbers from cutting a White man or woman's hair, and made it unlawful to bury African Americans in the same cemeteries as deceased Whites.

In September 1962, a federal court ordered the University of Mississippi to accept James Meredith, a 28-year-old African American, much to the vehement opposition of segregationists. The Mississippi governor at the time said he would never allow the school to be integrated with African Americans. This outraged Whites and set off several days of violence and rioting in Oxford, Mississippi. Meredith, accompanied by federal law enforcement officials, enrolled on October 1, 1962. The point that is important here is that U.S. Marshals escorted James Meredith into the University of Mississippi, with minimal or no protection by state or local police authorities (Hendrickson, 2003).

There are many cases throughout the 1960s where police authorities refused to protect racial minorities. In her book *Mississippi Challenge*, Mildred Pitts Walter describes police practices in the State of Mississippi during the 1960s:

> Good citizens averted their eyes. Law-enforcement officers, if not actually involved, did nothing to prevent the seizure of jailed suspects, and no mob leader is known to have been punished. Police officials refused to launch investigations when ordered to do so. Some victims were seized in daylight hours and blowtorched immediately after their trials for murder. Yet no one was able to identify the mob leaders (Pitts-Walter, 1992, p. 79).

Law enforcement's refusal to protect citizens is further exemplified by the many civil rights protesters in the 1960s who were regularly pelted with rocks and bottles from hostile White crowds while police authorities offered minimal or no protection (Pitts-Walter, 1992). In some cases, the police were the aggressors. One such case occurred in Canton, Mississippi in the late 1960s. In this case, the police used tear gas to disrupt a peaceful Civil Rights march (Katz, 1995). Images such as Birmingham, Alabama's public safety commissioner Eugene "Bull" Connor further exemplify how law enforcement was used by the power structure to maintain deplorable practices by any standards. Commissioner Connor was an outspoken proponent of racial segregation and without hesitation ordered the brutal use of police dogs and fire hoses to disperse Civil Rights demonstrators in Birmingham (Nunnelly, 1991).

Here is but yet another example of law enforcement's brutal tactics used against African Americans. In 1967, the Neshoba County Mississippi Sheriff Lawrence Rainey and his Deputy Sheriff Cecil Ray Price were two of the eighteen Mississippians convicted in 1967 of conspiring to violate the civil rights of three civil rights workers who were murdered in 1964. It was determined that the murders were carried out with the help of Neshoba County sheriff's officials and the Ku Klux Klan (Huie, 2000).

Consider a few more relatively recent cases. This incident occurred early one spring morning on March 3, 1991, in Los Angeles. That is when Rodney King, an African American man, was pulled over for a traffic violation. He had been speeding and took police on a 15-minute car chase. According to police, King emerged from his automobile in an aggressive manner that suggested he might have been high on drugs. Numerous officers confronted King and before handcuffing him, they delivered over 50 blows with their batons, numerous kicks, and two 50,000-volt shocks from a Taser stun gun. Twenty other police officers stood by and watched the beating. Listen to how King (2012) described the beating in his official memoir:

> Suddenly I was being hit with multiple baton blows to every part of my body—my knees, ankles, wrists, and head. The beatings continued to rain down on me (p. 45).
>
> How many bones did they have to break, how many quarts of blood did I have to lose before their fear died down? After forty plus baton blows, after a dozen kicks to the head, neck, and testicles, after not one but two Taser electrocutions, how could they possibly justify continuing to mutilate me because they were still afraid of me? (p. 95)
>
> Each baton hit and boot kick, each word I remembered the officers screaming at me, "You better run. We're going to kill you, nigger, run!" (p. 102).

A man named George Holliday, standing on the balcony of a nearby building, videotaped the incident. The next day, he gave his 81-second tape to Los Angeles TV channel 5. By the end of the day, the video was being broadcast by TV stations around the world. Four days later, all the charges were dropped on King and four officers were charged with felony assault and other beating-related charges.

The Independent Commission on the Los Angeles Police Department came out three months later documenting the "systematic use of excessive force and racial harassment in the LAPD." It also noted management problems and condemned the department's emphasis on crime control rather than crime prevention, which served to isolate the police from the public (Independent Commission's Report on the Los Angeles Police Department, 1991).

On April 29, 1992, the four police officers were found not guilty of committing any crimes against Rodney King. After the announcement of the verdict, the local police were caught fleeing several south central Los Angeles neighborhoods where large-scale riots had erupted. The National Guard was called in and the riots ended six days after they began. The collateral damage was the deaths of 42 people, the burning of 700 structures, the arrest of nearly 5000 people, and almost $1 billion in property damage.

Almost a year after the riots, LAPD Sergeant Stacey Koon and Officer Laurence Powell were convicted by a federal jury for violating the civil rights of Rodney King. The other two officers involved, Timothy Wind and Theodore Briseno, were acquitted. The 1991 *Report of the Independent Commission on the Los Angeles Police Department* (also called the Christopher Commission Report) was published in the aftermath of the notorious beating of Rodney King. The report stated:

> Within minority communities of Los Angeles, there is a widely held view that police misconduct is commonplace. The King beating refocused public attention to long-standing complaints by African Americans, Latinos and Asians that Los Angeles Police Department officers frequently treat minorities differently from whites, more often using disrespectful and abusive language, employing unnecessarily intrusive practices such as the prone-out (prone-out refers to the police practice of placing individuals who are being questioned on the street face down on the pavement), and engaging in use of excessive force when dealing with minorities. (Independent Commission on the LAPD, 1991, p. 70).

As the final pages of this book were being written, it was learned that on June 17, 2012, police in Rialto, California, found Rodney King dead in a swimming pool. He was 47 years old. Foul play was not believed to be involved in his death and the police were investigating the incident as a drowning.

The case of Malice Green is another case to consider. The incident occurred in Detroit in 1992. In this case, four Detroit police officers beat to death a Black motorist named Malice Green. Green was reportedly struck in the head numerous times by one of the officers with a heavy flashlight, which resulted in his death. Four Detroit police officers were charged in Green's death.

How can we forget the horrific case in 1997 of Abner Louima, a Haitian immigrant who was abused at the hands of New York City police officers? Louima suffered a torn bladder and intestine, which required several surgeries to repair the damage after New York police officers beat him and rammed the handle of a toilet plunger into his rectum and mouth at a Brooklyn police station. Several officers pled guilty or were convicted in federal court for violating Louima's civil rights.

The case of Tyisha Miller, a Black teenager who was shot and killed by Riverside, California police in 1998, also sheds light on something terribly wrong. In this case, police officers fired 27 shots at Miller after she was startled awake while sleeping in a disabled car. The teenager allegedly had a gun and, according to the police, reached for it when one of the officers broke the car window. The police claimed Miller fired at them first, but they later recanted that story.

Here is another case of the harsh realities of the American criminal justice system toward African Americans. The year was 2007, and the location was Jena, Louisiana, a small rural community of about 4000 citizens, the majority of whom are White. Six Black Jena high school students were arrested after a school fight in which a White student was beaten and suffered a concussion and multiple bruises. The six Black students were charged with attempted second-degree murder and conspiracy. The Jena Six, as they have come to be known, range in age from 15 to 17.

An all-White jury took less than two days to convict 17-year-old Mychal Bell of aggravated battery and conspiracy. Bell was the first of the Jena Six to go to trial. He was tried in adult court and faced up to 22 years in prison. Bell's lawyers argued that he was too young to be tried as an adult and that a 22-year prison sentence was excessive. There were also allegations that the prosecutors were biased. In fact, the judge was removed from the case for making disparaging remarks about one of the Jena Six defendants. Many of Jena's Black residents related that race has always been an issue in Jena and that it played a role in the harshness of the way the Jena Six's cases were handled. This case culminates from a series of racialized events that dated back several months, when a Black high school student requested permission to sit under a tree in the schoolyard, where usually only White students sat. The following day, three nooses were found hanging from the tree.

In November 2011, Kenneth Chamberlain, Sr., an unarmed 67-year-old African American was shot to death by White Plains New York police officers. Mr. Chamberlain, a retired veteran of the U.S. Marine Corps who suffered from a chronic heart condition and wore a pendant to signal Life Aid, had mistakenly triggered his medical alert, and although he told police he was OK and did not need assistance, he ended up in a 1-hour long standoff with police. Witnesses reported hearing the officers using the "N" word and screaming at Mr. Chamberlain to open the door. Police eventually broke into Chamberlain's apartment and shot him with a stun gun and a beanbag shotgun. The police said they were acting in self-defense because Chamberlain was emotionally disturbed and pulled a knife on them. Only recently did the Westchester District Attorney's Office announce that they would present the case to a grand jury.

You might be thinking that some of these incidents occurred many years ago. Why bring these incidents up now? You may also ask how are they relevant today, and how are they relevant to a discussion of racial profiling? For many racial minorities, this injudicious treatment is very relevant to the contemporary discourse centering on racial profiling. For many, the police represent a troubling part of their history. The police in many states enforced oppressive laws that resulted in devastation for many racial minorities. This not so glamorous portrait of history can assist in a better understanding of the perceptions and experiences of racial minorities with racial biased policing.

The Thin Blue Line

Bittner (1996) argued that the modern police officer emerged as the thin blue line, not against crime, but between Blacks and Whites. He contended that though the police did not create racism, their activities contributed to the magnitude of the gulf between Blacks and Whites.

American police reformers of the early years of the 20th century felt that it was necessary to overcome attitudes of contempt that middle-class citizens held toward the police. As a result, they literally had to sell the police to the people. It was during this timeframe that the police increasingly began to represent the values of the middle-class. Thus, there was an ever-growing police culture that they (the police) are the thin blue line, the last bulwark of defense against the forces of crime and disorder. The police role in turn was to separate the lawbreakers from the law abiders. Three elements are especially notable in regards to the police selling themselves to the middle class as the thin blue line to protect them from the criminal element:

1. At their best, the police employed highly sophisticated techniques of advertising, selling, and of course, public relations.
2. To police the "public" in a public relations sense, meant, essentially, policing middle-class adults and youth ("solid citizens" and their offspring).
3. No attempt was made to improve the "product"; the programs were designed solely to improve the police image; there was little or no provision to recommend or effect needed changes in departmental policy or procedure (Hunter, Baker, & Mayhall, 2004, p. 7).

The thin blue line proved to be counterproductive in policing racial minority communities. The thin blue line has perpetuated a warrior-like culture on the part of the police. The police are portrayed as protecting the middle-class from the offending lower class criminal type, which the middle-class has symbolized as those in the lower classes to engage in criminality and more often than not, they happen to be racial minorities. As a result, the thin blue line has been partly responsible for strained relations with many minority communities.

The War on Drugs

Let me begin this section with a story that unfolds in the small and rural farm town of Tulia, Texas in 1999. Thirty-nine African American residents were rounded up, arrested, and indicted on bogus drug charges (Blakeslee, 2005). An undercover police officer fabricated the drug charges. In the Tulia case, an 18-month drug sting led to the arrest of 46 of the town's 4699 residents.

Coordinated by the Panhandle Regional Narcotics Trafficking Task Force, the operation netted 38 narcotics trafficking convictions where some defendants received sentences as long as 90 years in prison (Post, 2004).

The sting operation earned undercover police officer Tom Coleman the coveted "Outstanding Lawman of the Year" award, presented by the Texas Narcotic Control Program. He was awarded status of Texas's best drug lawman. A Texas State District Court Judge has ruled that all 38 convictions should be overturned due to revelations that Coleman, the sole undercover officer in the sting, fabricated evidence and perjured himself while testifying against the defendants. Twelve of those convicted were immediately released. The remaining defendants were paroled or released since the judge's ruling.

In another story, a Black female who stood in federal court during her sentencing for possession of crack cocaine apparently got the best of federal sentencing Judge Richard A. Gadbois, Jr. when he said:

> This woman doesn't belong in prison for 10 years for what I understand she did. That's just crazy, but there's nothing I can do about it. Had the cocaine in the package been in powder rather than crack form, she would have faced a prison sentence of less than 3 years with no minimum mandatory. (Cole, 1999, p. 142)

Over the past 30 or so years, the War on Drugs, which has been primarily fought in poor and inner city communities, has resulted in significant increases in our nation's prison populations. Prior to the war on drugs being declared, approximately 300,000 inmates were serving time in our nation's prisons. After intensified efforts and enormous budgets were passed in support of the drug war, the corrections population soared to over 2 million. A great many of those locked up for drug crimes are racial minorities (Alexander, 2012).

In federal drug law enforcement, the drug war still seems to be primarily fought against racial minorities, or they are the ones investigated and targeted. In 2009, the U.S. Drug Enforcement Administration (DEA) reported that they had arrests totaling 29,896 individuals that same year. Of these, 20,693 were Black or Hispanic. Put another way, 69 percent were Black or Hispanic. Blacks represented 75 percent of the arrests for crack cocaine and Hispanics represented just over half (55 percent) of all arrests for powder cocaine (U.S. Department of Justice, 2011). Think about this for a moment: 69 percent of the DEA's arrests during 2009 were of Black or Hispanic, mostly male, suspects.

There have been billions of dollars funneled into local, state, and federal law enforcement budgets to fight the war on drugs. The expenditures to criminal justice agencies from the federal government for the war on drugs grew from an annual budget of $2.9 million in 1976 to $18.8 billion in 2002 (Engel

& Calnon, 2004). Federal funding sources such as anti-drug law enforcement grants encouraged local and state law enforcement agencies to intensify their drug enforcement efforts (Guerra-Thompson, 2001).

Money was used to hire additional police officers and to purchase paramilitary tactical equipment and powerful weaponry to effectively fight the war on drugs, and funding for prevention programs was given a lesser priority by police agencies. The author observed this in a small southern police agency in the 1990s. This particular agency asked the author and a colleague to be their outside evaluators as required by the community policing institute. When queried what they had purchased with the federal money they received, evaluators were told that they bought weaponry, body armor, camouflage or dark black military uniforms, and battering rams to make entry during a search warrant. There was no money used for prevention programs in this small community. Law enforcement had in turn produced results such as number of arrests and the amount of drug seizures in order to demonstrate to the grant funding agencies that drug enforcement efforts had been effective. The war was declared not only on drugs, but also on inner city and ghetto areas of the community, which were disproportionately targeted for drug enforcement activities as a matter of routine.

Intensified War Efforts

The get tough on drugs effort was intensified in 1986 with the passage of the Anti-Drug Abuse Act. The purpose of the Anti-Drug Abuse Act was to make it tougher on those who were involved in the illicit drug trade, and to strengthen law enforcement efforts both on the domestic and international front. A clause in the act gave the President of the United States the power to increase tariffs on products from countries that did not cooperate with the U.S. drug war efforts. The Anti-Drug Abuse Act also made it possible for the government to make civil forfeiture seizures of assets from drug offenders including but not limited to houses, cars, money, and other personal property that were deemed to be gained by illegal drug profits. Drug defendants had the burden to prove that they purchased the property from legitimate income and not drug proceeds. The Act also carved out some of the first laws against money laundering. Specifically, money laundering laws were primarily aimed at drug offenders who placed the proceeds of illegal drug sales into the U.S. banking system.

The Federal Anti-Drug Abuse Act significantly increased federal drug penalties. Federal drug sentencing guidelines were intensified, which over time would prove to be devastating on racial minority communities. Sentencing guidelines are used not only by the federal government, but also by many states that followed suit and enacted their own state-level sentencing guidelines.

Sentencing guidelines were established for three primary reasons: (1) to establish a more detailed criteria for sentencing criminal defendants, (2) to guide judges in making their determinations to appropriate sentences, and (3) to limit disparity and discretion on the part of the sentencing judge. Some see an underlying motive to sentencing guidelines. Written explanations are generally required if a judge departs from the guidelines. It is important to point out that until 1986 the federal government had no mandatory minimum sentences for drug offenses.

Perhaps the most controversial part of the Anti-Drug Abuse Act was the clear distinctions in minimum sentencing between offenders who possess powder cocaine and those who possess crack cocaine. In regards to crack cocaine, the U.S. Congress departed from its established kingpin and mid-level dealer categories. In turn, they divided the amounts necessary for powder-cocaine sentences by 100. That is, 50 grams of crack, instead of 5000 grams of powder cocaine, merited a 10-year minimum sentence, and 5 grams of crack, rather than 500 grams of powder, resulted in a 5-year sentence. If an offender were trafficking in 50 grams of powder cocaine, it would carry no mandatory sentence and often resulted in probation.

Think about this for a moment. Under the mandatory sentencing guidelines, an offender who was convicted of being in possession of 5 grams of crack cocaine (roughly the weight of a U.S. nickel coin) would be sentenced to a minimum mandatory federal prison sentence of 5 years, but an offender who was convicted of being in possession of 50 grams of cocaine powder would have no mandatory minimum sentence and probation is very probable.

While the 1986 Anti-Drug Abuse Act made it a federal crime to distribute drugs within 1000 yards of a school, in 1988 the act was expanded to include distribution of drugs within 100 feet of playgrounds, parks, youth recreational centers, neighborhood swimming pools, and video arcades (Gray, 2001).

Not only did this intensified war on drugs have a significant impact on racial minorities, but also the Violent Crime Control and Law Enforcement Act of 1994 proved to be one of the most ambitious and far-reaching crime bills in recent memory, which also proved detrimental for racial minorities. Signed into law in 1994, the act allocated over $30 billion for broad ranging criminal justice programming including the expansion of prisons, imposition of longer prison sentences, hiring what was an initial call for 100,000 more police officers, and funding prevention programs. The Violent Crime Control and Law Enforcement Act greatly increased the punitive actions of federal law enforcement including expanding the federal government's authority to impose the death penalty for certain types of drug distribution and other crimes, and the enactment of "criminal enterprise statues," which called for lengthy prison sentences (Gray, 2001).

In light of these unequal sentencing practices, lawyers argued before the courts that the different penalties for crack and powder cocaine are unconstitutional because of the impact they have on racial minorities. The courts largely rejected these arguments. Similarly, for many years Congress rejected recommendations by the U.S. Sentencing Commission to reduce the disparity between powder and crack cocaine sentences. However, recently the Fair Sentencing Act of 2010 took effect, which addresses the crack and powder cocaine sentencing disparities. In short, 28 grams of crack cocaine will now trigger a 5-year mandatory minimum prison sentence, and 280 grams of crack will trigger a mandatory minimum 10-year sentence. The 5-year mandatory minimum for simple possession of crack cocaine has been eliminated. The data below portrays the drug war efforts over the past few years by the U.S. DEA:

- The DEA arrested 29,896 suspects for drug offenses in 2009, a nearly 10% increase from arrests in 2008.
- From 2000 to 2006, the rate of arrests made by federal law enforcement increased by 8 times the rate of arrests by state and local law enforcement.
- Drug offenders' cases remained the most prevalent at adjudication and sentencing, in prison, and under supervision.
- Cocaine was the most common drug type involved in arrests by DEA in 2009.
- In 2009, marijuana was the most common drug in DEA matters referenced to U.S. attorneys in five border states.
- In 2009, defendants charged with violent (87%), immigration (95%), or drug trafficking (81%) offenses were more likely than other defendants were to be detained.
- Half of all suspects arrested by the DEA were age 31 or younger.
- Suspects arrested for offenses involving cocaine powder and crack cocaine accounted for 38 percent of all arrested by the DEA in 2009 (U.S. Department of Justice, 2011).

Collateral Damage

From 1986 through the next 20 years or so, we saw the industrialized prison complex grow significantly in the United States to close to 2 million persons. Federal and state prison populations soared with scores of inmates sentenced for drug crimes, the majority of whom were Black and Hispanic. The fact is that the majority of offenders sentenced under the crack cocaine guidelines were African American, whereas white offenders made up a much higher portion of those convicted for powder cocaine offenses. To further illustrate this point, roughly 75 percent of those arrested for powder cocaine happen to be White, and 90 percent of those arrested for crack cocaine are Black (Wimsatt, 1999).

Our nation's prisons are full of drug offenders and the majority of those are racial minorities. Look at the sobering data:

- Since 1971, there have been more than 40 million arrests for drug-related offenses. Even though Blacks and Whites have similar levels of drug use, Blacks are ten times as likely to be incarcerated for drug crimes.
- There are more Blacks under correctional control today, in prison or jail, on probation or parole, than were enslaved in 1850, a decade before the Civil War began.
- As of 2004, more African American men were disenfranchised (due to felon disenfranchisement laws) than in 1870, the year the Fifteenth Amendment was ratified prohibiting laws that explicitly deny the right to vote based on race.
- In 2005, 4 out of 5 drug arrests were for possession not trafficking, and 80% of the increase in drug arrests in the 1990s was for marijuana.
- There are 50,000 arrests for low-level marijuana possession a year in New York City, representing one out of every seven cases that turn up in criminal courts. Most of these arrested are Black and Hispanic men (Simmons & Ratigan, 2012).

The war on drugs has not only resulted in the mass incarceration of persons of color, but also many other long-term residual effects. The first as discussed previously is simply the disproportionate incarceration of racial minorities (primarily Blacks and Hispanics). The effects of conviction and incarceration will last in many cases for the rest of these individuals' lives, long after they are released from prison. They lose many of their fundamental rights including the right to vote. They are placed at a serious competitive disadvantage when trying to find work. The mere recording of a conviction on a job application is usually enough to have their application put to the bottom of the stack.

As collateral damage, the family of the offender who may be incarcerated for many years for the simple possession or selling of drugs suffers tremendously. Children are often raised by their mothers or by other family members. This exacerbates impoverished conditions and tears families apart. The constellation of factors associated with incarceration and post-incarceration will place these individuals at a significant disadvantage in trying to desist from their criminality and cope in a society where the deck remains stacked against them.

Policing and the War

As part of the war on drugs, police authorities have often been referred to in inner-city communities as an occupying army. The war on drugs has resulted in an alarming paramilitary presence in these communities. An aggressive paramilitary method of policing the drug war simply perpetuates brutality against the citizenry. Persons targeted as criminals in turn become more violent in their interactions with the police because of the potential for increased harm, while citizens (perhaps seen by the police as a criminal in wait) lose trust in the institution designed to protect them (Paul & Birzer, 2004).

Walker (1994) found that the American police authorities have fought the U.S. war on drugs by using one or more of three primary strategies. These strategies for the most part have impacted poor and racial minority communities, further alienating them socially and economically.

The first strategy, according to Walker, is police crackdowns. Crackdowns are when police authorities saturate small geographic areas of the community for short periods of time and shake things up. In essence, police intensify law enforcement activities in these areas perhaps because they receive intelligence information about drugs or other criminal activity in the area. The police make as many arrests as possible, enforce other types of code violations that may not be enforced as a matter of routine in other parts of the community, and stop anything and anyone that they deem to be suspicious. Inner city and ghetto areas are most often the target of police crackdowns.

The second strategy the police use is to increase the overall level of drug enforcement. Enhanced drug enforcement might be explicitly written into the police agency's short- or long-term goals and objectives. Increasing the overall level of drug enforcement may entail the police beefing up narcotics street enforcement units, undercover units and operations, or the use of special action teams that focus on street level crime and drugs.

Finally, Walker argued that police authorities might incorporate drug enforcement operations into the department's community policing strategy. The underlying motive here may have more to do with selling community policing to the rank-and-file police officer. That is to give the impression that community policing is real and tough police work. The police agency uses intensive street-level drug enforcement efforts as a venue to sell the community-oriented policing strategy to police officers who are already suspicious about the strategy and question its validity as real police work.

The objective of this chapter was to shed light on important factors that underpin racial minorities' perceptions of racial profiling in the United States. How racial minority citizens experience and give meaning to racial profiling are framed in the proper historical context. A history of racial discrimination and intolerance by the criminal justice system and police authorities has to be taken into account in any treatment such as this. I started this chapter by making the argument that in order to engage in a more constructive discussion about racial profiling, it is important to take a look at those factors in our history that perpetuate distrust that many racial minority citizens have of the police and the larger criminal justice system. In essence, why they remain suspicious of an institution, a criminal justice system, which in theory is there to protect those who need it most. I ask that you keep this in mind as you read the stories in this book of how racial minorities experienced racial profiling.

Discussion Questions

1. How does race coding lead to stereotyping and to a socially constructed symbolic racial minority offender?
2. What are some of the inherent problems with controlling for the variable of race in social science research?
3. How do historical injustices play a role in the perceptions of racial profiling by racial minority citizens?
4. What is the thin blue line and why is it problematic for police relations with the minority community?
5. How has the war on drugs impacted perceptions of racial profiling?

References

Alexander, M. (2012). *The new Jim Crow: Mass incarceration in the age of colorblindness*. New York: The New Press.

Barlow, D.E., & Hickman-Barlow, M. (2000). *Police in a multicultural society: An American story*. Prospect Heights, IL: Waveland Press.

Bittner, E. (1996). *Aspects of police work*. Boston: MA: Northeastern University Press.

Blakeslee, N. (2005). *Tulia: Race, cocaine, and corruption in a small Texas town*. New York: Public Affairs.

Carlson, D.K. (2004). Racial proofing seen as evasive, unjust. Wilmington, DE: Gallup Organization. Retrieved from http://www.gallup.com/poll/12406/racial-profiling-seen-as-pervasive-unjust.aspx

Center on Juvenile and Criminal Justice (2002). *Reducing disproportionate minority confinement: The Multnomah, County Oregon success story and its implications*. Center on Juvenile and Criminal Justice. Retrieved from http://www.cjcj.org/files/Reducing_ Disproportionate.pdf

Cole, D. (1999). *No equal justice: Race and class in the American criminal justice system*. New York: The New Press.

Engel, R.S., & Calnon, J.M. (2004). Examining the influence of drivers' characteristics during traffic stops with police: Results from a national survey. *Justice Quarterly*, 21(1), 49–90.

Federal Bureau of Prisons (2012). Quick facts about the bureau of prisons. Retrieved from www.bop.gov.

Fogelson, R.M. (1968). From resentment to confrontation: The police, the Negroes, and the outbreaks of the 1960s' riots. *Political Science Quarterly, 83*(2), 217–247.

Genovesse, E.D. (1976). *Roll Jordan roll: The world the slaves made.* New York: Vintage Books.

Gray, J.P. (2001). *Why our drug laws have failed and what we can do about it: A judicial indictment of the war on drugs.* Philadelphia: Temple University Press.

Guerra-Thompson, S. (2001). Did the war on drugs die with the birth of the war on terrorism? A closer look at civil forfeiture and racial profiling after 9/11. *Federal Sentencing Reporter* 14(3-4), 123–131.

Hadden, S.E. (2001). *Slave patrols: Law and violence in Virginia and the Carolinas.* Cambridge, MA: Harvard University Press.

Hendrickson, P. (2003). *Sons of Mississippi: A story of race and its legacy.* New York: Alfred A. Knopf.

Huie, W.B. (2000). *Three lives for Mississippi.* Jackson, MS: University Press of Mississippi.

Hunter, R.D., Barker, T., & Mayhall, P.D. (2004). *Police community relations and the administration of justice* (6th ed.). Upper Saddle, River, NJ: Prentice Hall.

Independent Commission on the Los Angeles Police Department (1991). Report of the Independent Commission on the Los Angeles Police Department (Christopher Commission Report).

James, A. (2008). Making sense of race and racial classification. In T. Zuberi and E. Bonilla-Silva (Eds.), *White logic white methods.* New York: Rowman & Littlefield Publishers, Inc., pp. 31–46.

Katz, W.L. (1995). *Eyewitness: A living documentary of the African American contribution to American history.* New York: Touchstone.

King, R. (2012). *The riot within: My journey from rebellion to redemption.* New York: Harper.

Leiber, M.J. (2002). Disproportionate minority confinement (DMC) of youth: An analysis of state and federal efforts to address the issue. *Crime & Delinquency, 48*, 3–44. doi: 10.1177/001112870204800101.

Lynch, J.R. (1968). *Facts of reconstruction.* New York: Arno Press.

Mauer, M. (1999). Race to incarcerate. New York: New Press.

Moss, E.Y. (1990). African Americans and the administration of justice. In Wornie, L. Reed (Ed.), *Assessment of the status of African Americans.* Boston: University of Massachusetts, William Monroe Trotter Institute, pp.79–86.

Nunnelly, W.A. (1991). *Bull Connor.* Tuscaloosa: University of Alabama Press.

Ogletree, C.J., Prosser, M., Smith, A., & Talley, W. (1995). *Beyond the Rodney King story: An investigation of police conduct in minority communities.* Boston, MA: Northeastern University Press.

Patterson, O. (1998). Rituals of blood: The consequences of slavery in two American centuries. New York: Basic Civitas Books.

Paul, J., & Birzer, M.L. (2004). Images of power: A critical analysis of the militarization of police uniforms and messages of service. *Free Inquiry in Creative Sociology, 32*, 121–128.

Pickett, J.T., Chiricos, T., Golden, K.M., & Gertz, M. (2012). Reconsidering the relationship between perceived neighborhood racial composition and Whites' perceptions of victimization risk: Do racial stereotypes matter? *Criminology, 50*(1), 155–186.

Pitts Walter, M. (1992). *Mississippi challenge.* New York: Bradbury Press.

Poe-Yamagata, E. (2009). *And justice for some: Differential treatment of minority youth in the justice system.* Darby, PA: Diane Publishing Co.

Post, L. (2004). Trouble in Tulia still resounds: As trial looms, role of solos emerges. *National Law Journal, 26*(31).

Puzzanchera, C., & Adams, B. (2011). Juvenile arrests 2009. *Juvenile offenders and victims: National report series.* Washington, DC: U.S. Department of Justice. Retrieved from ojjdp.gov

Quillian, L., & Pager, D. (2001). Black neighbors, higher crime? The role of racial stereotypes in the evaluation of neighborhood crime. *American Journal of Sociology, 107,* 117–167.

Quillian, L., & Pager, D. (2010). Estimating risk: Stereotype amplification and the perceived risk of criminal victimization. *Social Psychology Quarterly, 73,* 79–104.

Report of the National Advisory Commission on Civil Disorder (1968). *Kerner Report.* Washington, DC: United States Government Printing Office.

Russell-Brown, K. (2009). *The color of justice* (2nd ed.). New York: New York University Press.

Simmons, R., & Ratigan, D. (2012). *Occupy the dream: The mathematics of racism.* Justice Policy Institute. Retrieved from http://www.justicepolicy.org/news/3463

United States Department of Justice (2011). *Federal justice statistics, 2009.* Washington, DC: Office of Justice Programs (NCJ 234184).

Wadman, R.C., & Allison, W.T. (2004). *To protect and serve: A history of police in America.* Upper Saddle, NJ: Prentice Hall.

Walker, S. (1980). *Popular justice: A history of American criminal justice.* New York: Oxford University Press.

Walker, S. (1994). *Sense and non-sense about crime and drugs* (3rd ed.). Belmont, CA: Wadsworth Publishing.

Walker, S. (1999). *The police in America: An introduction* (3rd ed.). New York: McGraw-Hill.

Warren, P.Y. (2010). The continuing significance of race: An analysis across two levels of policing. *Social Sciences Quarterly, 91*(4), 1025–1039.

Williams, H., & Murphy, P.V. (1990). *The evolving strategies of police: A minority view.* Washington, DC: National Institute of Justice. Retrieved from https://www.ncjrs.gov/ pdffiles1/nij/121019.pdf

Wilson, W.J. (2009). *More than just race: Being Black and poor in the inner city.* New York: W.W. Norton and Company.

Wimsatt, W.U. (1999). *No more prisons.* Suffolk, NY: Soft Skull Press.

Wyatt-Brown, B. (1982). *Southern honor: ethics and behavior in the old south.* New York: Oxford University Press.

What about Congress, Data Collection, and the Court?

3

Larry King: "Have you ever been racially profiled?"
Colin Powell: "Yes, many times."

**Larry King interview with former Secretary of State Colin Powell,
July 28, 2009, CNN Larry King Live**

Introduction

This chapter is concerned with three issues: (1) how the U.S. legal system has dealt with allegations of racial profiling, (2) an examination of the issues that center on police stop data collection, and (3) the *Wren v. United States* Supreme Court decision. The chapter begins with an overview of proposed House Bill 118, which was introduced by Representative John Conyers of Michigan to the United States House of Representatives on January 7, 1997. The bill was titled the *Traffic Stops Statistics Act*, and it was the first known of its kind written to address racial profiling. The bill called for the United States Attorney General to carry out a nationwide study of traffic stops of motorists by U.S. police authorities. It passed with bipartisan support in the house and was referred to the Senate subcommittee where it stalled and never became law.

The second part of the chapter examines police stop data collection efforts and methods. The chapter culminates in a discussion of what many observers believe to be one of the most troubling cases decided by the Supreme Court. The *Whren v. United States (1996)* Supreme Court decision has had a significant impact on allegations of racial profiling. Do bad cases make good law? That is exactly what is argued in this chapter. It has been said that the *Whren* case was not the most ideal for the Court to make a finding of racial profiling.

While you read this chapter, you should ask two very important questions. Will the collection of police stop data result in the identification of suspected patterns of racial biased policing? If suspected racial biased policing practices are identified, will collecting police stop data be the panacea to end these practices? These important questions are taken up in this chapter.

Congressional Mandates

In 1997, United States Representative John Conyers of Michigan sponsored and introduced the *Traffic Stops Statistics Act* to the 105th Congress. The purpose of this bill was to mandate the collection of several categories of data on law enforcement traffic stops. The bill called for the United States Attorney General to take the lead role in data collection efforts. First, the Attorney General would perform an initial analysis of existing law enforcement stop data. This would include complaints alleging, and other information concerning, traffic stops motivated by race and other biases. Second, the collection of specified data on traffic stops from a nationwide sample of jurisdictions, including data on traffic infractions, identifying characteristics of the drivers, immigration status questions and inquiries, searches instituted and alleged criminal behavior that justified the searches, items seized, and citations or arrests resulting from the stops would be required. Last, the Attorney General would be required to report the results to Congress and to make the report available to the general public. The bill, along with several amended versions, failed to become law.

A summary of a revised bill titled the *End Racial Profiling Act of 2001*, introduced to the 107th Congress by Representative Conyers contained the following provisions:

1. Prohibits any law enforcement agency or agent from engaging in racial profiling.
2. Authorizes the United States, or an individual injured by racial profiling, to bring a civil action for declaratory or injunctive relief to enforce this prohibition.
3. Specifies proof that the routine investigatory activities of law enforcement agents in a jurisdiction have had a disparate impact on racial or ethnic minorities shall constitute prima facie evidence of a violation.
4. Authorizes the court to allow a prevailing plaintiff, other than the United States, reasonable attorneys' fees as part of the costs, including expert fees.
5. Requires federal law enforcement agencies to: (a) maintain adequate policies and procedures designed to eliminate racial profiling; and (b) cease existing practices that encourage racial profiling.
6. Directs that any application by a state or governmental unit for funding under a covered program include a certification that such unit and any agency to which it is redistributing program funds: (a) maintains adequate policies and procedures designed to eliminate racial profiling; and (b) has ceased existing practices that encourage racial profiling.

7. Authorizes the Attorney General to make grants to states, law enforcement agencies and other governmental units, Indian tribal governments, or other public and private entities to develop and implement best practice devices and systems to ensure race-neutral administration of justice.
8. Directs the Attorney General to submit to Congress a report on racial profiling by federal, state, and local law enforcement agencies (H.R. 2074, 2001).

Listed next are specific findings that were submitted as part of H.R. 2074 (*End Racial Profiling Act of 2001*). These findings were introduced into the U.S. House of Representatives in 2001.

1. The vast majority of law enforcement agents discharges their duties professionally, without bias, and protects the safety of their communities.
2. The use by police officers of race, ethnicity, or national origin in deciding which persons should be subject to traffic stops, stops and frisks, questioning, searches, and seizures is a problematic law enforcement tactic. Statistical evidence from across the country demonstrates that such racial profiling is a real and measurable phenomenon (H.R. 2074, 2001).
3. As of November 15, 2000, the Department of Justice had 14 publicly noticed, ongoing, pattern or practice investigations involving allegations of racial profiling, and had filed five pattern and practice lawsuits involving allegations of racial profiling, with four of those cases resolved through consent decrees.
4. A large majority of individuals subjected to stops and other enforcement activities based on race, ethnicity, or national origin are found to be law-abiding citizens and therefore racial profiling is not an effective means to uncover criminal activity.
5. A 2001 Department of Justice report on citizen-police contacts in 1999 found that, although African Americans and Hispanics were more likely to be stopped and searched, they were less likely to be in possession of contraband. On average, searches and seizures of African American drivers yielded evidence only 8 percent of the time, searches and seizures of Hispanic drivers yielded evidence only 10 percent of the time, and searches and seizures of White drivers yielded evidence 17 percent of the time.
6. A 2000 General Accounting Office report on the activities of the U.S, Customs Service during fiscal year 1998 found that Black women who were U.S. citizens were 9 times more likely than White women who were U.S. citizens to be X-rayed after being frisked or patted down and, on the basis of X-ray results, Black women who were U.S.

citizens were less than half as likely as White women who were U.S. citizens to be found carrying contraband. In general, the report found that the patterns used to select passengers for more intrusive searches resulted in women and minorities being selected at rates that were not consistent with the rates of finding contraband.

7. Current local law enforcement practices, such as ticket and arrest quotas, and similar management practices, may have the unintended effect of encouraging law enforcement agents to engage in racial profiling.

8. Racial profiling harms individuals subjected to it because they experience fear, anxiety, humiliation, anger, resentment, and cynicism when they are unjustifiably treated as criminal suspects. By discouraging individuals from traveling freely, racial profiling impairs both interstate and intrastate commerce.

9. Racial profiling damages law enforcement and the criminal justice system as a whole by undermining public confidence and trust in the police, the courts, and the criminal law.

10. Racial profiling violates the Equal Protection Clause of the Constitution. Using race, ethnicity, or national origin as a proxy for criminal suspicion violates the constitutional requirement that police and other government officials accord to all citizens the equal protection of the law.

11. Racial profiling is not adequately addressed through suppression motions in criminal cases for two reasons. First, the Supreme Court held, in *Whren v. United States*, 517 U.S. 806 (1996), that the racially discriminatory motive of a police officer in making an otherwise valid traffic stop does not warrant the suppression of evidence. Second, since most stops do not result in the discovery of contraband, there is no criminal prosecution and no evidence to suppress.

12. Current efforts by state and local governments to eradicate racial profiling and redress the harm it causes, while laudable, have been limited in scope and insufficient to address this national problem (H.R. 2074, 2001).

Some police authorities expressed opposition to the *Law Enforcement Traffic and Statistics Act* and its subsequent bills. According to these police groups, such a mandate would place an unfair burden on the police and would lengthen the time of many traffic stops. In addition, they argued that collecting information on personal characteristics would likely be considered highly offensive by many individuals. If an officer is uncertain of someone's ethnic background, for example, the officer would have to ask for this information and an uncomfortable situation could result (Harris, 2002).

The bill would not have required law enforcement agencies to greatly alter their practices. In fact, the bill presented several opportunities for police agencies. For example, if the bill would have passed, it had the potential to improve police–community relations in the sense that it would send a message to the community that police authorities have every intention of identifying and addressing biased policing practices. The bill called for provisions that fund law enforcement agencies during the initial startup of data collection and analysis. A contemptuous argument made by police authorities centered on their concern that they would encumber substantial costs relating to the collection and analysis of stop data. This is a valid argument. However, it is important to note that many agencies have demonstrated that they can design a comprehensive program of data collection and analysis of police stop data in a cost effective manner (Harris, 2002). It is certain that the collection of stop data will involve additional costs on the part of the law enforcement agencies (Grogger and Ridgway, 2006). This could be problematic in times where the police are increasingly asked to do more with less.

Collectively, the stop racial profiling bills introduced by Representative Conyers also included provisions that would ensure the confidentiality of citizens and law enforcement officers. Their identities would never be known. Numerous civil and human rights groups supported the bill. Many of these groups have long suggested that racial biased policing occurs frequently in minority communities and that America has turned a cold shoulder in dealing with the problem. A coalition of human and civil rights representatives crafted a letter, which was sent to the U.S. Senate urging them to pass the racial profiling legislation that mandates a program of police stop data collection. They wrote, "If the data is collected and used properly, it would go a long way towards helping millions of Americans regain the pride and trust in our law enforcement representatives that has been so sorely tested over the years" (American Civil Liberties Union, 2000, p. 1).

Despite the failure of the *Traffic Stops and Statistics Act* and its subsequent bills to become law, many individual states have passed their own data collection legislation. Moreover, many law enforcement agencies have arranged to voluntarily collect stop data. For example, the police departments in Miami-Dade, Florida, and San Diego and San Jose, California, voluntarily perform data collection, while the Pittsburgh police and the Maryland state police also collect racial data on police stops because of lawsuits. According to the Data Collection Resource Center at Northeastern University, all but just a few states are currently collecting police stop data (Data Collection Resource Center, n.d.).

What follows is a summary of a few selected states that have begun to collect racial data on motorist stops by police authorities. This is provided to give the reader an idea of how different states have approached the collection of stop data among their law enforcement agencies.

Missouri

In 2000, in an effort to identify and eradicate racially biased police practices, the State of Missouri passed legislation (Missouri Revised Statutes 590.650) that requires law enforcement officers to record specific data regarding motor vehicle stops. Missouri's state law requires all law enforcement officers throughout the state to report specific information including a driver's race for each vehicle stop. Law enforcement authorities are required to submit the data to the Attorney General. In turn, the Attorney General is required to compile the data and report to the Governor no later than June 1 of each year. There is a provision in Missouri's legislation that allows the Governor to withhold state funds for any agency that does not comply with the law. The Missouri legislation specifically requires law enforcement officers to record the following information on each motorist stop.

1. The age, gender, and race or minority group of the individual stopped.
2. The reasons for the stop.
3. Whether a search was conducted as a result of the stop.
4. If a search was conducted, whether the individual consented to the search, the probable cause for the search, whether the person was searched, whether the person's property was searched, and the duration of the search.
5. Whether any contraband was discovered in the course of the search and the type of any contraband discovered.
6. Whether any warning or citation was issued as a result of the stop.
7. If a warning or citation was issued, the violation charged or warning provided.
8. Whether an arrest was made as a result of either the stop or the search.
9. If an arrest was made, the crime charged.
10. The location of the stop.

Texas

In 2001, the Texas Racial Profiling Bill (SB 1704) passed and was signed into law. At the time, it was touted as being one of the toughest pieces of legislation passed up to that time in the United States (Applied Research Center, 2001). The bill requires that traffic citations include additional data on ethnicity and specific information on searches. The bill also calls on police authorities to implement a process for gathering citizen complaints on racial profiling. Mandated data collection was not intended to be a solution to racial profiling in Texas, but rather a first step in a long-term goal to eliminate racially biased police practices. The legislation was intended to provide a strong data-based tool that civil rights organizations could use to effectively advocate for more specific policy responses to racial profiling.

Phase II of the bill, also passed in 2001 (SB 1074), requires police authorities to report expanded information on all stops. For example, data is collected on pedestrian and traffic stops, whether or not a citation was issued, probable cause for conducting a search, if an arrest resulted from the search, and if contraband was seized. The Texas bill 1074 contains provisions to establish education and training programs (Applied Research Center, 2001). In all, the Texas legislation has three objectives:

1. Specifically prohibits racial profiling by police officers.
2. Mandates that each law enforcement agency in the state adopt a detailed written policy on racial profiling.
3. Requires law enforcement agencies to collect race data for traffic stops and creates a process by which citizens can file complaints about being targeted through racial profiling (Texas Senate Bill 1704, 2001).

Kansas

The State of Kansas recently initiated legislation that calls for the collection and analysis of police stop data. Specifically, the Kansas statute calls for the Governor, with the assistance of the Attorney General and the Kansas Commission on Peace Officers' Standards, to develop a request for a proposal for a system to collect and report statistics relating to the race, ethnicity, gender, age, and residency by county and state of those who come in contact with law enforcement activities (Kansas State Statute 22-4604). Proposals that are submitted must contain the following:

1. A system to collect data on a statistically significant sample of those persons who are arrested while operating a motor vehicle, and those who are stopped by law enforcement officers while a pedestrian. The sample must report the race, ethnicity, gender, age, and residency by county and state of such persons who were stopped.
2. A schedule and plan of implementation, including training.
3. Other factors that may be relevant to law enforcement officers in stopping or arresting individuals.
4. Civilian complaints received by law enforcement agencies alleging bias based on race, ethnicity, gender, age, or residency by county or state,
5. A survey of policies of law enforcement agencies relating to the investigation of complaints based on alleged race, ethnicity, gender, and age or residence bias.

At the conclusion of the study, the Governor and the Attorney General will make recommendations to the legislature if a data collection and reporting system should be expanded to other law enforcement agencies and whether the system should be made permanent. The Governor and Attorney General are also required under the statue to recommend improvements to law enforcement training and operations to address racial, ethnic, gender, and age or residency bias.

Washington State

In 2002, the State of Washington legislature passed Revised Code of Washington (RCW) Chapter 43.101, Section 43.101.410. The RCW addresses racial profiling policies, training, the complaint review process, and data collection and reporting. It reads:

1. Local law enforcement agencies shall comply with the recommendations of the Washington association of sheriffs and police chiefs regarding racial profiling, as set forth under (a) through (f) of this subsection. Local law enforcement agencies shall:
   (a) Adopt a written policy designed to condemn and prevent racial profiling.
   (b) Review and audit their existing procedures, practices, and training to ensure that they do not enable or foster the practice of racial profiling.
   (c) Continue training to address the issues related to racial profiling. Officers should be trained in how to better interact with persons they stop so that legitimate police actions are not misperceived as racial profiling.
   (d) Ensure that they have in place a citizen complaint review process that can adequately address instances of racial profiling. The process must be accessible to citizens and must be fair. Officers found to be engaged in racial profiling must be held accountable through the appropriate disciplinary procedures within each department.
   (e) Work with the minority groups in their community to appropriately address the issue of racial profiling.
   (f) Within fiscal constraints, collect demographic data on traffic stops and analyze that data to ensure that racial profiling is not occurring.
2. The Washington association of sheriffs and police chiefs shall coordinate with the criminal justice training commission to ensure that issues related to racial profiling are addressed in basic law enforcement training and offered in regional training for in-service law enforcement officers at all levels.

3. Local law enforcement agencies shall report all information required under this section to the Washington association of sheriffs and police chiefs.

Connecticut

The State of Connecticut recently passed Public Act 03-160 (The Alvin W. Penn Racial Profiling Prohibition Act). The law prohibits racial profiling and mandates the collection of police stop data from every police department within the state. It also mandates that every police agency establish policies prohibiting traffic stops and searches of motorists based solely on race, color, gender, age, ethnicity, and sexual orientation. The law requires that every police department in Connecticut collect and record the following data on traffic stops:

1. The number of people stopped for traffic violations.
2. Their identifying characteristics (age, race, color, ethnicity, and gender), based on the officer's perception and observations.
3. The alleged traffic violation that led to the stop.
4. Whether any arrest was made, search conducted, or warning or citation issued.
5. Any additional information police officers consider appropriate, provided this does not include any other identifying information about the person such as the person's operator's license number, name, or address (Alvin W. Penn Racial Profiling Prohibition Act, 2003).

The Alvin W. Penn Racial Profiling Prohibition Act requires that all police agencies submit an annual report on profiling prohibition data to the Chief State's Attorney and the African American Affairs Commission. However, in 2010, only 27 of the state's 169 police agencies submitted reports (Carter, 2011). There is currently an amendment (Bill 1230) before the Senate that would amend the law, in part, by mandating that police give drivers a copy of the form they use to collect the information. It would add fiscal penalties to departments found to be in violation of the law.

New York

Bill A2288-2011 is currently pending in the New York Senate. If passed, the bill will strengthen existing legislation prohibiting racial profiling by law enforcement authorities. This bill mandates the collection of data on traffic stops and creates a cause of action based on racial or ethnic profiling. A summary of the pending New York legislation is as follows:

1. Prohibits law enforcement agencies and law enforcement officers from engaging in racial or ethnic profiling.
2. Requires every law enforcement agency to promulgate and adopt procedures for reviewing complaints of racial or ethnic profiling and taking corrective measures. A copy of each complaint and a written summary of the disposition must be forwarded to the division of criminal justice services.
3. Requires each law enforcement agency to collect and maintain data with respect to traffic stops and persons patted down, frisked, and searched.
4. Requires every law enforcement agency to compile the data collected and forward an annual report to the division of criminal justice services by March 1 of each year.
5. Requires the division of criminal justice services in consultation with the Attorney General to promulgate necessary forms.
6. Requires every law enforcement agency to make documents required by this bill available to the Attorney General within seven business days of a demand.
7. Requires every law enforcement agency to provide all data collected from traffic stops to the division of criminal justice services. The division shall publish an annual report on law enforcement traffic stops without revealing the identity of any individuals.
8. States that inaction for injunctive relief and/or for damages may be brought by the Attorney General on behalf of the people against a law enforcement agency that has engaged in racial or ethnic profiling. A court may award costs and reasonable attorney fees to a prevailing plaintiff.
9. States that an action for injunctive relief and/or for damages may be brought by an individual who has been the subject of racial profiling against a law enforcement agency that has engaged in racial or ethnic profiling. A court may award costs and reasonable attorney fees to a prevailing plaintiff.

Police Stop Data

Earlier in this chapter, I asked you to consider two questions: Will the collection of police stop data identify patterns of racial profiling? Is the collection of police stop data a panacea? Take a moment to think about how you would answer these two questions. After you have completed reading the next section on data collection, think again about how you would answer these questions.

According to Northeastern University's Racial Profiling Data Collection Resources Center, racial profiling data is tracking the race, ethnicity, and gender of those who are stopped and/or searched by the police (www.racial-profilinganalysis.neu.edu). The collection of police stop data by law enforcement agencies varies from one agency to the next. Police executives reading this book are encouraged to review what kinds of data other law enforcement agencies are collecting and the protocol they use to collect it. If a data collection system is effective in one agency, examination of the components of that system can be adapted to your agency. It is also a wise practice to form a committee comprised of police personnel along with members of the community when designing data collection procedures.

The community's input, especially the minority community, can be invaluable. It also sends the message that the police organization is serious and places high value on their input. Obtaining views from the citizenry on racially biased police practices is an essential step for the police executive. In the past, this has been problematic because most dialogue between the police and community activist groups about racial profiling were often accusatory on the part of the community groups. This resulted in the police taking a defensive posture, which further exacerbated an already tenuous dialogue. Harris (2002) recommended extending an invitation to leaders to serve on the committee from groups such as the ACLU, the NAACP, and other civil rights and social justice groups.

Police authorities are very good at collecting data. Every time a police officer responds to the scene of a crime, he or she collects information (data) about the victim, suspects, witnesses, the time and location of occurrence, and other pertinent data. This information is then documented within an official police report, which is completed by the reporting officer. The police report becomes an official record. It will be read by investigators and, depending on the case, may potentially be read by attorneys, judges, probation and parole officers, and other actors in the criminal justice system. The point to make here is that collecting traffic stop data should not be that challenging for police authorities to take on. Ask any police officer and he or she will most likely tell you that writing reports is a substantial part of the job.

Police authorities may find it beneficial to approach the collection of stop data as a venue to more effectively understand their practices, to identify areas that would benefit from a change in standard operating procedure, and as a mechanism to send the message to the community that the police organization is serious about addressing biased policing practices. Moreover, it is important to ensure correct information is being collected on police stops that will assist police management in discerning if a police practice appears to be biased or disproportionally affecting a certain group. The U.S. Department of Justice published a comprehensive resource guide on racial profiling data systems (Ramirez, McDevitt, & Farrell, 2000). The guide offers a goldmine of information for law enforcement agencies, which serves the purpose of assisting law enforcement executives as they prepare a procedure for data collection. While the type of data that is collected among law enforcement agencies will vary somewhat, it will typically include the following:

1. The date and time of the stop including the duration of the stop.
2. The reason for the stop.
3. Number of occupants in the vehicle.
4. Was there a traffic citation or a written/verbal warning issued?
5. The race or ethnicity of the driver (based on the officer's observation).
6. The age and gender of the driver.
7. The year, make, and model of the vehicle.
8. The tag number.
9. Was the vehicle searched? If so, what if anything was found?
10. Was the driver arrested? If so, what were the charges?

The collection of police stop data has the potential to address several equally important issues. To start, data collection will provide the information that may potentially enable police and community leaders to better understand their policing activities. With this understanding, it is believed that police authorities will be in an advantageous position to examine and revamp policing strategies based on effectiveness, reconfigure deployment of police resources, and take other necessary measures.

Collecting data on police stops is inclusive of both the collection of the numbers and objective analysis of the data, which is often done through a partnership between the police department and outside experts. Data collection allows researchers and practitioners alike to gauge the proportionality of traffic stops based on racial factors. While recognizing the potential benefits of data collection, it is also important to point out some inherent shortcomings.

Simply collecting race-based data alone may do little to assist a law enforcement agency in answering questions about its practices. It is important to keep in mind that simply relying on aggregated data to identify disparate police stops of one race or another does not in and of itself substantiate that racial profiling is occurring (Liederbach et al., 2007). In order to make such a claim, additional data is required. For example, it would be important to have information on the use of discretion on the part of the officers prior to making a stop where racial profiling is alleged. In other words, was discretion involved, and if so, what were the circumstances centering on the discretion?

Simply relying on aggregated data may be problematic because of the nature of nondiscretionary police action. For example, suppose that a police officer stops a motorist after the motorist nearly caused an accident as the result of failing to stop at a red traffic signal light. After the stop, the officer determines that the motorist, a 24-year-old African American male, may be under the influence of alcohol because of an open beer bottle sitting in the center console, along with a strong odor of alcohol. While the officer is seizing the beer bottle, he observes a small baggie of what he believes to be cocaine on the passenger's side floorboard. The police officer arrests the driver. Given the facts of this hypothetical case, it would be difficult to substantiate a claim of racial profiling. This, of course, is one of the potential shortcomings when solely examining aggregated police stop data. In many cases, aggregated stop data does not tell the whole story.

Law enforcement authorities have long argued that after the data is collected they must arrange for the analysis and interpretation of what the data means. This can be costly, especially in an era of budget shortfalls and doing more with less. Furthermore, the analysis process may lead to more questions than answers, which can be frustrating for both the police and the community.

One other shortcoming as perceived by law enforcement authorities centers on the perceptions of law enforcement officers themselves. If law enforcement officers believe they are being monitored, they may disengage from police activity. In other words, officers would selectively reduce their traffic stops in order to avoid any behavior that might be perceived as racially biased. This could potentially have a devastating impact on public safety (Ward, 2002). Indeed, several cities that initiated data collection policies experienced reductions in the number of stops of and citations issued to the motoring public. For example, "the city of Houston and the states of North Carolina, Connecticut, and Missouri experienced significant reductions in the number of traffic citations issued and the number of stops made after data collection went into effect" (Ward, 2002, p. 734).

Some have questioned data collection systems that rely on police officers themselves to accurately report data from their stops. Ward (2002) expressed concern about relying on data provided by police officers used for identifying racial biased police practices. It will be crucial for police agencies to implement systems that have checks and balances built into the collection process in order to ensure the reliability of the data recorded.

Some national law enforcement organizations have approached data collection with caution. The IACP (International Association of Chiefs of Police) believes that data collection can play a role in reducing the incidence of biased enforcement actions. However, they do issue one caveat: In order reduce the incidence of biased enforcement actions, and to have reliable data to guide police protocol, it is imperative to ensure that data is being collected and analyzed in an impartial and methodologically sound fashion.

The collection and analysis of police stop data is one of several important steps in the investigation of possible biased police practices. Like any data in social science research, it is critical that police stop data be collected and analyzed using a scientific and reliable method. Not only should the researcher strive for reliable data, but also the data must be valid. If questionable data is collected and analyzed or if the methodology is flawed, the subsequent analysis will produce invalid results and thus be meaningless for future research and practice. It is also important that data collection and analysis be carried out according to a well-conceived plan that will ensure its validity. Statistical validity is an important objective to meet when analyzing police stop data. Statistical validity means that the researcher has chosen the correct statistical procedure and that the assumptions behind its use have been fully met (Neuman, 2012).

In addition to ensuring statistical validity, the findings from the analysis of police stop data must have both practical utility and political credibility (Walker, 2003). The findings have to be practical because if evidence of racially biased policing is discovered, it should point police authorities to effective solutions. Likewise, the collection and analysis must be politically credible. That is, it must answer the hard-pressed questions posed by the most incredulous community observers and activists. Many police executives grapple with how to best be politically credible. Unfortunately, some critics of the police will remain suspicious of the motives of the police in spite of their efforts to collect and analyze police stop data.

It may be helpful to offer a straightforward example in order to exemplify the complexities that undergird the collection and analysis of police stop data. Let us suppose that we have collected police stop data in a preselected 10 square block neighborhood. The objective of the data collection effort is to discern whether African American drivers are disproportionally stopped and ticketed. The data consists of traffic citations issued by the local police department. Assume that we were granted unlimited access to these data.

In the next step, a count was made of the race of the drivers who received citations over three months. Did more African American motorists receive traffic citations when compared to White citizens? Do you think the answer to this question will provide insight on racially biased policing? The short answer is no. The answer to this question tells us very little about the prevalence of biased policing. In fact, this hypothetical research raises more questions than answers. For one, it would be beneficial to have a benchmark against which the data can be compared. Second, the results only indicate how many citizens received traffic citations, and not the number who were actually stopped. There may have been 80 African Americans actually stopped by police authorities and only 40 received traffic citations. Moreover, the results of this hypothetical study does not inform us about discretionary police decision making after the stop was made. For example, how many motorists were searched after the stop and why were they searched? How many African American drivers were searched compared with White drivers? What were the results of the searches? Still other questions emerge. What are the traffic patterns in this particular neighborhood? What are the racial characteristics of persons driving each day in these neighborhoods? Do these racial characteristics change at different times throughout the day? Having the answers to these questions would be germane to any research that centers on racially biased policing.

The Racial Profiling Data Collection Resource Center at Northeastern University lists the following noteworthy advantages and disadvantages of police data collection. They report that data collection efforts:

1. Send a strong message to the community that the department is against racial profiling and that racial profiling is inconsistent with effective policing and equal protection.
2. Build trust and respect for the police in the communities they serve.
3. Provide departments with information about the types of stops being made by officers, the proportion of police time spent on high-discretion stops, and the results of such stops.
4. Help shape and develop training programs to educate officers about racial profiling and interactions with the community.
5. Enable the development of police and community dialogue to assess the quality and quantity of police-citizen encounters.
6. Allay community concerns about the activities of police.
7. Identify potential police misconduct and deter it, when implemented as part of a comprehensive early warning system.
8. Retain autonomous officer discretion and allow for flexible responses in different situations.

Disadvantages of a data collection system include the following:

1. Concerns about extra-budgetary expenditures associated with collecting data.
2. Developing a benchmark against which the data can be compared.
3. The potential burden an improved data collection procedure will have on individual officers in the course of a normal shift.
4. The potential for police disengagement from their duties, which may lead to officers scaling back on the number of legitimate stops.
5. The challenge of ensuring that officers will fully comply with a directive to collect stop data.
6. Ensuring that data is recorded on all stops made, and that the data collected is correct.
7. The difficulty of determining the race or ethnicity of the persons stopped.
8. Once data is collected and analyzed, the difficulty of making a definite conclusion about whether racial profiling exists, as this question requires more than a "yes" or "no" answer (Data Collection Resource Center, n.d.).

Data Collection Methods

From the earliest research centering on racially biased policing, there has been a fair amount of discussion on how to best study this complex phenomenon. For many, collecting police stop data is the answer to identifying patterns of biased-based policing. Collecting police stop data entails having police officers record pertinent information about each traffic stop they make during a tour of duty. The information that is required to be reported by officers may include the race of the driver and occupants, the reason for the stop, location, and whether a search was conducted, arrest made, and a citation issued. For others, data collection is only part of a much broader solution. There is also a concern that data collection procedures may result in police disengagement, or police officers scaling down the number of legitimate stops and searches they conduct. Of course, this could be detrimental for areas that experience disproportionally high crime rates. Unfortunately, many of these areas are inner city neighborhoods that are inhabited by a large number of minority residents.

The accuracy of data collection procedures have been called into question. For example, in some cases it may be challenging for police authorities to be certain that reporting requirements are not circumvented by police officers who fail to file required reports, or officers who may report erroneous information. There is also the question about how police agencies can ensure full compliance of data collection and reporting by police officers in the field, and how to deal effectively with officer resistance.

What remains for debate are the most effective methods that will assist police authorities in identifying biased-based policing, or those practices that may give the general perception of biased-based policing. The mere perception of racial biased police practices is often normalized in many minority communities, which makes the police authorities' task all the more difficult. It is also critical that the appropriate data collection methods be implemented that will assist police executives in improving fundamental police practice and reduce the perceptions of racially biased policing, while at the same time identifying early warning signs of racially biased police practices at the individual officer or unit level.

Benchmark Data

In order to increase the validity of police stop data, some researchers have begun to make use of benchmark data. Benchmark data "refers to control data against which stop data can be compared to determine if any racial or ethnic group is being stopped at a disproportionate rate" (Lamberth, 2003, p. 10). A benchmark is established when the researcher develops a valid profile of the race of drivers in a specific geographical area that is the subject of the investigation. This profile can then be used to check traffic stop data against the benchmark. Put another way, researchers develop comparison groups to produce a benchmark against which to compare their data (Fridell, 2004, p. 7).

A central problem for researchers is identifying the most accurate benchmark against which to compare the racial distribution of traffic stops (Grogger & Ridgeway, 2006). Past research has relied heavily on the use of official census data regarding race and ethnicity as a benchmark to compare against police stops (Batton & Kadleck, 2004; Lange, Johnson, & Vass, 2005). However, census data is not the most reliable data. The use of census data as a benchmark has been problematic in producing valid outcomes (Grogger & Ridgeway, 2006; Smith & Alpert, 2002; Alpert, Smith, & Dunham, 2004). One of the problems with census data is that it measures the geographic demographics of households. This data is considered static in nature (Lamberth, 2003). It is not a true reflection of the actual motoring public in a specific geographical area. Census data does not account for the dynamics of traffic flow in and out of an area. That is to say, some members of the motoring public may not live in a specific geographical area, but may travel in and out of the area for one reason or another. In reality, automobile traffic flow tends to be dynamic. Traffic fluctuates daily when citizens are driving to and from work, to school, to shopping centers, and the like.

Once again, many of the extant studies giving attention to racially biased policing have entailed collecting police stop data. After the stop data has been collected, statistical analyses are then conducted to see if an officer stopped a minority group more than it is represented in the community. Much of this research involves the collection and analysis of police stop data, and then comparing it back to neighborhood census track data of the community. By using this method there is a belief that it is possible to identify early indicators of racially biased police practices. Using population census data creates a host of problems. There are just too many variables and factors to make such a claim solely based on an officer stop data. What if the officer works in a primarily African American area of the community? It would only make sense that a large percentage of his on-duty police stops will be of African American citizens. Much more analysis would need to be completed to make a case of racially biased policing

Over time, these data collection strategies and analyses proved to be increasingly problematic and not a good way to identify racially biased policing practices. For one, a police officer who has stopped a disproportionate number of Hispanic or African American citizens in and of itself does not show that the officer is engaged in racially biased policing. There are simply too many factors that have to be taken into consideration. Second, simply collecting this type of police stop data fails to take into account the fluid dynamics of neighborhoods, and the members of the racial or ethnic groups that drive automobiles. That is, how many people travel into and out of a specific neighborhood at different times of the day? The volume of transient traffic in any given neighborhood may vary. For example, if there happens to be businesses or industry nearby, this will impact the traffic volume, while other neighborhoods may not experience the same amount of traffic volume. Neighborhood traffic patterns vary and depend on a number of factors that should to be taken into account when designing data collection methods.

One other hypothetical case is presented here to further illustrate the importance of carefully designed data collection strategies. Let us suppose that we have collected data in a specific area of the community. The data reveal that 55 percent of all traffic stops by the police are of African American drivers. Because 55 percent of all stops happen to be of African American drivers, this may seemingly be an early warning sign that something is not quite right. Can we say that this is a racial-biased police practice? The short answer is probably not. At least not until we have some additional data against which to compare the stop data. Put another way, we need to examine many other factors before making this determination. Merely knowing that 55 percent of traffic stops in a given neighborhood are of African American citizens tells us very little about racially biased policing. One method that would help to answer questions centering on the existence of racially biased policing in this hypothetical case is to establish a benchmark of the motoring public in order to compare the police stop data. While census data discussed previously is one form of benchmark data, it is the least reliable data to use when comparing the stop data. Collecting benchmark data has the potential to ensure the quality and effectiveness of police stop data. It is believed that the only effective way to determine the demographic of any given locality is to survey the traffic by race and ethnicity (Lamberth, 2003).

External Benchmark Data

It is well known that in many communities, citizens travel in and out of various neighborhoods at varying times for many reasons. Some are traveling to and from work, some to and from school, while others travel to and from a shopping mall, while others are just out taking an afternoon drive, and the like. The motoring public in any given community is dynamic. Consequently, traffic patterns vary greatly in a given community by area and by the specific time of day or night. Many researchers who study biased-based policing attempt to glean reliable data on the motoring public in a given community, neighborhood, or highway. Researchers accomplish this by carefully collecting external benchmark data.

External benchmark data involves collecting reliable demographic information pertaining to the motoring public in a specific neighborhood, roadway, highway, or other area of interest in order to compare police stop data. Ideally, benchmark data would include the number of automobiles that traveled in and out of a specific neighborhood at randomly selected times throughout the day and night, and the race, ethnicity, and gender of the drivers of those automobiles. Once this data has been carefully collected, it can be used to compare to police stop data. If the data reveals an officer or officers has stopped, for example, African American motorists at rates far beyond their driving rates as determined by benchmark data, this would give rise to a potential biased-based policing allegation and should be investigated further.

Traffic Surveys

In order to capture data that more accurately reflects true traffic patterns in a given community, it is necessary to collect carefully collected external benchmark data. In order to capture this data, some researchers have made use of traffic surveys. Traffic surveys capture the actual motoring public during randomized times throughout the day. Researchers also record the race and gender of the driver. The survey is carried out while the research team is in automobiles (generally best if they are surveying highways and interstates). Surveyors may also be stationary where they stand alongside a street or sit in their cars and record the number of cars that pass them, making note of the race and ethnicity of the driver. The collection times are typically randomized. That is, researchers randomize different times of the day when they will be surveying motoring vehicles in a given area. Randomized samples yield samples that are much more representative of the motoring public during specific times of the day. One way that researchers randomize the time and area they wish to survey is first to develop an accurate sampling frame. Let us hypothetically say that a 20-square block area is the sampling frame. Next, the researcher selects elements from the sampling frame according to a mathematical random procedure, and then locates the exact element to be included in the sample (Neuman, 2012, p. 154).

After the area to be studied has been randomized and selected for the traffic surveys, in order to collect benchmark data, researchers make several observations of the area in question at randomized times while recording the observed race of the driver of each vehicle during the observation period. Armed with the benchmark data that has been gleaned from traffic surveys, researchers are able to make comparisons against the benchmarked data with actual police stop data that has been collected by the surveyors. This is a much better way to discern if minority citizens have been stopped at disproportional rates as members of the driving public. In neighborhoods that have minimal traffic flow throughout the day, there may not be a need to collect benchmark data and population census data may be sufficient.

A traffic survey was used by researcher John Lamberth as part of the *State v. Pedro Soto* (1996) case. This case centered on the arrests by New

Jersey State Police of 17 Black citizens while they were traveling on the New Jersey Turnpike. The 17 defendants claimed their arrests on the New Jersey Turnpike between 1988 and 1991 were a result of discriminatory enforcement of the traffic laws by the New Jersey State Police. The defendants consolidated motions to suppress evidence under the equal protection and due process clauses of the Fourteenth Amendment. The windshield survey entailed stationing observers by the side of the road in randomly selected periods of 75 minutes from 8:00 a.m. to 8:00 p.m. The objective was to count the number of cars and the race of the occupants. It was determined by the windshield survey that out of 40,000 New Jersey turnpike drivers that were observed, 13.5 percent were Black motorists. In addition, a violator survey was conducted. The violator survey was held over 10 sessions in 4 days between Exit 1 and Exit 3 on the New Jersey Turnpike. The researchers traveled with the cruise control calibrated and set at 55 miles per hour, which in this case was 5 miles per hour over the legal speed limit. Researchers observed and recorded the number of vehicles that passed them, the number of vehicles they passed, the race of the driver, and whether the driver was speeding. Fifteen percent of the violators were Black.

As pointed out previously, traffic surveys are much more reliable compared to census data. If designed correctly, they have the potential to provide accurate estimates of the motoring public. However, the traffic survey does have a few shortcomings. First, they are very expensive and time consuming to conduct (Grogger & Ridgeway, 2006). The lead researcher is responsible to train observers who will spend many hours in the field observing traffic. Traffic surveys may also suffer from observer error, especially in multi-ethnic environments where there may only be literally a few seconds to identify the race/ethnicity of the driver (Grogger & Ridgeway, 2006). For example, the observer records a motorist as a Hispanic male when actually he is an African American. In some cases, this may be an unavoidable error short of stopping and asking the motorist his or her race or ethnicity.

Internal Benchmarking

One other approach that police agencies can use to monitor police stops is the use of internal benchmarking data. Internal benchmarking data is data that the police agencies collect on the stop practices of officers. It can be useful for determining patterns of behavior or other explanations. In other words, police officers or specific police units are monitored and their stops are compared to some baseline. For example, we could look at police officers working in similar areas of a community and establish that the typical officer writes 20 speeding tickets per month. Twenty speeding tickets becomes the baseline for comparison. If an officer writes more than 20 tickets per month, it by no means indicates that he or she is engaging in biased-based policing practices, but it would be an early warning indicator for police management. The officer's stop behavior could then be monitored over time. The advantage of collecting internal benchmark data is that these data can track an officer's behavior over time. Internal benchmarks have the potential to be a very useful early intervention system.

Police supervisors have a significant role in internal monitoring systems. It is critical that supervisors monitor the stop habits of their officers. Oftentimes supervisors at the rank of sergeant or lieutenant are in the best position to observe first hand specific patterns of behavior of individual officers and individual police units. If a supervisor notes that an officer is stopping an unusually high number of automobiles, this is an early warning. The supervisor could then more fully investigate the matter in order to discern who it is that the officer is stopping and for what reason. An officer who has stopped 50 automobiles during a one-month period and only issued 10 citations should warrant a query by his or her supervisor. It may very well be that the officer likes to give citizens the benefit of the doubt and resolves the traffic encounter with a verbal warning. Nevertheless, this indicator should be monitored over time. As will be reported later in this book, many minorities report that they are stopped by police authorities and extensively peppered with accusatory questions while never receiving a traffic ticket. This raises many questions in the minds of the minority citizen about the officer's motive for the stop.

Search Data

Another type of internal benchmark is the search habits of officers. This data can be very useful as an early warning indicator. Typically, an external benchmark is not needed when examining search patterns because the agency can use written citations of a specific officer or special unit and then examine search patterns of those traffic violators who have been issued a citation. The issue here is whether minority drivers who are cited by the police are subjected to more searches when compared to White drivers. It would also be beneficial to examine the hit rates of searches where evidence of a crime is found such as a drugs or drug paraphernalia.

Some organizations that track racial profiling suggest that linking citation information with search data can be beneficial in discerning information about both the quantity and quality of searches. This protocol can be easily designed by adding a few lines on the back of the citation for information regarding a search, if one was conducted. If because of the search, evidence was found, then the arrest report or evidence report would logically be linked to the citation.

Final Thoughts on Data Collection

The collection of police stop data should be conducted with diligence. It is highly advisable for police executives to seek the advice from experts who have experience designing studies and analyzing data. An old adage in research is apropos to collecting police stop data: garbage in – garbage out. If data is collected that is not reliable, or if it has been collected using questionable methods, it is useless. The result is wasted time and resources of the department. Perhaps, more importantly, it leaves the police agency and the concerned citizenry with lingering questions centering on whether there may be biased police practices occurring within the community. With that said, simply collecting data on police stops may shed light on what may turn out to be racially biased police practices, but it is far from a panacea. As will be argued in forthcoming chapters, rigorous qualitative studies are sorely needed in constellation with police stop data to really make sense of what the data means.

The collection of police stop data may have implications for the line level police officers who may conclude that the department does not trust them and this is just another way for the administration to monitor their activities. Police executives should be mindful of this when planning a stop data collection program. The chief of police or agency executive should address the rank and file to inform them of the purpose of the data collection system and specifically how it will impact their jobs. It is important that the chief of police or law enforcement executive deliver this message for three primary reasons. First, it sends the message to the rank and file police officer that this is an important mandate; second, it conveys that the chief of police is very much aware of the need for data collection and is able to communicate directly to the rank and file the advantages of such measures; and third, it sends an implicit message to the rank and file that racial profiling will not be tolerated.

Did the Supreme Court Sanction Racial Profiling?

The *Whren* Decision

As discussed in the previous section, data collection is an important step in addressing racial profiling (Ward, 2002; Harris, 2002). While data collection is critical in order to attract attention to biased police practices, data collection alone will be insufficient. The answer, in part, lies with the courts.

The U.S. Supreme Court has not made it any easier to address suspected racially biased police practices. In fact, they may have exacerbated the problem. The problem specifically centers on the *Whren v. United States* (1996) Supreme Court decision. While racial profiling is an unacceptable police practice, the 1996 Supreme Court decision in *Whren v. United States* allows the police to stop motorists and search their vehicles if police reasonably believe probable cause exists that the occupants are trafficking illegal drugs or weapons. The *Whren* decision has had a significant impact on minority drivers, especially African American drivers.

Consider the facts of the *Whren* case. Two plainclothes vice police officers were patrolling in a Washington, DC drug area. The officers observed a Nissan Pathfinder occupied by two Black males, James Brown, the driver, and Michael Whren, the passenger. The Pathfinder was stopped at a stop sign for what police called an "unusually" long time. Later, the officers would testify that the Pathfinder was stopped for a little more than 20 seconds in duration. Officers determined a traffic violation had been committed when the car stopped too long at the stop sign and then sped off. The vice police officers immediately stopped the truck and claimed to have warned the driver about the traffic violation. When the officers approached the truck, they observed Whren, the passenger, to be in possession of a white baggie, which the police officers believed to be crack cocaine. The officers overheard Michael Whren say, "Pull off! Pull off!" and then place one of the bags inside of a hidden compartment (Hall, 1996). Both Whren and Brown were arrested and charged with possession of illegal drugs, and subsequently indicted on federal drug charges. What do you think so far? Were the officers correct in the decision to stop the Pathfinder? If you were the police officers in this case, would you have done anything different?

Prior to trial, Whren moved to suppress the evidence arguing that the stop was not justified because there was neither a reasonable suspicion nor probable cause to believe he had engaged in illegal drug activity. This is an important argument made to the court. Remain aware of this argument as you read the facts of this case further. The trial court denied the motion to suppress and at trial, the defendants were convicted of drug-related crimes. Whren appealed the case but an appellant court agreed with the trial court. The U.S. Supreme Court granted *certiorari** and affirmed both lower courts on the basis that the stop was reasonable.

In other words, the U.S. Supreme Court found the police had probable cause to believe Brown committed a traffic violation, and the police officer acted reasonably by stopping the vehicle. In its ruling, the Court held that even though the accused, James Brown and Michael Whren who were Black, contended that police officers might decide which motorists to stop based upon impermissible factors such as race, and even though the constitution prohibits selective enforcement of the law based on considerations such as

---

* *Certiorari* is a Latin word used by the U.S. Supreme Court in the context of appeals. It is also granted by a state supreme court in order to review a lower court's decision (Roberson & DiMarino, 2012). *Certiorari* is the name given to limited appellate proceedings for re-examination of actions of a trial court, or lower appeals court, and while common, it is not an automatic right of litigants.

race, the constitutional basis for objecting to intentionally discriminatory application of laws is the Equal Protection clause, not the Fourth Amendment.

The Equal Protection Clause of the Fourteenth Amendment of the U.S. Constitution prohibits states from denying persons within its jurisdiction the equal protection of the law. In essence, the laws of a state must treat an individual in the same manner as others in similar conditions and circumstances. The equal protection clause is not intended to provide "equality" among individuals or classes but only equal application of the law. In other words, the result of a law is not relevant, as long as there was no discrimination in its application. Thus, by prohibiting the states the ability to discriminate, for example, on the basis of race, the equal protection clause of the Constitution is crucial to the protection of civil rights.

While the *Whren* case appears to put its stamp of approval on racial profiling, the case in and of itself is inundated with bad facts with which to make such a profound ruling (Birzer & Birzer, 2006). Do bad facts make good law? Is the Whren decision good law? Especially salient is the fact that the Washington, DC plainclothes vice police officers were in a high drug area where they know, or have reason to know, that drugs are prevalent. Furthermore, they waited while a traffic infraction was committed. Without question this was a short wait because it is well settled that traffic laws are so heavily regulated that any person is likely to commit a traffic infraction even when not trying to do so (Birzer & Birzer, 2006; Withrow, 2007).

In the *Whren* case, the claimed traffic infraction consisted of aggregate events such as temporary license plates on the vehicle, the youthful appearance of the occupants, and because the Pathfinder waited at the stop sign "too long." Think about this for a moment. One could not reasonably argue that there was no probable cause to believe that a traffic offense had been committed (sitting too long at the stop sign), which was the basis for the stop. In addition, the vice squad police officers were patrolling a high drug area, and they observed Black defendants in a Nissan Pathfinder who committed a traffic infraction. It is important to point out that even if the police officers engaged in racial profiling as suggested by *Whren*, it would not be as clearly evident by the facts of his case. In this case, too many factors are present that enable the police officers to shield themselves from accusations of racial profiling.

Consider, for instance, that the same Black defendants were in an upscale Black neighborhood or leaving a mall or even on a heavily traveled U.S. highway and crossed the centerline, or committed a minor traffic infraction. Would they be subjected to such reasonable suspicion or probable cause? Possibly, yes; however, it would be more difficult for a police officer to hide behind the predictable nature of a "high drug area" regardless of whether the officer's intentions are truly racially motivated. The *Whren* court could not then effectively shield themselves behind the fact that a criminal defendant should make a Fourteenth Amendment Equal Protection challenge rather than a Fourth Amendment challenge, which is intended to protect a person from unreasonable searches and seizures (Birzer & Birzer, 2006).

Some have argued that the *Whren* ruling should be reversed (Jernigan 2000). The irony here is that even if *Whren* were reversed, the same problem would still exist. The police may stop any motorist for any traffic infraction, regardless of severity (with or without the *Whren* decision). Prior to the 1996 *Whren* decision, law enforcement authorities as a matter of routine used pretextual stops to detain motorists. A pretextual stop is when law enforcement authorities stop a motorist for a traffic violation (often a minor traffic violation) in order to investigate a motorist further. The traffic violation does not have to be the underlying motive for the stop. In other words, law enforcement authorities may use the traffic infraction as the primary purpose of the stop, with the intention to conduct further investigation of the driver, which may or may not result in the search of a vehicle or an occupant, seizure of contraband, and ultimately additional charges.

The *Whren* decision further complicates the allegations of racial profiling. Consider the police worldview for just a moment. There is no denying that a case for pretext stops can be made as a venue for effective police work. The ability of the police to stop a motorist suspected of a serious crime, such as transporting illicit drugs or guns, is crucial.

Take the hypothetical case of a police officer who receives a tip from a concerned citizen who lives in a neighborhood prone to drug and gang violence. The concerned citizen tells the police officer that every day between 4:00 p.m. and 7:00 p.m. he notices numerous vehicles drive up to a certain house and stay for a few minutes and leave. The officer takes into consideration the neighborhood density of crime, along with the fact that his experience has taught him that oftentimes persons buying drugs will fit the method of operation that the citizen described. That is, they will drive to a location to purchase drugs, and then leave rather quickly. Police officers typically refer to these locations as "dope houses" or "drug houses."

Given the facts presented in the preceding paragraph, is it unreasonable for the police officer to investigate further and stop motorists for traffic infractions as they leave the residence? Should it matter how minor the violations appear to be in order to investigate the possibility of a drug buy? Let us assume that the officer stops two motorists as they leave the residence, one for lane change violation, and the other for failing to use a turn signal. Both motorists in this case are Black. Based on these facts, do you think this would give rise to racial profiling? Was racial profiling involved here? I hope that you can begin to see just how complex the nature of racial profiling can be.

The *Whren* decision creates a paradox of sorts. On the one hand, the decision grants police the authority to stop motorists based merely on a pretext, a pretext that in some cases the police may need in order to perform essential law enforcement duties and keep communities safe. On the other hand, the *Whren* decision itself may be an invitation for police to engage in racially biased police practices. With the U.S. Supreme Court's affirmation of pretextual stops under the *Whren* decision, the test for reasonableness is not the underlying motive for the stop, but rather if the traffic violation occurred (Pampel, 2004). This means that if a police officer observes a motorist commit a traffic violation, no matter how minor, he or she can stop the motorist even though the underlying motive for the stop is something different from the traffic violation, and may search the car if probable cause exists. Moreover, any illegal substances (e.g., guns, drugs) seized as a result of the search are admissible in a court of law if they were seized within the framework of the Fourth Amendment of the U.S. Constitution (Withrow, 2007). Given this ostensibly open invitation to stop citizens based on merely a pretext, even the most objective data collection techniques on police stops will be hard pressed to identify outright racial profiling. As Gumbhir (2007) notes,

> …because the *Whren* decision allows for the presence of a law violation to override other considerations (at least in terms of the Fourth Amendment), the institution has preserved and protected an opportunity for racial/ethnic discrimination, and as such is complicit in the differential treatment that is almost sure to follow (p. 59).

Would Have, Could Have, Should Have

The U.S. Supreme Court in delivering the *Whren* decision complicated the matter of racial profiling. The decision makes it almost impossible to identify an officer who is engaged in racially biased police practices because he or she can hide behind the pretextual stop. The *Whren* decision allows the police to stop anyone for the most trivial traffic infraction, even though that may not have been the real motive for the stop. Later in the book when the data from the racial profiling study is reported, consider the many African American and Hispanic citizens who were stopped for trivial traffic infractions such as lane straddling, failing to use a turn signal 100 feet from an intersection, making a wide turn, cracked taillight, burned-out tag light, defective windshield wiper, and, in one case, failing to use a turn signal when pulling away from the curb. The *Whren* decision has created an almost impossible mandate for those attempting to identify and eradicate racial profiling, whether real or perceived. What is the answer? How can we effectively deal with impact of the *Whren* decision while at the same time not compromise public safety or make it more difficult for police authorities to do their job? The answer lies in the courts.

Birzer and Birzer (2006) argued that it is incumbent upon the U.S. Supreme Court to carve out a test to properly identify racial profiling even in the most subtle situations. The *Whren* court considered the "would have" and "could have" test, which are both, by their very nature, subjective. The "would have" test is valid only if a reasonable officer "would have" made the stop in the absence of an invalid purpose. This is alarming. Is it possible to know what a reasonable officer would have done in a similar situation? Or as Pampel (2004, p. 80) points out, "trying to establish whether an officer had the proper state of mind when making a stop would present a difficult, if not impossible, task for the court."

While the "would have" test considers reasonableness, the "could have" test begs the question of whether an officer legally "could have" stopped the car in question because of a suspected traffic violation. The *Whren* Court rejected the "would have" test because of its subjectivity and certified the "could have" test as objective. Both tests mingle subjectivity with objectivity because they involve police officers' subjective thinking. Subjectivity is the core of personal opinion, bias, and, ultimately, prejudice. The U.S. Supreme Court should have been put on notice that the nation was in a legal quandary and in need of a wholly objective test for racial profiling, especially in light of the Fourth and Fourteenth Amendments, which guard against unreasonable search and seizure and guarantee equal protection afforded to each citizen, respectively.

What Would a New Test Look Like?

As noted previously, Birzer and Birzer (2006) argued that the Supreme Court should carve out a test to identify racial profiling. So what would such a test resemble? Do you have any ideas? Imagine that you are a Supreme Court Justice. How would you carve out such a test? How would you balance the need for fundamental fairness so that racial minorities can drive on the roadways and highways with fear of being racially profiled while at the same time ensuring that effective law enforcement practices that are fundamental to public safety are not jeopardized? This deserves some serious consideration. It is one thing to be critical of the *Whren* decision and to yell and scream without any effective solution. We typically call that griping and the field is full of those critics who often just gripe without going out on a limb and proposing something. They have nothing constructive to say.

It is another thing to have some idea that may work or resolve the problem. What is attempted next is a new test applied to racial profiling. With the current *Whren* decision in place, basically law enforcement officers have the green light to racially profile persons as long as they use a pretext or something else to stop them. This is where the line gets murky.

In 1986, the U.S. Supreme Court made a profound statement in the case of *Batson v. Kentucky* (1986) when it seemingly eliminated racial profiling on juries. If the issues in the *Batson* and *Whren* cases were compared, it would be evident that the right of a Black person to serve on a jury is just as equal to the right of a Black person to be free from unreasonable searches and seizures and racial profiling. No right of the two is tantamount to the other. Perhaps the creation of a test similar to the *Batson* test may be the beginning of accurately identifying racial profiling.

In the *Batson* case, prosecutors used their peremptory challenges during jury selection to strike prospective Black jurors from cases where their defendant was Black. The U.S. Supreme Court in its reversal of the lower court created a three-prong test wherein: (1) the defendants must first show that they are members of a cognizable racial group and that the prosecution has exercised peremptory challenges to remove from the venire, members of the defendants' race; (2) the defendants may rely on the fact that peremptory challenges are a jury selection practice that allows those who are minded to discriminate to do so; and (3) the defendants must show that these facts and other relevant circumstances raise an inference that the prosecutor used that practice to exclude the prospective juror on account of race. The burden then shifts to the prosecutor to show a race-neutral reason for excluding the prospective juror (*Batson v. Kentucky*, 1986).

In applying the *Batson* test to the *Whren* facts, *Whren* would be required to establish first that he is Black, a member of a cognizable racial group, and that the vice squad police officers used a permissible minor traffic infraction to stop, detain, and seize him. Second, *Whren* would have relied on the fact that the discretion that police have in making traffic stops allows those police officers who are inclined to discriminate to do so. Third, *Whren* would have established the fact that this particular "high drug area" is made up mainly of Blacks and the fact that traffic laws are so heavily regulated that almost anyone could commit a traffic infraction irrespective of how minor the traffic infraction may be. Finally, the vice squad police officers used their unbridled discretion to discriminate against Black motorists based on race. The burden would then shift to the government to show a "race-neutral" reason for its actions. Such "race-neutral" reasons should be a clearly articulated prong-test in which the government must convince the court by a "clear and convincing" burden of proof that the law enforcement officer did not engage in racial profiling.

If the defendant does not meet the first three factors discussed above, then the burden never shifts to the government. When the defendant meets the three factors, the burden shifts to the government and it must show by clear and convincing evidence a race-neutral reason for its actions. If the police show a clear and convincing race-neutral reason for their actions, then it is not racial profiling. However, it is racial profiling if the police fail to show a clear and convincing race-neutral reason for their actions, and the defendant meets the initial burden.

The *Batson* test offers some level of objectivity such that it may be applied universally in most racial profiling cases. There would be little room to address this issue on a case-by-case basis if the proper test were applied in a proper manner. It is most appropriate that the burden of establishing racial profiling fall not only on the government, but the defendant as well. Neither party should be allowed the privilege of shielding themselves from such burdens by reliance on "high drug areas" or cover-ups for wrongs.

Batson also announced policy reasons that, even today, may be transferable to racial profiling. As a matter of policy, the consideration of the *Batson* test to racial profiling issues will not undermine the contribution of police enforcement of drug laws and the administration of justice. In reality, various studies as depicted in this chapter have shown that pretext stops have been used to racially profile motorists. Trial courts should be sensitive to the racially discriminatory nature of pretext stops and, thus, enforce the mandate of equal protection and further the ends of justice.

The *Batson* decision is not without limitations. For example, some have contended that the *Batson* holding does nothing to address the problem of racial profiling of juries and that it is ineffective at stopping even blatant racists as long as they can manufacture a "neutral explanation" after the fact. In other words, because peremptory challenges need not be rational, the most irrational reason, if deemed credible, suffices to defeat a *Batson* challenge. Courts have accepted explanations that the juror was too old, too young, made too much eye contact, appeared inattentive or headstrong, nervous, too casual, and the like (Cole, 1999).

So how do we avoid this in a new test carved out from *Whren*? First, the court has to acknowledge that the perplexity of racial profiling is about race. The court should come to terms with the fact that race does matter in the criminal justice system. Historically, the courts and the criminal justice system have conveniently passed on engaging in this discourse. Butler (2002, p. 327) eloquently made this point. He writes:

> Americans seem reluctant to have an open conversation about the relationship between race and crime. Lawmakers ignore the issue, judges run from it, and crafty defense lawyers exploit it. It is not surprising, then, that some African American jurors are forced to sneak through the back door what is not allowed to come through the front door: the idea that race matters in the criminal justice system.

There is no clearly defined relationship between *Batson* (the right to serve as a juror) and *Whren* (the right to be free from all unreasonable searches). Both cases dealt with mistreatment of minorities on the basis of race. *Batson* was faced with a similar dilemma (race) as *Whren* and carved out a test. It is suggested that the same can be done with *Whren*. The crucial point, though, is that this new test should be policy driven as in *Batson*.

The issue of racial discrimination is very difficult to prove simply because it boils down to a question of intent. While it is true that, in a general sense, a person often intends the consequences of his or her actions, it is virtually impossible to determine by any objectivity what a person is thinking inside of his or her head. This has always been the problem with proving any form of racial discrimination and ultimately will be the challenge in proving racial profiling. As previously noted, the U.S. Supreme Court should be put on notice that the nation is in a legal quandary and in need of a wholly objective test for racial profiling.

Discussion Questions

1. Summarize some of criticisms that law enforcement made of the End Racial Profiling Act of 2001.
2. What were some of the central features of the End Racial Profiling Act of 2001?
3. What are some of the advantages for a police agency to collect stop data?
4. Regarding the collection of police stop data, explain the concept of establishing benchmarks.
5. What are some of the arguments made in the *Whren* Supreme Court decision that may make it difficult to identify racial profiling?

References

Alpert, G.P., Smith, M.R., & Dunham, R.G. (2004). Toward a better benchmark: Assessing the utility of not-at-fault traffic crash data in racial profiling research. *Justice Research and Policy, 6*(1), 43–70. doi: 10.3818/jrp.6.1.2003

Alvin W. Penn Racial Profiling Prohibition Act, Connecticut Public Act No. 03-160 (2003).

American Civil Liberties Union (2000). Coalition letter to the Senate on the traffic stops and statistics act. Retrieved from: http://www.aclu.org

Applied Research Center (2001). *Preventing racial profiling by police: SB 1074, State of Texas*, 2001. Retrieved from http://www.arc.org/pdf/176pdf.pdf

Batton, C., & Kadleck, C. (2004). Theoretical and methodological issues in racial profiling research. *Police Quarterly, 7*(1), 30–64. doi: 10.1177/1098611103254102

Birzer, M.L., & Birzer, G. (2006). Race matters: A critical look at racial profiling, it's a matter for the courts. *Journal of Criminal Justice, 34*, 643–651.

Butler, P. (2002). Racially based jury nullification: Black power in the criminal justice system. In S. L. Gabbidon & H. T. Greene (Eds.), *African American classics in criminology and criminal justice*. Thousand Oaks, CA: Sage, 323–347.

Carter, A. (2011, April 4). Conn. considers bill to strengthen anti-profiling laws. *New Haven Register*. Retrieved from http://nhregister.com

Cole, D. (1999). *No equal justice: Race and class in the American criminal justice system*. New York: The New Press.

Data Collection Resource Center at Northeastern University, (n.d.). *Reporting and analysis benchmarks*. Retrieved from http://www.racialprofilinganalysis.neu.edu/index.php

End Racial Profiling Act of 2001, H.R. 2074, 107th Cong. (2001).

Farrell, A., McDevitt, J., & Buerger, M.E. (2002). Moving police and community dialogues forward through data collection. *Police Quarterly, 5*, 359–379.

Fridell, L.A. (2004). *By the numbers: A guide for analyzing race data from vehicle stops*. Washington, DC: Police Executive Research Forum.

Grogger, J., & Ridgeway, G. (2006). Testing for racial profiling in traffic stops from behind a veil and darkness. *Journal of American Statistical Association, 101*, 878–887.

Gumbhir, V.K. (2007). *But is it racial profiling? Policing, pretext stops, and the color of suspicion*. New York: LFB Scholarly Publishing LLC.

Hall, J.C. (1996). Pretext traffic stops: Whren v. United States. *FBI Law Enforcement Bulletin, 65*, 28–32.

Harris, D.A. (2002). *Profiles in injustice: Why racial profiling cannot work*. New York: The New Press.

Jernigan, A.S. (2000). Driving while black: Racial profiling in America. *Law and Psychology Review* 24, 127–135.

Lamberth, J.A. (2003). *Racial profiling study and services: A multijurisdictional of traffic enforcement and collection in Kansas*. Washington, DC: Police Foundation.

Lange, J.E., Johson, M.B., & Vaas, R.B. (2005). Testing the racial profiling hypothesis for seemingly disparate traffic stops on the New Jersey Turnpike. *Justice Quarterly, 22*, 193–223.

Liederbach, J., Trulson, E., Fritsch, E.J., Caeti, T.J., & Taylor, R.W. (2007). Racial profiling and the political demand for data: A pilot study designed to improve methodologies in Texas. *Criminal Justice Review, 32*, 101–120.

Neuman, W.L. (2012). *Basics of social science research: Qualitative and quantitative approaches* (3rd ed.). Boston, MA: Allyn and Bacon.

Pampel, F.C. (2004). *Racial profiling*. New York: Facts on File, Inc.

Ramirez, D., McDevitt, J., & Farrell, A. (2000). *A resource guide on racial profiling data collection systems: Promising practices and lessons learned*. Washington DC: United States Department of Justice.

Roberson, C., & DiMarino, F.J. (2012). *American criminal courts*. Upper Saddle, NJ: Prentice Hall.

Smith, M.R., & Alpert, G.P. (2002). Searching for direction: Social science, and the adjudication of racial profiling claims. *Justice Quarterly, 19*, 673–703.

Walker, S. (2003). *Internal benchmarking for traffic stop data: An early intervention system approach*. Washington, DC: United States Department of Justice, Office of Community Oriented Policing Services.

Ward, J.D. (2002). Race, ethnicity, and law enforcement profiling: Implications for public policy. *Public Administration Review, 62*, 726–735.

Withrow, B.L. (2007). When Whren won't work: The effects of a diminished capacity to initiate a pretextual stop on police officer behavior. *Police Quarterly, 10*, 351–370.

Cases Cited

State v. Pedro Soto, 324 N.J. Super. 66; 734 A.2d 350 (1996).
Whren v. United States, 517 U.S. 806 (1996).

Phenomenology as Method in Racial Profiling Research

4

"Phenomenology asks, what is this or that kind of experience like?"

Max van Manen, *Researching Lived Experience* **(1990)**

Introduction

The primary objective of this chapter is to describe the method used to collect the data reported in this book. If you are accustomed to reading primarily quantitative treatments of racial profiling studies, this chapter will be quite different. The data collected, analyzed, and validated is much different from quantitative ways, which employ statistical analysis techniques. The overall purpose of why a qualitative inquiry was selected is twofold: (1) to describe the essence of how minority citizens experienced what they believe to be racial profiling, and (2) to describe how they gave meaning to their experiences. Collecting police stop data cannot effectively answer these two questions. Ask yourself this question before reading on: Do you think that the answers to these two questions could be answered using a quantitative approach?

There is a corollary purpose in this chapter, too. The student who has limited knowledge of research methods will be introduced briefly to qualitative research methods and phenomenology. Phenomenology is one of many approaches used in qualitative research. Other unique approaches include ethnography, ethnomethodology, autoethnography, life story, case study, grounded theory, and narrative studies. This introduction to qualitative methods will not be terribly exhaustive, but just enough so that you will understand the procedures and the way that racial profiling was studied. I hope that this chapter will motivate you to want to learn more about the many qualitative research approaches that may be used to study racial profiling and other social phenomenon. Moreover, if you do use one of the many approaches to qualitative research, you should expect your experiences to be rewarding.

The experiences of citizens who perceive that they had been racially profiled by police authorities are the centerpiece of this study. Perceptions by minority citizens of racially motivated police stops have the potential to reveal a great deal from the minority citizens' perspective. The mere perception of racially biased police stops can be disastrous for police relations with the minority community and may actually increase distrust of the police (Weitzer & Tuch, 2002). Mistrust of the police, in turn, has the potential to further fracture and exacerbate the already strained relationship the police have with many communities of color.

Perception and experience are important variables to study. Social scientists can learn much from how citizens perceive and experience what they believe to be racial profiling. As you will soon discover, qualitative research methods are much more than simply collecting and reporting anecdotal stories of perceived racial profiling from citizens. Many published books that give attention to racial profiling simply report anecdotal stories without subjecting the data to sound analyses. While books that report anecdotal stories of perceived racial profiling are important and do indeed provide some cursory descriptions of racial profiling, they lack sound methodological and analytic procedures, thus making the data somewhat limited in understanding this complex phenomenon.

Framing the Study

Sorely missing in the literature are studies of racially biased policing that have used a qualitative method. To be clear, many studies examining racially biased policing were conducted using quantitative research methods. In quantitative research, the data is in the form of numbers and measurements. Thus, in racially biased policing research the quantitative data is often represented as police stop data, benchmark data, population census track, and demographic data. However, as some scholars have correctly argued, quantitative treatments of racial profiling are not without their fair share of methodological issues. For example, Schafer, Carter, and Katz-Bannister (2004, p. 160) pointed out that conceptualizing racial profiling is problematic. They write:

> Within the debate over racial profiling, it's unclear what this practice involves. For example, is racial profiling envisioned as: officers stopping some drivers (e.g., Hispanic males) at a disproportional rate with other drivers under equal circumstances (e.g., when speeding more than ten miles over the speed limit); officers using different standards for violations which invoke traffic stops (e.g., only stopping White drivers for serious violations, while stopping minority motorists for even the most minor infraction); or, officers stopping some drivers under pretext or false pretense?

Because a majority of studies of racial profiling have made use of quantitative methods, the objective of the present research was to use qualitative methodology in order to describe the minority citizenry's experiences with racial profiling. In other words, this work focused on how minority citizens experience what they believe to be racial profiling. I made use of a phenomenological approach to accomplish this objective. Before proceeding, perhaps it may be helpful for the reader who has not taken a college research methods course or for the research novice who is conceptualizing qualitative methods to briefly introduce qualitative research.

Alternative Epistemology

Epistemology refers to the nature of knowledge, or simply, how we know what we know. In this book, the epistemology centers on the method used to understand and deconstruct the experiences of minority citizens with racial profiling. The method entails in-depth interviews and focus group sessions with those citizens who say they have experienced it. What I attempt to do is lessen the distance between the participants and myself, and to provide thick and rich descriptions of their experiences with racial profiling. Moreover, the research reported in this book describes in detail how minority citizens ascribe meaning to these experiences.

As Alford (1998, p. 85) instructed, "Such meanings are inferred from observations of behavior in natural situations, from interpretations of texts, depth interviews that interrogate individuals about the way in which they interpret experiences and social relationships." From the rich descriptions and meanings offered by participants, the underlying essential, invariant structure (unifying description) of their experiences was written. In order to accomplish this, a qualitative research method using a phenomenological approach was used. This specific approach will be discussed later in this chapter.

Much of what is learned about racial profiling experiences comes from listening to hours of stories told by story participants, followed by much reflection and introspective. Likewise, each participant was asked to engage in much reflection and introspective as he or she relayed the stories. Reflection and introspective is central to understanding and giving meaning to our experiences. It is a process that is "integral to human existence, occurring continuously throughout the lifetime of every human being" (Georges & Jones, 1980, p. 108).

The Paradigm Divide

A paradigm is a framework for doing business, a specific way of seeing the world, a thought or a pattern. The social sciences have been divided for some time on how best to investigate social phenomenon. Many argue for qualitative approaches. Still many more argue for a quantitative lens as the way to study phenomenon. Still others make the case for using both approaches. In this study, one approach is no better than the other. Using a method that can best glean the answers to the research questions is preferred. How persons experience what they believe to be racial profiling can best be answered by a qualitative method using a phenomenological approach. Moreover, because I was interested in developing the unifying experience that racial minority citizens had with racial profiling, I choose a phenomenological approach.

Quantitative researchers take a specific stance on what they believe constitutes the nature of reality. For example, quantitative research reflects the traditional scientific approach, which draws largely from positivism. Criminal justice and criminology researchers have largely accepted the assumptions of positivism that a single reality exists consisting of inter-related variables. With positivism, researchers amass facts to describe a situation with the aim of uncovering law-like relationships that help explain aspects of this reality. Positivism, with its emphasis on the sta-tistical analysis of data, has driven a great deal of research in criminal justice and criminology. According to Lincoln and Guba (1985, p. 28), positivism rests on at least five assumptions that are increasingly difficult to maintain:

1. An ontological assumption of a single, tangible reality "out there" that can be broken apart into pieces capable of being studied inde-pendently; the whole is simply a sum of the parts.
2. An epistemological assumption about the possibility of separation of the observer from the observed, the knower from the known.
3. An assumption of the temporal and contextual independence of observations, so that what is true at one time and place may, under appropriate circumstances (such as sampling), also be true at another time and place.
4. An assumption of linear causality; there are no effects without causes and no causes without effects.
5. An axiological assumption of values freedom; that is, that the meth-odology guarantees that the results of an inquiry are essentially free from the influence of any values system (bias).

Despite the prevalence of quantitative methods in the criminal justice and criminology literature, some concern exists that these procedures may not be adequately addressing the research needs for the field. This concern is framed in part on the argument that quantitative techniques do very little to offer a more complete explanation of the phenomenon under study. Or, as DiCristina (1997, p. 191) argues, "quantitative research may have an explana-tion, but this is not the same as being justified." Ferrell, Hayward, and Young (2008) made a more poignant point regarding the field's traditional research method. They write:

The methodological terrain of contemporary criminology is so barren, its conventional methods so inadequate for addressing the human pathos of crime and control, so wanting in any sense of intellectual elegance and innovation, that the discipline today seems a sort of methodological kakistocracy—an upside down world where the worst matters the most. (p. 161)

Traditionally, researchers select random samples from a specific population of interest, isolate and control variables, run complex statistical analyses, and attempt to generalize the results to the population under study. The researcher's role in this process is distant, neutral, and arguably value-free. One problem with this approach is that the researcher is removed from and has minimal or no interaction with the very persons, phenomenon, or problem he or she wishes to study and understand. This is troubling.

In criminal justice and criminology, many research questions require a qualitative approach. Quantitative approaches alone may not be sufficient for researchers attempting to understand the complexities of what I attempt to understand here—racially biased policing. Many years ago, Polsky (1967, p. 122) said this about the quantitative dominance in criminology: "This is where criminology falls flat on its face." Cromwell (2006) reminds us that the field of criminology has sometimes suffered from a distance between student and subject of the study. He makes an astute observation about medical training. Professor Cromwell observed that it would be impossible to train a physician without contact with a sick person. An important part of medical training is taking patient case histories, listening to their symptoms, and forming tentative diagnoses. Would it not make sense that researchers who study such things as crime, criminals, the criminal justice system, and racially biased policing have contact with the very persons they study?

Venkatesh (2008) observed that most researchers do not seem interested in meeting the very people about whom they write. He asserted, "It isn't necessarily out of animosity—nearly all of them are well intentioned—but because the act of actually talking to research subjects is seen as messy, unscientific, and a potential source of violence" (Venkatesh, 2008, p. 3). Professor Venkatesh knows a little something about meeting the people about whom he writes. He spent the better part of a decade hanging out with some of the roughest gangs in Chicago.

Qualitative Research

The objective of qualitative research is to understand a social phenomenon or problem at the very deepest level. The study reported in this book represents a qualitative method that was used to study minority citizens who said that they have been racially profiled by the police while driving in their automobiles. Specifically, a qualitative method using a phenomenological approach (discussed later in the chapter) was used. Qualitative methods attempt to uncover patterns in the data and to give a voice to those individuals who have experienced racial profiling.

Qualitative research is about providing an understanding of why something occurs or exists rather than how it occurs or exists. It is an ideal way to explore and understand phenomenon, or to make sense of a person's or group's reality perceptions of an issue. This usually involves directly asking questions of people who have experienced the phenomenon. It may also entail that the researcher spend time in the field observing social behavior.

Qualitative research is also concerned with the nature of reality or ontology. Ontology is a term frequently used in qualitative literature and simply means the nature of reality. In qualitative research, an ontological assumption centers on the fact that there are many realities that people experience. These realities are subjective. Information from a wide variety of sources is collected and combined in a meaningful way in order to understand these realities. Researchers use quotes and themes in the words of participants and provide evidence of different perspectives in order to make sense and understand reality (Cresswell, 2007). In racial profiling research, it is important to understand the phenomenon from those who experienced it. Each person has multifaceted experiences with racial profiling. It is the researcher's task to make sense of these experiences, which will in turn deepen our level of understanding.

Qualitative research methods provide much flexibility when compared to quantitative approaches. The data collection may take the researcher on several different paths as the study evolves. Moreover, in studies that use qualitative research methods, the data is not quantified or subjected to statistical manipulation. The data is described in the form of words. This is a distinct difference between quantitative and qualitative research. Because perceptions are subjective, researchers go into the field and get next to people, interact with them, and interview them at the site where they experience the issue or problem under study. In criminal justice and criminology, this means that crime, criminals, social control agents, probation officers, judges, and other actors within the system are studied in the field, in their natural habitat, as opposed to bringing them into a contrived situation. The up close and personal information gathered by directly talking to people and seeing them behave or act within their context is a major characteristic of qualitative research (Creswell, 2007).

One can open up any one of the numerous qualitative research methods textbooks on the market and find eloquently crafted definitions of qualitative research. Two such definitions are provided from Denzin and

Lincoln (2005), and Creswell (2007). According to Denzin and Lincoln (2005, p. 3):

> Qualitative research is a situated activity that locates the observer in the world. It consists of a set of interpretive, material practices that make the world visible. These practices transform the world. They turn the world into a series of representations, including field notes, interviews, conversations, photographs, recordings, and memos to the self. At this level, qualitative research involves an interpretive, naturalistic approach to the world. This means that qualitative researchers study things in their natural settings, attempting to make sense of, or interpret, phenomena in terms of the meanings people bring to them.

For Creswell (2007, p. 37), qualitative research is defined like this:

> Qualitative research begins with assumptions, a world view, the possible use of theoretical lens, and the study of research problems inquiring into the meaning individuals or groups ascribe to a social or human problem. To study this problem, qualitative researchers use an emerging qualitative approach to inquiry, the collection of data in a natural setting sensitive to the people and places under study, and data analysis that is inductive and establishes patterns and themes. The final written report or presentation includes the voices of participants, the reflexivity of the researcher, and a complex description and interpretation of the problem and it extends the literature or signals a call for action.

Inductive and Deductive Reasoning

Qualitative research makes use of inductive reasoning because researchers begin not with a theory or hypothesis, but rather with something to observe, a particular social situation or group of people (McIntyre, 2005). Inductive reasoning begins when the researcher makes an observation of a phenomenon or problem of interest. After the observation, a generalization is made about the observation, and a theory is constructed that explains the observation. Using an inductive approach, the qualitative researcher asks questions like, who are these people, what are they doing, and why? In turn, the answers to these questions help to formulate theories and hypotheses. By using inductive reasoning, qualitative researchers work back and forth between the preliminary themes and the database until they establish a comprehensive set of themes.

Deductive reasoning is used in quantitative studies and follows the logic of the scientific model. Deductive reasoning works from the more general to the more specific. It begins with a theory and then narrows down to specific hypotheses that make statements about the relationship between two or more variables. A hypothesis is an educated guess that provides a tentative explanation of the problem. A theory is simply an interrelated set of variables formed into propositions or hypotheses (Creswell, 2009). In quantitative research, the researcher is concerned with analyzing the implications of a hypothesis. In other words, the implication of the hypothesis is examined by gathering data and statistically testing the data to see if it is relevant to the hypothesis.

Multiple Data Sources

In studies that use qualitative methods, it is common for researchers to use multiple data sources. Multiple data sources may include direct observations of the phenomenon, the researcher's personal experience and involvement in the phenomenon, photographs, interviews, art, social artifacts, focus groups, and the like. This study of racial profiling made use of multiple data sources. The data included in-depth interviews, focus groups, official reports, and diaries written by the participants, email communication, electronic blogs, and the like.

The Discovery of Meaning

The qualitative researcher engages in an in-depth examination of the multiple meanings of individual experience, and then attempts to understand how those meanings are socially and historically constructed (Creswell, 2007). Qualitative research is beneficial when the objective of the research is to understand the day-to-day social life and routine of people, organizations, or societies. Qualitative work seeks to understand the essence of social life and what it is like to experience a phenomenon. The researcher's ability to interpret and make sense of what he or she sees is critical for an understanding of social phenomenon (Leedy & Ormrod, 2001). Qualitative researchers answer questions by examining various social settings and the individuals who inhabit these settings. They develop a holistic picture of the problem under study. In some studies, researchers are interested in how humans arrange themselves and their settings, and how inhabitants of these settings make sense of their surrounds through symbols, rituals, social structures, social roles, and so forth (Berg, 2001). Qualitative research studies share some common characteristics:

- A humanistic bent
- Curiosity
- Creativity and imagination
- A sense of logic
- The ability to recognize diversity as well as regularity
- A willingness to take risks
- The ability to live with ambiguity
- The ability to work through problems in the field

- An acceptance of the self as a research instrument
- Trust in the self and the ability to see value in the work that is produced (Corbin & Strauss, 2008, p. 13)

Phenomenology

The rich descriptions of racial profiling reported in this book were the result of a qualitative method using phenomenological approach. Few researchers in criminal justice or criminology have used this approach. Moreover, a review of the literature on racial profiling did not reveal any studies where a phenomenological approach was used.

Qualitative phenomenology represents an innovative way to study social phenomenon. Simply put, phenomenology is the study of lived experience. This is what is attractive about phenomenology. It is another approach to further our understanding of racial profiling. Phenomenology attempts to gain a deeper understanding of the nature and meaning of our experiences (Van Manen, 1990). The aim is to determine what an experience means for persons who have had the experience (Moustakas, 1994). A phenomenological approach was selected for this study in order to capture the essence of how racial minority citizens interpret, process, and give meaning to experiences of racial profiling.

Phenomenological studies are useful when the researcher is interested in discovering the lived experiences and perceptions of a phenomenon of a specific person or group. Based on in-depth interviews and other data sources, the objective is to identify what is perceived to be the central underlying meaning of the descriptions provided by the participants. In other words, the aim is to describe as accurately as possible the phenomenon, reframing from any pre-given framework, but remaining true to the facts.

Before moving on to discuss specifics about the research reported in this book, it is appropriate to share with you how Moustakas (1994) described the common features that distinguish qualitative research approaches like phenomenology from traditional, natural science, quantitative research methodologies. These features include:

1. recognizing the value of qualitative designs and methodologies, studies of human experiences that are not approachable through quantitative approaches
2. focusing on the wholeness of experience rather than solely on its objects
3. searching for meanings and essences of experience rather than measurements and explanations
4. obtaining descriptions of experience through first-person accounts in informal and formal conversations and interviews

5. regarding the data of experience as imperative in understanding human behavior and as evidence for scientific investigations
6. formulating questions and problems that reflect the interest, involvement, and personal commitment of the researcher
7. viewing experience and behavior as an integrated and inseparable relationship of subject and object and of parts of the whole (Moustakas, 1994, p. 21)

In order to study the experiences of racial minorities with racial profiling these features make perfect sense. They all underscore the importance of how individuals experience phenomena and how they make sense of their experiences. Although there are differences in the breadth of research focuses among those that make use of qualitative research, there is one common bond: "Understanding the complexity of the phenomenon of interest to them" (Peshkin, 2009, p. 416). It is in this spirit that I propose that it is both timely and necessary to examine racial profiling through a qualitative lens.

Selecting Participants

Participants were carefully selected using two types of sampling strategies. The first sampling strategy used was the criterion. This sampling strategy works well when a study is framed as qualitative phenomenology. Criterion sampling selects individuals to be studied who have experienced the phenomenon (Creswell, 2007). Specifically, the requirements were:

- Participants had to be a member of a racial or ethnic minority group, 18 years of age or older.
- Participants had to have experienced what they believed to be racial profiling by police authorities while driving within the past 5 years (in some cases the 5-year time limit was waived due to the rich context of a participant's story).

The research also employed a snowball sampling strategy. This is a sampling technique where the researcher "identifies cases of interest from people who know what cases are information rich" (Creswell, 2007, p. 127). In this study, the participants were asked to identify others who have experienced what they believe to be racial profiling and may be willing to participate in the study. About 57 participants were identified using a snowball sampling strategy and the other 31 participants contacted the researcher as a result of seeing an advertisement or hearing about the study. Figure 4.1 depicts the schema of sampling strategy followed.

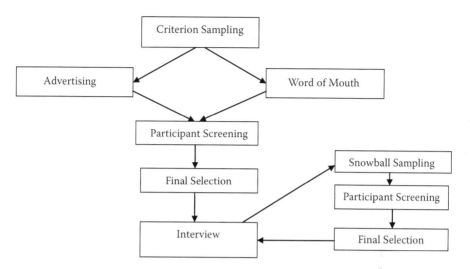

Figure 4.1 Participant selection protocol.

Advertising

There were many strategies used to advertise the study. Participants were solicited using electronic advertisements, Facebook, electronic blogs, and newspaper advertisements (specifically, several newspaper publications that have a minority readership). To assist in soliciting participants, the researcher employed the help of countless community leaders, law enforcement leaders, NAACP local chapters, various human rights organizations across the state of Kansas, the Human Rights Commission in this state, Center for Peace and Justice, and several other organizations.

Screening

Because it was desired to collect data that could provide the richest context to minority citizens experience-perceived racial profiling, a significant amount of screening was done. First, potential participants underwent an initial phone screening to ensure that they fit the criteria for the study. Much effort was given to screening out those persons who were involved in criminal activity at the time of their perceived racial profiling. Moreover, those persons who were determined to merely have an "axe to grind" with police authorities were not considered for the study. For example, on one occasion a citizen reported that he had been racially profiled by the police. Upon further screening it was discovered that he had been involved in a hit and run accident and was subsequently arrested. The data from this initial screening was not used. On many occasions, individuals contacted the researcher to simply complain about how they were treated by police authorities in various situations. After concluding they did not fit the criteria for the study, these persons were advised that they should contact the internal affairs investigation unit or the law enforcement executive in the specific jurisdiction.

A Portrait of the Participants and Setting

There were well over 100 persons interviewed for this study. In the end, there were 88 interviews that were used in the final analysis. Sixty-six individuals were interviewed about their experiences with perceived racial profiling and 22 citizens were divided up and participated in four separate focus group sessions. A focus group entails assembling a group of participants who are then interviewed together and encouraged to share their experiences with and opinions about a specific phenomenon (Lauer, 2006). Although you probably would not know it because of the quantitative hegemony in the social sciences, focus groups received recognition many years ago in social science research due in part to sociologist Robert Merton and his colleagues' classic work, *The Focused Interview* (Merton, Fiske, & Kendall, 1956). Today, focus groups have become widely accepted and are used in many studies (Morgan, 1996).

Focus groups were used for three primary reasons: (1) to promote self-disclosure and dialogue among participants regarding racial profiling, (2) to discuss themes and their associated meanings that were fleshed out of individual interviews with participants, and (3) to establish the trustworthiness or validly of the data. In other words, focus groups were used in part to ensure that the data was valid. Trustworthiness will be discussed further in Chapter 6.

Recall that 66 participants agreed to interviews regarding their experiences with perceived racial profiling by police authorities. Each interview ranged from 20 minutes to 2 hours in length. The majority of the participants were interviewed multiple times over several months. Of the participants interviewed, 40 were Black (28 males and 12 females), 25 were Hispanic (15 males and 10 females), and one participant was an Asian male. Of the 23 participants who were selected to participate in focus group sessions, 14 were Black (9 males and 5 females), and 8 were Hispanic (4 males and 4 females). Collectively, the average age of these participants was 38, and their ages ranged from 18 to 68. Tables 4.1, 4.2, and 4.3 illustrate the demographic makeup of the study.

Table 4.1   Interviews and Focus Groups—African American Participants

Participant Race/Ethnicity	Interviewed	Focus Group	Total
African American Male	28	9	37
African American Female	12	5	17
Total	40	14	54

Table 4.2 Interviews and Focus Groups—Hispanic Participants

Participant Race/Ethnicity	Interviewed	Focus Group	Total
Hispanic Male	15	4	19
Hispanic Female	10	4	14
Total	25	8	33

Table 4.3 Interviews and Focus Groups—Asian Participant

Participant Race/Ethnicity	Interviewed	Focus Group	Total
Asian Male	1	0	1
Total	1	0	1

The study's participants represent a large cross-section of occupations, including a parole officer, a corrections officer, a high-ranking school administrator, several school teachers, numerous business owners, a retired corporate executive, college students, several ministers, numerous laborers, youth and substance abuse counselors, one security guard, one banking employee, several health professionals, social workers, and several unemployed citizens. I collected data over a 17-month period starting in early 2009 and ending in late 2010.

Data was collected across the state of Kansas. Kansas is an interesting state, referred to as the sunflower state (named after the state flower). The state bird is the meadowlark. Thomas Frank, in his book *What's the Matter with Kansas?*, describes Kansas like this:

Kansas is Midway, USA; it's the setting for countless Depression-era documentary photographs; it's the home of the bright boy in the mailroom who wants to be a player on Wall Street. It's where Dorothy wants to return. It's where Superman grows up. It's where Bonnie and Clyde steal a car and Elmer Gantry studies the Bible and Russian ICBMs destroy everything and the overchurched anti-hero of *An American Tragedy* learns the sinful ways of the world (Frank, 2004, p. 29).

As Kansas officially opened to settlement by the U.S. government, abolitionist free states from New England and pro-slavery settlers from neighboring Missouri convened on the territory to determine if Kansas would become a free state or a slave state. As these forces collided, the area was a mass of violence in its early days and was known as Bleeding Kansas. The abolitionists who waged bloody battles with pro-slavery forces eventually prevailed in 1861. The state embodies large metropolitan areas like Wichita to the south-central part of the state, and Johnson County to the east. Kansas is the subject of folklore and old western stories of Wyatt Earp who spent time as a law officer in Dodge City and Wichita. Politically, Kansas is predominately conservative and the state has been consequently identified as a red state.

According to the U.S. Census, Kansas is home to some 2,818,747 citizens. With regard to gender, it is just about an equal split of males and females. The median age of Kansans is just about 35 years. About 86 percent of the state's population is White, while Black or African Americans represent 6 percent, Asian Americans about 2 percent, and the remaining 6 percent account for a sundry of other races (i.e., Native American, Pacific Islander, etc.). About 9 percent of the state's population is Hispanic or Latino of any race (U.S. Census Bureau, 2010).

There are 342 law enforcement agencies in Kansas that employ 10,227 persons, of which 6761 are sworn officers. These agencies range in size from small and rural police and sheriff's departments employing only a handful of officers to the largest department, the Wichita Police Department, which employs over 800 sworn officers. There are departments in eastern Kansas such as Overland Park that employ 304 officers, and the Johnson County Sheriff's Department, which staffs 481 deputies. In the northeast part of the state, the Topeka Police Department employs 354 police officers. Topeka, a community of about 122,000 citizens, is the state capital, and is located about 50 miles west of Kansas City, Missouri.

Kansas does not have a state police but rather a highway patrol. The Kansas Highway Patrol employs about 500 troopers who are spread out across the state. The highway patrol is tasked primarily with traffic enforcement and other law enforcement responsibilities on the state's roads and highways. The Kansas Bureau of Investigation, which boasts in its mission statement that it is dedicated to providing professional investigative and laboratory services to criminal justice agencies and the collection and dissemination of criminal justice information to public and private agencies for the purpose of promoting public safety and the prevention of crime in Kansas, employs 82 special agents.

Participants were interviewed regarding their experiences with what they believe to be racial profiling from 16 communities across Kansas (see Table 4.4). These communities were selected for two reasons: (1) I attempted to collect data from all areas of Kansas (north, east, west, and south), and (2) participants were identified in these specific 16 communities. The reference point used was Wichita, Kansas, which is the state's largest city, and its location is readably identifiable to most of the state's residents. Wichita is in the south-central region of Kansas and is 30 miles north of the Oklahoma state line.

Table 4.4 Participant Representation by City

City	Location Reference	Region in Kansas
Dodge City	154 miles west of Wichita	Western
Emporia	88 miles east of Wichita	East Central
Florence	29 miles northwest of Newton	North Kansas
Great Bend	118 miles northwest of Wichita	Northwest
Hesston	48 miles north of Wichita	North Central
Kansas City	62 miles east of Topeka	Northeast
Leawood	5 miles east of Overland Park	Eastern
Liberal	83 miles southwest of Dodge City	Western
Maize	14 miles northwest of Wichita	South Central
Manhattan	58 miles northwest of Topeka	Northeast
Mulvane	17 miles south of Wichita	South Central
Newton	27 miles north of Wichita	South Central
Overland Park	13 miles south and west of Kansas City, KS	Eastern
Spearville	17 miles northeast of Dodge City	Western
Topeka	59 miles east of Emporia	Northeastern
Wichita	30 miles north of Oklahoma state line (I-35)	South Central

Treatment of Data

In the event that that you are not familiar with how qualitative researchers analyze their data, let me offer a few notes on the general process. The analysis will vary somewhat depending on the specific qualitative approach used. For a most informative overview of analysis strategies for different qualitative approaches, it is recommended that you read Creswell (2007).

To start, it is important to recognize that qualitative data analysis does not use statistics or numbers as used in quantitative analyses. Common sense may lead you to believe that qualitative research is easy. Qualitative analysis is actually a difficult and complex endeavor. The difficulty lies in the fact that the researcher may be faced with making sense of, reducing, simplifying, and abstracting and interpreting what can start out as a voluminous amount of data, including but not limited to interview and focus group transcripts, observational notes, memos, photographs, and other information.

As you have learned in this chapter, qualitative data analysis typically culminates in thick and rich descriptions based on narratives, interviews, and observations. In any qualitative analysis, the researcher has a responsibility to map out for the reader exactly how the data was analyzed and how validity was established. Statistical data analysis follows a somewhat safer, step-by-step process in comparison to qualitative research. The type of statistical analysis is determined based on a specific level of measurement. In other words, different variables may have to be measured using different statistical procedures. For example, racial profiling surveys where respondents answered Likert scaled questions would be analyzed at a lower level of measurement than the number of police stops in a specific area. What this means is that the data will dictate the type of statistic that can be used. Thus, in statistical analysis a uniform protocol must be followed.

Qualitative analysis is not that straightforward and may involve a multifaceted approach. Creswell (2009) reminds us that qualitative data analysis involves making sense out of text and image data, preparing the data for analysis, conducting different analyses, moving deeper and deeper into understanding the data, representing the data, and making an interpretation of the larger meaning of the data. Miles and Huberman (1994) suggested that there are some general analytic practices that can be used across different qualitative approaches. These practices were helpful in this racial profiling study. They include:

- Affixing codes to a set of field notes drawn from observations or interviews
- Noting reflections or other remarks in the margins
- Sorting and sifting through these materials to identify similar phrases, relationships between variables, patterns, themes, distinct differences between subgroups, and common sequences
- Isolating these patterns and processes, commonalties and differences, and taking them out to the field in the next wave of data collection
- Gradually elaborating a small set of generalizations that cover the consistencies discerned in the database
- Confronting those generalizations with a formalized body of knowledge in the form of constructs or theories (Miles & Huberman, 1994, p. 4)

Analyzing Phenomenological Data

Because I framed this qualitative study using a phenomenological approach, I followed a few techniques that are appropriate for phenomenology. Qualitative phenomenological methods recognize and seek to describe the intrinsic relation of the person to the subject matter. Keep in mind that the aim of the phenomenological approach as used here was to determine what the experience of racial profiling means for the persons who had the experience and are able to provide a comprehensive description of it.

Giorgi (1985) identified two levels of phenomenological data: naïve descriptions and the structure of the experience. The racial profiling data primarily fell into two levels. First, the original data was comprised of naïve descriptions obtained through open-ended questions and dialogue (interviews and focus groups). On a higher level, the data was described in terms of the structure of the experience based on reflective analysis. Giorgi (1985) maintains that in Level two, the researcher engages in some interpretation of the participant's account or story. I part slightly from this tradition and allowed the participants whenever possible to interpret what the experience with racial profiling means to them.

The data analysis technique used in this study was adapted and modified from the one discussed in Moustakas (1994). A qualitative data analysis program (NVivo version 8) was used to assist in organizing, sorting, and analyzing the data. The raw data in this study included transcriptions from interviews and focus groups, audio recordings of interviews and focus groups, interview memos, analytical memos prepared by the researcher after each interview and focus group, electronic dialogue with participants, and written records provided by participants (e.g., copies of official complaints that were filed by participants to police and other human rights organizations). Data analysis was carried out using a six-step process as:

Step 1: Once data collection was completed, the transcripts, interview memos and all other written material were read in order to first ensure that they contained adequate data to be useful in the analysis.

Step 2: The data were then examined and relevant information separated from irrelevant information. All relevant information was broken into small segments of significant statements that each reflected a single, specific thought.

Step 3: The significant statements were then carefully re-read and overlapping and repetitive statements were eliminated.

Step 4: The segments were then grouped into meanings that depict what participants described as racial profiling.

Step 5: Clusters of themes were organized from the formulated meanings. Specifically, the data were examined and the various ways considered in which racial profiling was experienced by participants, and these were clustered into themes. The objective in this stage of the analysis was to allow for the emergence of themes common to all the participants' descriptions.

Step 6: In the final step of the analysis, the clusters of themes were used to develop an overall description. The overall description is referred to as the essential, invariant structure. The essential, invariant structure describes the one unifying meaning of all the descriptions provided by the participants.

Discussion Questions

1. How are qualitative research methods useful in furthering under-standing of racial profiling?
2. What is the objective discussed in the chapter of using a phenome-nological approach in the study of racial minorities' experience with racial profiling?
3. What is criterion sampling and how was it used in this racial profil-ing study?
4. Why is it important to carefully screen participants in qualitative studies of racial profiling?
5. How would a qualitative researcher carry out a study of racial profil-ing compared with a quantitative researcher?

References

Alford, R.A. (1998). *The craft of inquiry: Theories, methods, evidence.* New York: Oxford University Press.

Berg, B.L. (2001). *Qualitative research methods for the social sciences* (4th ed.). Needham Heights, MA: Allyn and Bacon.

Corbin, J. & Strauss, A. (2008). *Basics of qualitative research (3rd ed.).* Los Angeles: Sage.

Creswell, J.W. (2007). *Qualitative inquiry and research design: Choosing among five approaches* (2nd ed.). Thousand Oaks, CA: Sage.

Creswell, J.W. (2009). *Research design: Qualitative, quantitative, and mixed methods approaches.* Thousand Oaks, CA: Sage.

Cromwell, P. (2006). *In their own words: Criminals on crime* (4th ed.). Los Angeles: Roxbury.

Denzin, N.K., & Lincoln, Y.S. (2005). *The Sage handbook of qualitative research* (3rd ed.). Thousand Oaks, CA: Sage.

DiCristina, B. (1997). The quantitative emphasis in criminal justice education. *Journal of Criminal Justice Education, 8,* 182–197.

Ferrell, J., Hayward, K., & Young, J. (2008). *Cultural criminology.* Los Angeles: Sage.

Frank, T. (2004). *What's the matter with Kansas?* New York: Henry Holt and Company.

Georgi, A. (1985). *Phenomenology and psychological research.* Pittsburgh, PA: Duquesne University Press.

Georges, R.A. & Jones, M.O. (1980). *People studying people: The human element in fieldwork.* Berkeley, CA: The University of California Press.

Lauer, P.A. (2006). *An educational research primer: How to understand, evaluate, and use it.* San Francisco: Jossey-Bass.

Leedy, P.D., & Ormrod, J.E. (2001). *Practical research: Planning and design.* Upper Saddle River, NJ: Prentice Hall.

Lincoln, Y.S., & Guba, E.G. (1985). *Naturalistic inquiry.* Newbury Park, CA: Sage.

McIntyre, L.J. (2005). *Need to know social science research methods.* Boston: McGraw-Hill.

Merton, R.K., Fiske, M., & Kendell, P.L. (1956). *The focused interview*. Giencoe, IL: Free Press.

Miles, M.B., & Huberman, A.M. (1994). *An expanded sourcebook: Qualitative data analysis* (2nd ed.). Thousand Oaks, CA: Sage.

Morgan, D.L. (1996). Focus groups. *Annual Review of Sociology, 22*, 129–152.

Moustakas, C. (1994). *Phenomenological research methods*. Thousand Oaks, CA: Sage.

Neuman, W.L. (2012). *Basics of social science research: Qualitative and quantitative approaches*. Boston: Pearson.

Peshkin, A. (2009). Understanding complexity: A gift of qualitative inquiry. *Anthropology and Education, 19*, 416–424.

Polsky, N. (1967). *Hustlers, beats and others*. New Brunswick, NJ: Aldine Transaction.

Schafer, J.A., Carter, D.L., & Katz-Bannister, A. (2004). Studying traffic stop encounters. *Journal of Criminal Justice, 32*, 159–170.

U.S. Census Bureau (2010). Kansas census data 2010. Washington, DC: Retrieved February 19, 2012 from: http://www.uscensus2010data.com/20-kansas-census -2010-data

Venkatesh, S. (2008). *A rogue sociologist takes to the streets: Gang leader for a day*. New York: Penguin Press.

Van Manen, M. (1990). *Researching lived experience: Human science for an action sensitive pedagogy*. Albany, NY: The State University of New York Press.

Weitzer, R., & Tuch, S.A. (2002). Perceptions of racial profiling: Race, class, and personal experience. *Criminology, 40*(1), 435–451.

Experiencing Racial Profiling

5

"Make me wanna holler the way they do my life."

Marvin Gaye, 1971, *Inner City Blues*

Introduction

The purpose of this chapter is to report how racial minorities experience racial profiling. The descriptions reported here are more than just anecdotal accounts. As discussed in Chapter 4, these accounts of racial profiling have been examined using qualitative analysis techniques framed in phenomenology. The analysis identified six dominant themes, and fleshed out the unifying experience (essential, invariant structure) of racial profiling experienced by racial minorities. Perhaps more importantly, the data reported in this chapter shed light on how racial minorities give meaning to their racial profiling experiences.

Constructing the Stop

After interviewing and conducting focus groups with the 87 racial minority citizens, data saturation was reached. Data saturation is the point in the research when additional collected data becomes redundant. In other words, the researcher begins to hear and see the same contextual themes repeated in each interview; thus, continuing the data collection would reveal redundant information.

After the transcripts, memos, and other documentation were carefully read and recorded, 370 significant statements that described racial minorities' experiences with racial profiling were extracted from the raw data. From these 370 significant statements, 257 were taken out because they were repetitive and overlapping. This left 113 significant statements that were coded for use in the analysis. The 113 significant statements were then clustered to form six dominant thematic categories. These six themes reveal a great deal about how citizens experience what they believe to be racial profiling. The richest significant statements and narratives were extracted from the transcripts and interview memos in order to illuminate, support, and give meaning to these themes. The objective here is to give a voice to those minority citizens who

Table 5.1   Common Themes and Their Associated Meanings

Common Themes	Associated Formulated Meanings
Emotional/affective	Embarrassment
	Heightened alertness upon seeing police
	Increased anxiety
	Anticipation of being stopped
	Frustration
	Anger
	Fear
	Helplessness
	Lasting emotional trauma
Symbolic vehicle	Driving an expensive car
	Customized apparel (rims, paint, window tint)
	Driving older model car with customized apparel referred to as a "Hoopty"
Nature of the violation	Perceived minor traffic violation
	Pretextual stop
Officer demeanor	Ambiguous about why being stopped
	Accusatory
	Demeaning
	Impersonal
Normative experience	Accustomed to being stopped
	A part of life in minority community
Routine	
Race and place	Driving in affluent White neighborhoods
	Driving in police-targeted areas
	Driving in economically disadvantaged areas

otherwise would never be heard in the public square. Let us take a look at the six dominate themes outlined in Table 5.1.

Theme 1: Emotional/Affective

Participants reveal much about their emotional experiences as a result of being stopped by the police for reasons they believe to be based solely on their race. For many, these emotions had a lasting impact. Some participants began to sob as they struggled to tell their stories. This theme carried with it several associated meanings to include embarrassment, heightened alertness upon seeing police, increased anxiety, anticipation of being stopped, frustration, anger, a sense of helplessness, and lasting emotional trauma.

The participants spoke of the embarrassment of being stopped by the police. They told stories of being made to stand alongside the street while their vehicles were being searched. They spoke of the humiliation of having other motorists stare at them as they drove past. Participants felt a sense of embarrassment because they wholeheartedly believed that they did not do anything wrong, and that the sole reason they were stopped was for driving while Black or Brown. This seemed to be exacerbated by the reason for the stop (e.g., cracked windshield, failure to use turn signal within 100 feet of an intersection, cracked brake light, tinted windows, etc.). There was a pervasive feeling among participants that the police use a pretext such as a cracked windshield as a reason to stop them, when the real underlying motive may be that they suspect other criminality, which according to participants is perpetuated by race, clothing and appearance, type of car, or geographical area. In order to cope, many participants said they purposively avoid driving in areas where there is a high probability that the police will be present.

Listen to how some of the participants describe the feeling of embarrassment and humiliation when stopped by the police. The following descriptions were taken verbatim from the taped transcripts, interview memos, and written reports furnished to me by the participants.

Sharla, a Black woman in her early 40s who is employed as a parole officer, recalls one memorable encounter that she and her family had with the police. Sharla and her family were stopped one summer evening at about 12:30 a.m. They had been playing cards at a friend's home and as they were driving back to their home the police stopped them.

During the encounter, she questions the treatment her family received by the police. Sharla's husband was driving a 1987 Cadillac, which he takes great pride in keeping in pristine condition. Sharla was sitting in the front passenger seat, and two of their friends along with their toddler grandson were sitting in the backseat. All were Black with the exception of the grandson who Sharla described as bi-racial. Listen to Sharla tell the story.

> My husband was driving and we noticed the police were following us for a long time. The police officer signaled his red lights and we heard the siren and we pulled over. He walked up to the car and asked for my husband's driver's license. My husband gave him the license. He [the officer] then asked where we were headed to. My husband said, well why do you need to know, why did you pull me over? Then the officer said do you have your registration? So my husband pulls it out and gives it to him. My husband asked the officer again why we were being stopped. And then my husband asked, "What did I do wrong?" The officer was like just stay right here, as if we were going to go somewhere. So he goes back to his car and he never told us what he stopped us for. Finally he walked back to our car and we noticed two other police cars drive up and I was like what the hell, what's going on? So he comes back to the car. Now I begin to question him and was asking like what is the problem? He says well your car is reported stolen. We were like what! What are you talking about! So then he tells us we need to get out of the car, first he tells my husband to step

out of the car. So my husband steps out of the car and he [the police officer] says well I'm going to have everybody step out of the car.

By this time there were five other police cars that had driven up, so there were a total of like seven police officers. So he asks my husband to step back, does his procedure and asks him if he can search the vehicle. I started talking then and said no, why do you need to search our vehicle? If it was reported stolen why are you searching the vehicle? And I want to know who made the report? So then he says, well ma'am, I'm not addressing you and you need to be quiet. I said No, I will not be quiet. This car is registered to us—you see who it is registered to, my husband. The owner is driving the car so how can it be stolen. The officer got really upset with me because I was arguing with him and asking him questions. He said that I was being argumentative and that if I did not shut up he was going to put me in the back of the police car. So now my husband is angry because he [the officer] just threatened to put me in the police car for trying to find out what's going on. My husband started yelling that you just pulled us over because we are Black. After several more minutes it was over, all of sudden the officer said we could get back in our car and were free to leave. We did not even get an apology. As we were walking back to our car one of the officers said, I suppose you are one of the ones that are going to say we racially profiled you too. We just got back in the car and got out of there.

My husband drove right down to the substation to file a complaint. He told the supervisor that we don't appreciate this and my family was embarrassed, all these people were watching us and they just randomly picked us. My husband told the police supervisor at the substation that he wanted to see the stolen car report. They never did produce the report.

Sharla describes the embarrassment she experienced for her as a parole officer to be standing alongside of the road while police officers searched the car. Sharla said, "There were cars driving by and slowing down to get a look." She said, "We were all standing out on the side of the street at 12:30 a.m." A few days after the interview I received a follow-up email communication from Sharla. She wrote that she forgot to mention that after the stop, "they did not receive a ticket." She also wrote, "They [the police] never knew I was a parole officer until they asked for my driver's license and saw my badge." Sharla writes verbatim in her email,

They [the police] wanted to know what the badge was for and I told them I was a parole officer. One of the officers must have recognized me and he told me that he asked me to issue a warrant over the phone a while back and he told the officer who was standing there—the one that had stopped us—that he remembered me from the parole office.

Read DeMarcus' story. DeMarcus is a Black male in his late 20s, employed as a youth care worker, and is college educated with a master's degree. He describes the embarrassment he felt when he, his wife, and their small child were stopped while driving on a highway a mile or two north of Liberal, Kansas. DeMarcus began the interview by telling me that even though he has never been in trouble or arrested, being stopped by the police is just "part of his world." He said, "I have just gotten used to it."

DeMarcus had flown into the Liberal airport from Albuquerque, New Mexico where he had been visiting family. His wife (who is White) and their biracial daughter picked him up at the airport. As they left Liberal and began driving to their home located in central Kansas, they were stopped by a Kansas State Trooper. DeMarcus describes the incident.

> We were on the highway just outside of Liberal, Kansas, we were on our way home. I saw the police car pass us going the opposite direction. I noticed that he immediately made a U-turn and started to follow us. He really followed us for a while, maybe a mile or two, and then stopped us. He was a young White trooper. He told me the reason he was stopping me was because I was following a semi-truck too close. I thought to myself, what! He asked for my driver's license—and then with no explanation he asked me and my wife to get out the car. He separated us at opposite ends of the car. He started going back and forth between us asking us questions. It seemed like he was purposively trying to mix up our stories. He kept asking where we were coming from and where we were going and this and that. He kept asking the same questions over and over. My daughter was still in the back seat and she was scared.
>
> After a while he asked me if he could search my car. I told him well you're not going to find anything in the car except my bag of clothing. He then said, where did you guys say you were coming from again, did you say you were from Texas? I was like no! I told you Albuquerque, and he was like are you sure you didn't say Texas? I said no I didn't tell you Texas. So he kept trying to use that line over and over again and he had us out there for a good 45 minutes. My wife started getting irritated. She told him this is against the law—you can't do this! He didn't say anything. Yeah, he searched and the first thing he went for was my bag. I have a big Nike duffle bag, big duffle bag for school and you know he's digging through clothes and shoes. You know he searched the car, let us go, and no ticket, not nothing...Even though you're like I don't want him to search my car because you're not going to find nothing...This whole thing made me feel bad, I was upset, it was just, you know, really embarrassing. I have learned not to argue with them [police] when I get stopped. If you do they make it hard on you. There is just not a dammed thing you can do about it.

DeMarcus believes the reason he was stopped was that the officer saw a Black male and White female driving along the highway and probably thought that they were drug smugglers. He concluded that the trooper kept trying to trip them up on their story by saying, "are you sure you didn't say you were from Texas?" DeMarcus is convinced that his race prompted the suspiciousness on the part of the trooper coupled with the fact that he was just leaving a rural airport located in a predominantly White community. He said the officer used the pretext of following the semi-truck too close as the reason to stop him even though, according to DeMarcus "he [trooper] could probably care less about that charge."

I asked DeMarcus about seemingly and without hesitation giving the trooper consent to search his car. He replied,

> Yeah, I found that by telling them no, it creates more of a headache. They get upset and they try to hold you longer. So it's kind of like something you just want to get it done and over with.

It is interesting that DeMarcus justifies giving the trooper consent to search his car "to get it over and done with." This seems to portray a routine and seemingly normative response to law enforcement's request to search. This normative response was so compelling in this study that it became a dominant theme and will be discussed later in this chapter.

DeMarcus explains, "It was embarrassing to be stopped like this and standing along the highway with my wife and little girl while he searched our car and asking if I had any guns or drugs in the car."

Jada, a Hispanic woman in her early 30s, describes her experience this way:

> I was embarrassed that someone who knows me would drive by and see me standing along the street with the police searching my car. You know there must have been 4 or 5 police cars. You know that you haven't done anything and it hurt so badly and you can't do anything about it. You know what, this all boils down to being a Latina driving a customized car in America. You learn to expect this.

David, a 29-year-old Hispanic manufacturing worker, further illuminates this theme by explaining the embarrassment he felt when stopped by two police officers for a cracked taillight.

> They kept asking me what gang I was in. I told him I have never been in a gang. They kept on asking me back-to-back questions. I was embarrassed because it was in the parking lot of where I work and all my friends were watching.

Of the many minority citizens who shared their stories with me, perhaps the following excerpt from the interview of Tony, a 60-year-old Black male who retired several years ago from a professional corporate management job, most effectively illustrates the "emotional/affective" theme. Tony seemed to struggle to tell me his story. He stopped several times during the interview in order to regain his composure. It was clear to me after spending a considerable amount of time talking with Tony that his experience affected him deeply and emotionally. Although Tony's experience occurred about one year prior to the time I interviewed him, the emotional scars from the incident remain fresh. He is convinced that authorities would have handled the situation differently with a White person.

According to Tony, he was stopped by authorities because he looked suspicious. He was not charged with a crime nor was he issued a citation. Tony does not live in Kansas but frequently visits his elderly mother who resides in Wichita. It was during one of these visits that he says he was profiled because he is Black. Speaking in a measured tone, Tony recalls the incident, which sheds light on the embarrassment and humiliation he felt. As you will see from the following excerpt, he specifically uses the words *embarrassment* and *humiliation* to describe how he felt.

> I have never been so embarrassed in my life. This was humiliating. I am 60 years old, retired from middle management, and this happened to me. I have never been stopped in my life until this incident. I drove to [location purposively taken out] to purchase a newspaper and a cup of coffee to start my day. Over the past year I have done this many times, it is part of my routine. I drove on this day only because I had a lot of running around to do during the day. I usually walk for daily exercise...Basically they approached me and asked what business I had there. I informed them that I was merely having my morning coffee and reading the newspaper. All of a sudden with no warning or provocation, the officer abruptly told me to stand up and put my hands behind my back. At this point, I was just incredulous and couldn't believe what was happening. I was horrified and embarrassed because it was totally public humiliation being marched out of a public venue for no apparent reason and treated like a common criminal in view of others. I stood up and turned around, complying totally with his unwarranted demands. At this point, I just couldn't believe what was happening to me. It was like I was having an out of body experience. In 60 years, I've never managed to get myself handcuffed. I've never been arrested. I've always been the consummate and quintessential lawful citizen. It was very degrading with the unwarranted abrupt treatment of being bullied and having my rights to public accommodations violated...As I was being led out, I remarked to the officer [name purposively taken out] that if I was of a different color, I am sure this matter would have been handled differently. He accused me of playing the race card...I complained about how embarrassed I was about being led out of a public place in handcuffs for no reason or cause. He [the officer] didn't seem to be too empathetic.

Tony was checked for warrants and was released without as much as a ticket. Tony said the incident bothered him tremendously. Tony was a polished and articulate man. He very much looked and exhibited the mannerisms of a corporate executive.

Many participants describe feeling increased anxiety while driving and seeing the presence of a police car. For example, one participant remarked, "I started driving really conscientiously when I saw the police car." Another participant, Javier, a Latino from Dodge City in his early 20s, described it this way: "I noticed the officer pull a U-turn and start to follow me. When I first saw him I really got nervous and in the back of my mind I knew he was going to start following me."

Certainly, many drivers may experience increased anxiety regardless of race upon seeing a police car, but these data seem to suggest it has more significance for minority citizens. It appears to be even more profound for African American participants.

Participants reveal a defensive and cautious attitude upon seeing a police car. Participants were always alerted to the police presence and they would peer in their rearview mirror watching to see if the police car was going to start following them. Because research has pointed out that minority citizens often hold deeper suspicions of the police when compared to White citizens, this may in part explain the increased anxiety (Birzer, 2008; Birzer & Smith-Mahdi, 2006; Parker, Onyekwuluje, & Murty, 1995).

Rodney, a college-educated Black man in his late 20s, provides further context to what many racial minority citizens experience while driving:

> For many of us, especially African American males, we laugh and joke about it, but this is a serious matter. Whenever I drive past the police, I find myself getting nervous even though I've done nothing wrong. We get a scary feeling when driving past the police, even when we've done nothing wrong. There's something about driving past the police that makes you scared and it turns you into the perfect driver. Whenever I'm driving and I spot the police, I'm aware of where they're at. I'm constantly checking my mirrors to keep an eye on them. A lot of my Hispanic friends said that they too find themselves with the scary feeling whenever law enforcement presence is around. A lot of times, because we constantly check our mirror, it makes us look suspicious and gives them a reason to pull us over. A lot of African American males tend to keep conversations to a minimum with law enforcement once they've been pulled over. The thinking behind this is if I'm quiet, I'll get off with a warning, and if I express my emotions, I'm being defiant. So, for us, the anticipation of being stopped is very real. It's almost like you get accustomed to being pulled over, but no matter how many times you've been stopped the scary feeling inside of you still is there each and every time.

The sense of anxiety that participants described while driving and spotting a police car led to the "anticipation of being stopped." There is a subconscious feeling among participants that they could be stopped. Rita, a Hispanic woman in her late 20s, describes the anticipation of being stopped this way: "As I was driving, I saw the police officer sitting in the parking lot and I was mindful of his next potential move." Another participant said this:

I saw him [the police officer] sitting in the parking lot and he stared at me as I drove by. I knew there was a good chance he would start following me. I was about maybe a block away and I saw him pull out and come in my direction. He followed me for about two more blocks and I remember thinking, OK he is going to stop me any minute. That's just a fact when you are Black and driving late at night.

Participants racially constructed the anticipation of being stopped. In other words, they believe that because they are members of a racial or ethnic group, they are more likely to be stopped by the police. Thus, they are at a heightened state of alert upon seeing a police car. One participant, Charles, a Black man in his 40s, provided rich context for this racialization. During the interview with Charles, he described an experience while driving in an affluent and predominantly White neighborhood.

If I notice an officer pass me going the opposite direction, I automatically look in my rearview mirror. I have had things happen like this in the past. This one time I saw an officer and I really got nervous and in the back of my mind I knew he was going to start following me, and he pulled a U-turn and did. You know I am a Black man driving in this area and you see a police car, what do you think is going to happen.

Participants often describe feeling frustrated and angry when stopped by the police for what they believe to be racial profiling. The participants usually control the frustration and anger because they know if they openly exhibit emotion it will make matters worse. Many participants described a sense of helplessness or, as one participant put it, "there is not a damn thing I can do about it." One participant said:

They [the police] always ask if they can search my car, they let me know that I have a choice. So I let them search because I know I had nothing to hide. I knew if said no, he would have called more officers and it would have been worse. You know there is nothing you can do, and you better not say anything or they will make it tough on you.

Theme 2: The Symbolic Vehicle

The symbolic vehicle continues to emerge in this research as a robust theme. In particular, the association between the Black male as assailant and the vehicle that he drives has come to symbolize something terribly distorted in the worldview of the police. I think that we cannot deny the macro-racialization of racial profiling. Whites often dismiss these macro trends, or they often discount the complaints from racial and ethnic minorities about racial profiling. Glover (2009, pg. 48) argues that mainstream criminology has tended to dismiss or downplay allegations of racial profiling. In essence, mainline criminology has accused communities of color of distorting and exaggerating the extent of racial profiling. Some may interpret this as siding with the White majority sentiment.

Mainline criminological research seems to dismiss some racial profiling actions as the result of a few bad apple cops who were allowed to enter into policing. The problem with this is the fact that we overlook the potential contaminating macro effects of racism. Historical perspectives are relevant here.

Many of the participants describe being stopped or profiled by the police because of what they were driving; that is, the type of car they happened to be driving. Participants were stopped because of miscellaneous violations such as a tag light burned out, a tail light burned out, failure to use their turn signal, and the like. They indicated that what initially would attract the police to them was the fact that they were driving a gangster type of car, or a car that the police would commonly associate with a minority. For example, a low rider, a Cadillac, and a Buick Seville, among others, are often mentioned.

Participants describe the frustration and anger of being stopped for what they say is stereotyping because of their race coupled with, in some cases, the type of car they drive. This was the case with Ana, a 34-year-old Hispanic female and former correctional officer now employed as an advocate for crime victims. Ana describes the anger and frustration she felt during an incident she had with police authorities. Ana also questions the officer's motive for stopping her.

> I was driving a 1985 Cutlass Supreme low rider. It had gold plates. My family is in the business of customizing cars. My brother borrowed my car that day because he had a job out of town and my car got better gas mileage. My son had a doctor's appointment and I had to get him there. I asked my brother if I could use his car because my son needed medicine. He said, no sweat, take my Cutlass, we just painted it, but it's ready. My brother said to take his wife's tag and put it on the car. That tag had not been registered because they were restoring the car and they hadn't used it in forever.

Ana recalls that this was a one-time thing and that she just wanted "to get from point A to point B and back with no problems." She continues her story.

> The car had very expensive rims and sits low to the ground. I saw the sheriff's car traveling in front of me. I was behind him a little ways. I made a turn onto [location purposively taken out] and noticed that the sheriff's car made a U-turn and got behind me and started following me. Now I am a very good driver and I was thinking to myself that this can't be happening. I know from my friends that they will stop you if you're driving a low rider because they

think you are just gang banging Mexicans. He followed me for a while, maybe a mile or so and then stopped me. By this time, I was pretty upset about what was happening. When he came up to the car I told him you better have a good reason to stop me. He told me he was randomly running tags and that he ran my tag and it was not assigned to the vehicle. I remember thinking he is stopping me because I'm driving a low rider which they associate with Mexican gang members. I got upset and yelled at him. I was yelling that this is not a serious thing and why did you turn around and follow me in the first place. He told me to get out of the car because I was being verbally aggressive. I kept on questioning him about why he turned around and started to follow me. He then grabbed me and forcibly pulled me from my car and handcuffed me. I remember that he searched me in front of his video camera. He searched my car and impounded it and he refused to let my brother pick it up. I think that he was maxing out his authority because I was so angry and not very cooperative with him. I asked if I could pull it into a parking lot and he said no. I know my actions might have made this worse, but I watched the whole thing play out and I knew what was going on. He turned around to follow me just because I am Hispanic driving a low rider. I was embarrassed that someone I know would see me standing alongside of the road in handcuffs. I lived in the area where I was stopped.

Ana believes she was profiled because of her Hispanic ethnicity coupled with the fact she was driving a customized Cutlass Supreme low rider. She said, "We were traveling the other direction and there is no way he could get behind me unless he intentionally braked to do so. That's why I feel I was profiled."

In the symbolic vehicle theme, participants describe how they believe police authorities hold stereotypical beliefs about the type of vehicle that minority citizens drive as well as the appearance of their vehicles. For example, participants believe if you are Black and driving an expensive car, this will attract increased police suspicion because of the belief that the vehicle is too expensive for a Black citizen to drive. One participant said, "They stopped me because I was Black and driving a nice car. They probably think I am not supposed to drive a nice car. If I was driving my Kia I would have never been stopped." Another participant, Michael, a Black male in his early 30s, is convinced he was stopped by the police and peppered with interrogating questions for simply being Black and driving a newer model Mercedes. In another interview, Rick, a 28-year-old Black male said, "You know, it was just the type of car I was driving." During the interview with Rick, it was revealed he was driving a 1995 Chevy Caprice with customized rims and tinted windows. Another participant, Angela, who is a Black female in her early 50s, described being stopped by police authorities for driving a nice car.

It's like they think you are not supposed to be driving this nice car. It's like we are still in slavery. They never issue me a ticket so I think it had to be because I was Black and driving that nice Jaguar. You know the thing is that I never got a ticket. They would just check me out and let me go.

In a follow-up phone interview with Angela, she reported being stopped on many occasions while driving in her Jaguar. She reiterated that not once did she receive a traffic citation. In her own words:

They never issued me a traffic ticket so I think it had to be because of my race driving that car. If you are Black and driving a nice car, you are going to get stopped by the police. I can tell you I drove a Kia for years and never got stopped. When I purchased the Jaguar, I swear to you I was stopped three times within a few weeks.

Participants highlighted that the make and model along with the appearance of their car will attract police attention because it is perceived as the type of car a minority would drive. There is a belief that the police construct the "symbolic vehicle" based on stereotypes. According to participants, the "symbolic vehicle" would include customized apparel such as wheel rims, nice paint job, sits low to the ground (low rider), window tint, gold around the tag, etc. Participants believe the police associate certain cars with Black and Hispanic drivers. Cheryl, a Black female in her early 30s and employed as a beautician, explains:

I drive a 1999 Cadillac with lavender paint. I got stopped and he never gave me a reason why he was stopping me. I had my sister in the car. He asked to search my car and I said no. I was not given a ticket and after I refused to let him search he let me go. I think the reason I was stopped was because I was driving a 1999 Cadillac with lavender paint and tinted windows. This is the kind of car they associate with a minority driver and that will get you stopped. It's almost like if you are a Black person you aren't supposed to be driving that nice of a car.

One other participant describes being stopped by the police because of the association of his ethnicity and the type of car he drives. Albeto, a Hispanic male in his early 20s who works as a laborer in the construction industry, explained that he is stopped frequently because he believes police authorities associate the appearance of his car with criminality (gangs and drugs). Albeto said, "I was driving a customized Cutlass Supreme. I think the officer was just sizing me up because I was driving this car, it sits low and they think these cars are associated with Mexican gangs." Another Black male participant describes his experience.

I remember another time a police officer stopped me. I was walking into my apartment, I think he must have been following me. He called me and said he heard that my license was suspended. My license was not suspended. I heard from a friend who knows some police officers in Hesston that they will stop you if you are Black and driving a car that fits what they call a drug dealer's car. Maybe it's the rims, tinted windows or something like that. Even when I had the tinted windows on my car, I always drove with my windows down to avoid getting stopped. I had tint but you could still see through my windows.

An interview with Melvin, a Black man in his early 20s, reveals it wasn't necessarily a customized car that resulted in him being stopped, but rather for driving an expensive car. Melvin was stopped for a turn-signal violation. Here is how Melvin describes it:

When the police officer walked toward my 2005 Cadillac CTS, he says, is this your car? The officer didn't ask for my driver's license, instead he wanted my insurance. I think the reason for this is because he thought a young African American male can't drive a nice car. After he looked at my insurance, he then asked me for my driver's license. I thought it was fishy but being an African American sometimes you have to bite your tongue when it comes to certain situations.

Perhaps the story that most effectively illustrates the symbolic vehicle theme was one shared by Darryl, a 62-year-old Black male who is employed as a custodian. This story is especially salient because the officer interjects the symbolic gesture of race and ethnicity along with the symbolic vehicle into the context of the stop. Here is how Darryl describes it, verbatim.

I was driving my Ford F-50 two-toned extended cab pick-up truck. I noticed the police officer driving in the opposite direction. As we passed each other, I noticed he looked directly at me and seemed to be surprised. It was kind of strange. I just had a feeling I would be stopped. I watched in my rear-view mirror and sure enough, he did a U-turn and turned on the red lights. I immediately pulled over and stopped...There were two White police officers in the police car. They approached on each side of the truck. He asked for my driver's license. I asked him why I was being stopped and he said for having tinted covers over my headlights. Now listen, you know this was at ten o'clock in the morning. I received a ticket for driving with covers over my headlights. I didn't realize this was even a violation because they're sold in just about every automotive store. As he was giving me the ticket, he kind of looked my truck up and down and said your truck kind of looks like the kind of truck a Mexican would drive.

Theme 3: Nature of the Traffic Violation

Another dominant theme fleshed out of this study is one that I named "Nature of the Violation." In this theme, participants deconstructed the pretextual basis of their being stopped by police authorities. In other words, participants revealed that the police routinely use, in their words, "petty" or "minor" traffic violations to stop and "harass them" because of their race.

As discussed in Chapter 3, the U.S. Supreme Court decided that pretextual stops by police authorities are legally permissible. In the 1996 decision *Whren v. United States*, the Supreme Court decided that the police could stop motorists and search their vehicles if probable cause exists, for example, that the occupants are trafficking illegal drugs or weapons. Under the *Whren* decision, police can stop motorists for a traffic violation even though the traffic violation may not be the underlying motive for the stop. Regardless of the legality of this police practice, participants feel that they are routinely stopped for "minor traffic offenses" and that the police often use these minor traffic offenses as a reason to single them out and profile them.

Participants related that many of the stops they had experienced at the hands of the police over their lifetimes often concluded without a traffic citation being issued. The irony here is that many citizens would probably view this as a desirable outcome. Who would argue that not receiving a traffic citation is the desirable result of a traffic stop? However, to racial minority citizens this seems to reinforce the racialized aspect of being stopped. The absence of a traffic citation reinforces their suspicions of a racially motivated stop. Professor Karen Glover (2009, p. 97) made note of this in her research on racial profiling. She writes, "The traffic stop, innocuous as it appears to some and especially when no citation is issued, is a micro-level occurrence that demonstrates the state's reach on a macro-level."

In one interview of a Black male named Arnold, who was in his late 40s, he describes being stopped on at least six different occasions in a short period of time while driving through the eastern Kansas communities of Leawood and Overland Park. Arnold says he was not stopped for a traffic violation per se, but rather he was stopped and just "checked out," in what he describes as "routine practice." Arnold travels from the Kansas City, Missouri area to Overland Park frequently to pick up a White co-worker. Listen to how he describes his experiences.

> When they stopped me it wasn't even for a traffic violation, at least they never told me I violated any law, they just said they were checking me out. I never got a ticket. It was a routine. They would always ask where I was headed and where I was coming from. They asked for my license and proof of insurance. Sometimes they would ask if they could search my car. A couple of times I would get out, they would have me stand at the back of the car and they would

search my car and have me open up the trunk. The older I get the more I just learn that it is easier just to let them do their thing so I can get on my way.

In 60 (65%) stops reported by participants, traffic citations were not issued. On the other hand, 32 (35%) stops resulted in a traffic citation or an equipment fix-it ticket being issued. Thirty (35%) stops were for what participants described as "being suspicious" or for "tinted windows." The 87 participants I interviewed in this study reported 92 stop incidents of what they believed to be racial profiling. Table 5.2 shows the reasons participants were stopped and whether a traffic citation or written warning was issued.

As I was writing the final pages of this book, DeMarcus, the 29-year-old Black male participant who previously interviewed on several occasions, called to report that he believed that he was recently racially profiled by the police. I interviewed DeMarcus the following day. The interview is reported here because it adds additional context to the "Nature of the Stop" theme.

DeMarcus was driving his 9-year-old daughter to school one morning just before 9:00 a.m. He was driving a 2001 midnight blue Chevrolet Monte Carlo. He described the car as having tinted windows and customized chrome rims. DeMarcus saw a highway patrol car traveling in the same direction about 50 or so yards in front of him. For DeMarcus, what happened next reinforced that he was singled out and profiled based on his race. Here DeMarcus describes the stop:

I was turning out of the parking lot and I saw the highway patrol car pass me. As soon as he passed, I pulled out onto the road. He was in front of me about 50 yards. He then pulled over to the side of the road and waited for me to pass him. I went by him and then he pulled out and started to follow me. I thought to myself, what now? He followed me for a while. I think he was probably checking out my tags. Then he stopped me. I pulled over. I saw him walking up kind of cautiously to the passenger's side of the car and then he changes directions at the last minute and walks over to the driver's side of the car. He bent over to look into my car and I saw his hand on his gun. I remember thinking this is the same trooper that stopped me a few months back about tinted windows on my Caprice.

"Do you know why I pulled you over?" The trooper asked.

"No, I don't," DeMarcus said.

"Have you had your window tint checked out lately?" The trooper asked.

"No, I haven't," DeMarcus said.

"That's why I am stopping you to check out your tinted windows, they look kind of dark," the trooper said.

"I will need to see your driver's license and proof of insurance. If you have your registration, let me see that too," the trooper said.

DeMarcus hands the requested documents over to the trooper.

"Just sit tight and let me check them out," the trooper said.

Table 5.2   Stop and Citation Information as Reported by Participants

		Citation Issued	
Reported Reason for Stop	Number of Reports	Yes	No
Suspicious	15	3	12
Tinted windows	15	5	10
Brake light out	9	4	5
Just checking you out	6	0	6
Cracked taillight	5	1	4
Driving in known drug area	4	1	3
Making a wide turn	4	2	2
Speeding	4	2	2
Tag not assigned to vehicle	4	3	1
Failure to use turn signal	3	1	2
Failure to stop at stop sign	3	3	
Expired tag	2	2	
Cracked windshield	2	2	
Check out tag	2		2
Illegal lane change	2	2	
Defective headlight	2		2
Report of stolen vehicle	1		1
Fit description of stolen vehicle	1		1
Following too close	1		1
Suspended driver's license (cleared at scene)	1		1
Tinted covers on headlights	1	1	
Defective windshield wipers	1		1
Failure to yield to emergency vehicle	1		1
Inattentive driving	1		1
Failure to signal 100 feet when making a turn	1		1
Failure to signal when pulling away from curb	1		1
Total	**92**	**32**	**60**

Note: Citation category inclusive of written warnings and equipment fix-it tickets.

"How long will this take? I am taking my daughter to school and I don't want her to be late," DeMarcus said.

"I will get you out of here as soon as possible," the trooper said.

The trooper leaned over once more and peered into the car. After a few seconds, he walked back to his patrol car and returned with the tint meter. DeMarcus continues,

He told me my tint was too dark and he started to walk back to his patrol car. I said again that I was taking my daughter to school and did not want her to be late. He said, I'll get you out of here as soon as possible. He went back to his car and he was back there for a while, he took his time. My daughter was 30 minutes late to school. He gave me a ticket for the window tint and told me that if I did not take care of it my license would be suspended. My thing is if he is going to pull me over for tint, then you have to stop and pull everyone over. I was so mad. I dropped my daughter off at school and went home and just sat there. I was really bothered by this. I called down to the courthouse and talked with someone in the traffic office. I asked her if she could tell me how many people this trooper has stopped for tinted windows. She told me she could not release that information but she could tell me that in the county [which has a population of about 33,675] there were 24 tickets issued for window tint so far this year [the author notes that the month of this stop was in early December].

As DeMarcus reflects back on the experience, it is clear that he is in emotional turmoil over this incident. He describes vividly as a youth growing up in Arizona and seeing his mother stopped and her car searched because, according to DeMarcus, she was Black and driving through an affluent White neighborhood. He recalls his mother being interrogated by the police about what she was doing in the area and then released without so much as a warning. DeMarcus recalls standing alongside the road with his brothers and sisters as the police searched his mother's car.

DeMarcus has White friends who drive cars with tinted windows in the same community where he resides and the police never stop them. He believes they are given a pass because they are White. He is convinced that the police are attracted to the appearance of certain cars because they are associated with minority drivers. After the association is made, the police follow until the driver has committed a traffic violation. According to the citizens interviewed, the police stop them based on a pretext, which they say usually amounts to a minor traffic infraction.

Perhaps the irony of DeMarcus' story is something he said during the interview. He said, "I tried to control my anger when he stopped me because I did not want my daughter to have a bad impression of the police." This admission is striking in light of his experiences with what he believes to be racial profiling, and along with the experience of seeing his mother stopped and searched during his youth. In spite of these experiences, he finds it necessary to protect his daughter from negative views of the police.

Theme 4: Officer Demeanor

Participants reveal during their contacts with police authorities that the police would often "talk down to them." Participants spoke of being "treated like a criminal." The fact is that most African Americans can "readily point to an encounter with the police where they were treated with discourtesy, hostility, or worse" (Hacker, 2003, p. 230).

Listen to how Peter, a Hispanic male in his mid-30s and a former U.S. Army Demolition Expert who holds a master's degree, describes his experience. As a preface to Peter's story, he was traveling in a large city in Kansas, and on a major throughway at about 5:00 p.m. His children, both of Hispanic ethnicity, were in the backseat. He was driving a black 1998 Dodge Neon with tinted rear windows. The car had a clear plastic film cover over the license plate. The officer stopped Peter for the tinted windows.

Peter was in a hurry when he left his residence because he had to pick his wife up from work. In the rush of getting his children out the door and into the car, Peter left his driver's license at home. During the stop, the police officer confirmed that Peter had a valid driver's license. Here is how Peter describes his experience.

> I didn't feel like I was doing anything wrong and I really think this was a racially motivated stop. He [the officer] acted superior, talking down to me, and his voice, his words, the way he talked and acted was aggressive. He treated me like I was inferior. I thought the way he treated me was awful and if they are getting away with this with me, what else are they getting away with?

As Peter continues to tell his story, the emotionally laden context of the stop is revealed. I sensed that this incident was emotionally charged for Peter. He continues:

> My kids were frightened and they thought something was going to happen to me. You know, he didn't have to talk to me like that in front of my kids. They were afraid and saw law enforcement as bad people because of this situation. I mean, I was angry, but I didn't want my kids to see me that way, they [police] are not all bad, even if I think this one was wrong.

Peter believes his incident was racially motivated. For Peter, this was reinforced by the police officer's comments about what Peter believes is his Hispanic heritage. Peter explains further in the following passage.

> When he [police officer] came back up to the car, he said that he wasn't going to give me a ticket for the tint being too dark, but instead he was going to give me a ticket for you know those plastic film covers you can get to put over your license plate. He was still asking about my driver's license. I think I asked him why he still thought I didn't have a driver license even after he confirmed it in the computer. He told me that usually when he pulls people over like me they usually don't have a driver's license, or it's suspended and they start coming up with excuses as to why they don't have a license on them.

After the officer used the term "people like me," Peter recognizes that he may have just been profiled because of his Hispanic heritage. Peter is upset and questions the officer regarding the statement. He continues:

I said, wait a minute! People like me! I asked him what he meant by people like me. He seemed surprised that I was questioning him, and then he really tried to explain himself. I think he knew I caught him. I really believe that he didn't think I was going to challenge him on that statement. He really started to change his tune after that.

Peter was greatly troubled by the stop. He believes the officer was pushing his weight around. Peter has never been in trouble with the police and spent many years in the military. After his discharge from the military, he enrolled in college and earned a master's degree. Peter said, "The officer kept repeating to me that not having your driver's license on your person is an 'arrestable offense'." I asked Peter to explain why he felt that this incident was racial profiling. Peter believes that when the officer used the term "people like me," that the officer was making an association to undocumented Mexicans living in the United States. He said that the officer knew he was caught and did not expect Peter to challenge him. Peter believes that the officer used the threats of arrest to make it seem like he was doing Peter a favor or cutting him a break. The motive, Peter believes, is so that he (Peter) would not make an issue out of the seemingly bigoted remark.

The following narrative describes Teresa's experience of being stopped by police authorities one evening and talked down to for looking suspicious.

I was driving home from the gym and was just exiting off [street name omitted]. I saw him following me in my rearview mirror. He followed me for a short distance and then stopped me. Right away he started to treat me like a criminal. I asked him why he stopped me and all he kept asking was if I know this person and do I know that person. He looked at my gym bag on the floor board and said what do you have there? He picked it up and started to search it. I was very angry at this point and I asked him, just what is your problem with me and I asked him again why he was stopping me. He did not say anything. He just continued to look through my bag and in my car without my permission. He finally said I am stopping you because you look suspicious. Now let me tell you, I drive a 2001 Mitsubishi Diamante, it's not suspicious. The only thing I can think of is that I am Hispanic and was wearing a hoodie because I just left the gym. He was probably thinking gang member.

William, an African American male in his mid-20s, describes his experience with a police officer. William said the officer talked down to him. William was stopped for tinted windows but he says it was really because he is Black. William questions if the incident would have been handled differently if he were White.

> The officer was not polite to me at all. Maybe if my tattoos were showing this would give him a reason to fear me or question his safety around me, but they weren't because I was fully covered. He said I don't look like the picture on my driver's license and that I memorized my driver's license. I was speechless, I couldn't believe this was happening, he wouldn't stop harassing me, no matter what I said, and he kept being an asshole to me. Then he tried to make me think he was doing me a favor, yeah, cutting me a break or something because he said he could have cited me for having dark tint on my windows.

William continues the interview and begins to talk about the way the police talk to minority citizens.

> When they do stop us, they should know that the worst thing they can do when stopping a Black person is talking down to them. They disrespect us. They shouldn't talk down to us. Just treat us like human beings.

Stacie, a Black female in her early 30s, complains about the manner in which police talk to minority citizens. "It's like when they stop a person of color they are automatically suspicious and always begin the contact with little demeaning remarks." She believes this is a common experience among racial minorities. Stacie illustrates one such incident where the police officer talked to her in what she describes as a very demeaning manner. She thought the officer was very inappropriate. Here is how she describes it:

> I had just dropped off a friend at his house and was driving home when I noticed a police car start to follow me. I keep my eye on the rearview mirror and he kept following me. This went on for about three blocks and then he stopped me. He said he was stopping me for a cracked windshield. I couldn't believe it. I can tell you it was a tiny crack on the passenger's side of my car. I am not even sure how he noticed this...The only reason he stopped me is because he was driving around in a bad neighborhood looking for someone to stop. I was a lone Black female driving in the area so I was stopped. He was very rude from the start and told me to shut the fuck up when I started asking questions about why he stopped me. He really talked down to me.

During one focus group session with a group of African Americans, the discussion was centered on the officer demeanor theme. Luther, a male participant in his mid-20s, suggested if the police were polite and improved their communication skills when dealing with racial minority citizens it would minimize many negative perceptions of the police. He said, "It's all in the way they talk to us." Luther admits he has a past arrest history along with several what he referred to as "run-ins with the police." He said an officer's communication during the initial contact could go a long way. Luther suggested in some of his encounters the officer's demeanor escalated his reaction, which in some cases resulted in him arguing with and challenging the police. Here are a few remarks taken verbatim from another focus group participant.

> In the academy, if they were to train them to be polite and then take action, it would kill a lot of problems. None of them know how to communicate. They don't even talk to us right. You are automatically a threat to them. I think a lot of Black men get offended because they [the police] make them feel like less than a man, especially in front of other people. If you run from them you get a case, if you say something smart to them, you get a case. You can't talk smart to them or question or challenge them about anything. There is nothing you can do. If you try to, it makes the situation worse.

Theme 5: Normative Experiences

Many participants accept racial profiling as a normative part of their lives. There is a pervasive feeling that the chances of being stopped by police authorities for the most minor traffic infraction are very real among racial minority citizens. While this feeling was widespread among all participants in this study, it was especially prevalent among Black male participants. During one focus group session with eight African Americans (6 males and 2 females), one participant, a Black male in his early 60s, when asked about what he thinks of when he hears the term racial profiling replied, "I think about Black men." Another participant underscored this sentiment and said, "I've really gotten used to being stopped, it's just a part of life for a Black man." Another participant replied, "Getting stopped by the police is a reality in our neighborhood. White communities don't understand because they don't face this like we do. It's a matter of fact to us." Recall Arnold, the African American who shared the many incidents of being stopped in eastern Kansas. Arnold said, "It's just a routine fact of life, at first I really had a lot of rage built up inside, but as I have matured in life, I learn to accept it as the norm."

Perhaps the most revealing statement that underscored the normative experience is the one volunteered by Cory, a Black male participant in his late 20s. Here is what Cory said:

> It's almost like we are in slavery. Every time we are driving around, we got to watch out because we might get stopped. You know I have become so used to the possibility of being stopped it's like an everyday thing. You get used to it after a while. When I see a police officer, I automatically begin to think that I may be stopped. It is always there in the back of your mind, it's automatic, you just think about it when you see the police car.

Cory's narrative is troubling. Here we have an African American male in his late 20s, an American citizen, equating the experience of potentially being stopped by police authorities to slavery. He captures how a great many minority citizens feel. Participants constructed an almost normative expectation of being stopped by the police. The "normative experience" theme was strong throughout this study and was often intertwined with the other themes.

Several participants actually use the "norm" to describe being stopped. For example, during an interview of one Black male participant, he used the word "norm" on two occasions, in a matter of fact style. Notice that in that last sentence of his narrative, he suggests a "we against them attitude."

> Too many Black males in a car will strike up suspicion. That's the norm. My friends refuse to let other Black people pile up in a car or they will get stopped. That's the norm. It's just not worth the hassle. Why take a chance and give them a reason.

Theme 6: Race and Place

The "race and place" theme centers on participants' belief that there is a greater likelihood being stopped in certain geographical areas of the communities. This theme is binary in nature. First, there is a sense among participants that they are more likely to be stopped in what they describe as predominately White and affluent neighborhoods. Second, participants describe what they call as an increased chance of being stopped in economically disadvantaged areas including areas that have been targeted by the police.

Participants describe how they consciously avoid driving through some affluent White neighborhoods for fear that they will attract police attention. This theme was discussed during one focus group. A Black male focus group participant who is employed as a house painter recalls driving through an affluent White neighborhood and being followed for several blocks by the police. He believes it was simply because he was Black and "out of place." He explained that he had a residential paint job that he was finishing in the neighborhood. He routinely makes it a habit of not driving through some neighborhoods in order to avoid police scrutiny, even if it means driving several blocks out of his way. Many participants in this study described altering their routes in order to avoid police attention.

As illustrated in the following interview with Tina, a 36-year-old Black female employed as a school paraprofessional, race and place is very real.

> I was trying to find my friend's house. My friend is White and lives in a White area of town. It's a pretty nice area. I'm driving around this neighborhood in broad daylight and I see in my rearview window this police car following me. I thought to myself, here we go again. My 11-year-old sister is in the car with

me. I was driving a big yellow 2000 Buick. I know it stands out. I kept driving thinking he would get off of me but after a couple of blocks he stopped me. He told me he was stopping me for a cracked windshield. The crack was only about two inches and was on the passenger's side. He asked for my driver's license and proof of insurance. What really surprised me is when he asked if I had any drugs or weapons in the car. I said no, I don't. He was like looking at my driver's license. I had my 11-year-old sister in the car and he is asking this. He used the windshield as an excuse to stop me. I'm pretty sure he stopped me because he saw this Black woman driving a yellow Buick around in this White neighborhood. I got a warning for the cracked windshield and he told me I could go.

Tina questions how the police officer could notice the small crack in the windshield. She believes that he must have really been searching for something to stop her for. For Tina, this racialized the stop. In other words, the pretext of using the cracked windshield as a reason to stop her racialized the stop. Tina believes that there is a perception among the police that if a Black person is driving through an affluent White neighborhood, that he or she must be up to something criminal.

The race and place theme not only reveals a heightened awareness among participants of being stopped in White affluent neighborhoods, but also neighborhoods disproportionally impacted by crime including those that are economically disadvantaged. Participants discuss being stopped by police authorities for driving in lower income areas, many of which have high crime rates. In an interview with Betty, a 49-year-old African American minister, who is proud of the fact that she has her own church, recalled being stopped by the police while driving through what she described as a "rough part of the community." Here is how Betty describes it verbatim:

It was about 7:00 or 8:00 one night. I was driving home when I saw a police car in my rearview mirror following me. I think that they followed me for a couple of blocks. You know they were probably calling in my tag. I was driving a 2000 Nissan Pathfinder and there was nothing special about the Pathfinder. The windows were slightly tinted. After a couple of blocks, sure enough, they stopped me. There were two officers in the car. They were walking up on both sides of my Pathfinder. When they came up to the window, I said, I know why you are stopping me but there is nobody in here but me and Jesus. One officer said can I see your driver's license. And then I asked him, why are you stopping me? He said, ma'am just give me your driver's license. I pulled my driver's license out and said, I know why you are stopping me, you thought you had a car full of gang bangers, but you had no idea you were stopping a 49-year-old minister. I told him that I just left work and that I had to work late that night. Then the officer who was standing on the passenger's side of the car must have recognized me as being a minister and called me by name. I said, yep that's me but I know you guys do this all of the time. Yep, I could tell that he had egg all

over his face. Then the other officer said that my tag light was out. I know that
this was a bogus stop and that's the best they could come up with. When it was
all said and done, they gave me a fix-it ticket and told me when I get it fixed to
have a police officer sign off on it.

Betty believes that the officers made the up the tag light violation because
they are aware that many young Black males are unlikely to file a complaint.
Betty indicated she was driving in a rough area of the community and the
police have knowledge that most people they stop in the neighborhood are
poor and cannot fight back. Betty continues with her story:

The next day I stopped in the QuikTrip to get something to drink and I see the
same two officers that stopped me the night before. I went up to the officers
and said hey, do you remember me? You gave me a bogus ticket last night.
You said my tag light was out and it works just fine. I asked him if he wanted
to sign the bogus ticket. I told him I want you to go out there and write off on
this ticket because I did not have a defective tag light. I saw that the officer who
knew me looked a little embarrassed. Then the other officer said I don't know
what you are talking about and then he says you better watch the way you are
talking to us.

Betty said the officer went outside and checked the tag light, which
was working properly, and signed off on the ticket. Betty recalls asking
the officer after he signed the ticket, "How many times do you all do that
each night?" Betty believes that the officers thought they were stopping a
young African American male. She told me, "I know if it would have been
a Black male and he had friends in that car they would have been all over
them." Betty said she ministers to many young Black males and she hears
the same thing over and over about the police stopping them for bogus
reasons. Betty continues:

You know they [police] might get lucky every now and then, and find someone
with an old ticket they didn't or couldn't afford to pay and then they get to take
them to jail. It happens all of the time.

For Betty, what was particularly striking is the fact that the officer who
recognized her as being a minister apologized to her. Betty describes the apology, "[T]the officer that knew who I was, got me to the side at the QuikTrip
and said, pastor I am sorry, I was riding with him and that was him." For
Betty, the apology reinforced her suspicions of the police.

What is salient in Betty's case is that she also seems to try to understand the police perspective. Betty explains, "I can see both sides here. To
the police, you have this young Black male driving around in this car with
expensive rims that probably cost five or six thousand dollars, and he doesn't

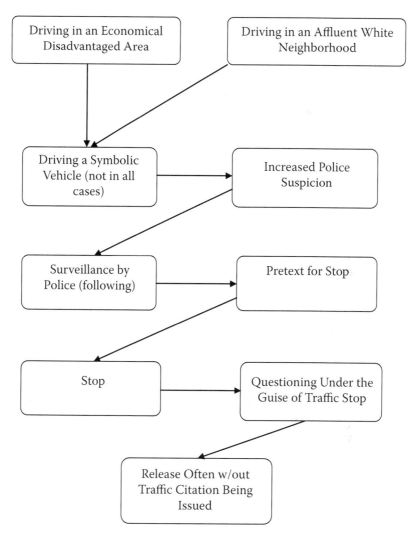

Figure 5.1 Race and place model as constructed by participants.

have a job." Betty is quick to point out that she still believes this is not a reason to stop young Black males but she can certainly see the police view.

Figure 5.1 is a visual construction of participants' descriptions of the race and place theme.

Coercion and Appearance

The research identified two weaker but important themes, which were named "Feeling Compelled" and the "Symbolic Appearance." These two themes are included in this discussion because they provide additional contextual

Table 5.3   Search Details

Type of Search	Number	Number of Searches Where Evidence Was Found
Gave police consent to search	24 (67%)	0
Search incidental to arrest (consent was not asked)	12 (33%)	3[a]
Total searches	36 (40%)	3

N = 91 stops
[a] In 3 searches, small amounts (1 gram or less) of marijuana were seized.

information regarding the manner in which minority citizenry experience what they believe to be racial profiling.

Feeling Compelled

Motor vehicle searches are a possible extension of racial profiling. If the police requested to search the participants' automobiles, they would most likely consent because if they did not, the police would make it worse for them. Participants believe if they did not consent to the search, then they would be accused of hiding something, which would lead to a lengthier detention time and additional police interrogation.

Of the 92 stop incidents studied, in 36 (39%), the police conducted a search of the participants' automobiles. Table 5.3 provides information regarding the 36 searches.

Symbolic Appearance

Predictors such as dreadlocks, tattoos, the way they wore their ball cap, wearing hoodies, and specific types of clothing were verbalized by participants as contributing to what they called "stereotypical views" of a symbolized criminal element such as drug dealers or gang members. According to participants, being a minority and looking a certain way is a pretext for heightened police suspicion. For example, participants explained that wearing their baseball hats slightly tilted on their heads would result in increased police scrutiny. Participants related that wearing the hat to the side of one's head or slightly tilted is a symbol that they reject the status quo, a status quo that many participants said was unfair to them. Wearing the hat in a tilted manner on one's head appears to have evolved into a fad among youth.

Black male participants were not only more structural in their explanations of the impact of appearance and its relationship to being stopped by the police, but also they seemed to be far more critical and devastated by what they believe to be a systematic practice of being stopped for how they look in constellation with their race. For example, in regards to wearing a tilted ball cap, Black male participants related to the author that if they see a police car they will either remove their baseball hat or adjust it to a straight position on their head to avoid attracting police attention.

Recall the discussion in Chapter 2 of the incident in Sanford, Florida where George Zimmerman, who was reported to be a neighborhood watch captain, shot an African American teenager to death. In part, the controversial shooting centered on Zimmerman's equating that the African American teenager looked suspicious and specifically told police dispatchers that he was wearing a hoodie. Many of the participants I talked with in my study related that the hoodie is a sign of fashion and not criminality. Some told me that the wearing of the hoodie, especially by African American males, is a sign that you are cool and that there is a desire for anonymity, to not be noticed.

Participants revealed that if you are a minority and wear clothing a certain way, for example, baggy clothing or sagging, as it was referred to (especially trousers), then this would lead to increased police suspicion. I queried the participants about why wearing baggie clothes would subject them to police attention. They explained that the police would automatically assume they were a member of a gang or a drug dealer. It is also important to keep in mind that while many gang members do wear their pants baggie or let them sag, not all persons who wear baggie clothes are gang members. Traditionally, in prison, sagging pants meant that you were advertising your availability for sexual conduct. However, because of changing times that is not always the case now.

The sagging pants came as part of the hip-hop culture in the late 1980s and early 1990s. African American males who liked that type of music participated in it as a fashion statement. With the advent of gangster rap, many gang members became enmeshed in the hip-hop culture and adopted the fashion. At the time, Hispanic males wore their pants abnormally high. According to Professor Gregg Etter, a nationally known gang expert, a Hispanic gang cop from Los Angles told him that the Hispanic bangers wore their pants so high that they had to unzip to brush their teeth (personal communication, July 21, 2011). As the popularity of the music crossed cultures, the fashion statement of sagging crossed racial lines. Hip-hop and rap fans of all races began to sag. Many law enforcement officials and many municipal officials began to identify the fashion with unruly or unlawful behavior. Some cities and most schools have outlawed sagging pants as being gang related.

However, in the mid 1980s in Wichita, Kansas, there was a gang called the Playboy Gangster Crips. Members of the gang began to start to wear their hair in a flattop haircut. During this time, very few if any African American males wore their hair in that style. The Playboy Gangster Crips also had a playboy bunny razored into the side of the hairdo. This was unheard of at the time. However, in six or eight months both of these practices were all the rage among young African American males. Sports teams, school mascots, girlfriend's names, etc. began to show up in the sides of their flattop haircuts.

When some sports figures began to wear the fashion, it exploded. This type of hairdo had become a fashion statement. According to Professor Etter,

> One of the things that I teach my students is that you cannot identify a gang member on solely one thing, an exception might be a tattoo that displayed Crips, Bloods, or Skinheads. Another might be a motorcycle jacket that said Hell's Angels on the back. Generally, it takes more than one criteria to identify a gang member. (Gregg Etter, personal communication, July 21, 2011)

You may recall the Columbine school shootings in Colorado. The two shooters identified themselves as being part of the "Trench Coat Mafia." Schools all over America panicked and began to ban trench coats. We tend to automatically assume if A, then B. It is not always true. A young teen wearing a Kansas City (KC) Royals ball cap in Kansas City is probably a baseball fan. A young teen wearing the same ball cap in some neighborhoods in Chicago may be affiliated with the Simon City Royals (a Folk Nation gang). The totality of the circumstances makes the identification.

Skolnick (1966) proposed that because of the inherent dangers in police work, police officers develop a symbolic assailant of sorts. As part of police socialization, the police officer learns that individual behavior cues may be a sign of danger for a police officer. Skolnick (1966, p. 45) informs us that the police officers develop "a perceptual shorthand to identify certain kinds of people as symbolic assailants, that is, as persons who use gesture, language, and attire that the policeman has come to recognize as a prelude to violence."

What flowed out of this research was strikingly similar to Skolnick's thesis, that is, the participants believe that the police have constructed a symbolic assailant that includes race, clothing, and vehicles. Thus, they believe that if you are a racial minority and you fashion baggie trousers, wear your hat tilted or wear a hoodie, or drive a certain type of car, you then have significantly increased your chances of being stopped and scrutinized by police authorities.

Perhaps one reason participants believe that the police construct a symbolic criminalized racial minority assailant is because the police themselves have a tendency to label racial minorities in a criminalized manner. Labeling theory was developed in the 1960s and focuses on the linguistic tendency of majorities to negatively label racial minorities or those seen as deviant from norms, and is associated with the concept of a self-fulfilling prophecy and stereotyping (Becker, 1973). For example, the police may falsely view racial minorities as being more likely to transport illegal drugs (this is a false prophecy). They may believe that because some drugs in the United States get here via Mexico, then minorities, especially Hispanics, are more likely to be involved in transporting illicit drugs. This false prophecy leads to a heightened suspicion when stopping, for example, a Hispanic motorist. In the case of several of my interviews with participants, this seems plausible.

Consider the case of Alex who was stopped by police authorities on a rural western Kansas road who when questioned what he was doing in the area told the officer that he was lost. In this case, we have a lone Hispanic male, stopped for speeding, who tells the police officer he is lost, he does not live in the area, and the police officer doubts his story—the heightened sense of awareness is established because Alex is Hispanic. The labeling effect takes over, that is, Alex is Hispanic and may be transporting drugs. This is supported by the police officer's actions when he radioed for additional officers and a K-9 unit. The officer asks to search Alex's car (this further reveals the suspicion on the part of the police officer). Alex gives consent to search his vehicle. As Alex describes, the police searched as if they were determined to find something. This would seem to indicate that the police officers had already formed the conclusion that Alex was transporting drugs and their goal was to find them.

Unifying Experience

The essential, invariant structure is the one unifying meaning of all the descriptions provided by the participants. The unifying experience was constructed by taking the clusters of themes that emerged in this study, and then developing the overall description. During validation procedures using member checks, the essential, invariant structure was adjusted and perfected several times as a result of feedback provided by participants. Table 5.4 depicts the essential, invariant structure describing the one unifying meaning of all the descriptions.

Berry's Story

In concluding this chapter, let me relate Berry's story to you. He is an African American male in his late 40s. His encounter with the police is compelling. Berry's encounter sheds light on three salient factors in the racial profiling discourse. First, it clearly illuminates the problems with the pretextual stop for seemingly minor traffic infractions, which probably are not enforced to the same extent in White middle- to upper-class neighborhoods. The second factor is the coercive language used by the police officer in an attempt to get Berry to consent to a search of his automobile. The third factor is the retaliation that the police may use on a citizen who refuses a consent search. This

Table 5.4   Unifying Experience of Perceived Racial Profiling Experiences

Incidents in which participants believe they were racially profiled by police authorities often began with a heightened awareness of the police car presence. The police follow participants for great distances before stopping them. This results in increased anxiety on the part of participants. Participants were humiliated, helpless, embarrassed, and frustrated, and the encounter with the police often left them angry and emotionally drained. In some cases, the emotional effect lasts for a considerable time after the stop. Minority citizens believe the type of car they drive will result in increased police suspicion. For example, driving a customized car (rims, tint, low rider, or flashy paint) or simply driving an expensive car such as a Mercedes, BMW, or Lexus is perceived to attract greater police suspicion. Participants perceive that the police form a stereotype of the symbolic minority vehicle and use the traffic infraction as a pretext to stop them. The stop is most often described as a minor traffic infraction. During the stop, participants say the police are demeaning and accusatory, asking many questions such as "Do you have any weapons or drugs on you?" "Where are you coming from?" and "Where are you going?" In many cases, the police do not give participants an immediate reason for why they are being stopped. Many ethnic and racial minorities learn not only through their own but others' experiences that their chances of being stopped by the police are greater when compared to White citizens. There is a normative expectation of being stopped. It is similar to a routine, always watchful for a police car and always mindful of the possibility of being stopped. Participants become conditioned to tolerate it and are reluctant to show emotion, or even to inquire about the reason for the stop because they do not want to make the situation worse. When police ask for consent to search participants' automobiles, many consent because they feel compelled, and if they refuse to consent to the search, it may make their situation worse.

retaliation may be a long detention and the assurance that a traffic citation will be issued.

Berry is a former police officer turned academic administrator. His encounter with the police occurred on a spring day in 2011. Berry was driving a rental car through what he admits was a high-crime neighborhood. He was navigating the rental car through the neighborhood looking for an address. It had been many years since Berry had been in this particular inner city neighborhood, which is made up predominately of African American residents. Berry drove slowly as he peered at addresses. He pulled over to let other traffic pass because he was not sure of the location he was trying find.

When Berry pulled into the neighborhood, he saw the police but continued to look for the address. The officer suddenly started following Berry. Berry pulled over to let the officer pass. The police cruiser drove by and Berry slowly pulled out and continued driving and looking for the address. Without warning, the police officer was following him again. Berry related that he came to a stop at the next intersection, which was marked with a stop sign. He signaled to turn. After he turned the corner and within a matter of seconds, the officer stopped Berry. In Berry's words, "He immediately lit me up." The officer told Berry that the reason he was being stopped is because he was "acting suspicious." Listen to how Berry described what happened next.

> He asked me what I was doing in the area, I told him. He then asked me about the car, which was an orange 2011 Dodge Charger with Missouri tags. I guess the car draws attention, it has ever since I was given it on Friday but being a rental, there are no defects other than as the officer said, the tags were not on file. I told him it was a rental. He asked me why I had a rental. I told him that my car was being repaired. He asked me by whom and why. I told him that I drive a 2009 Hyundai Genesis and that the rear night vision camera is not working. I believe he asked me what I did. I told him that I'm an administrator at a local college and until a couple of years ago I was a police officer. He thought about it for a while and then asked me if I had anything illegal on me. I said I better not, having been a police officer before.
>
> He then asked me if he could search me and the car. By this point, I was incredulous because I was dressed in a baseball cap, t-shirt, gym shorts with no pockets and flip-flops. There was no way I could conceal anything on me and I know there's nothing suspicious about my demeanor. He had no probable cause: no smell of marijuana, no smell of alcohol, the interior of the car was clean. I said no. He said that he would get a canine unit. He then said that he was going to write me for not signaling within 100 feet when making a turn. I threw my hands up and said, "Ohhhhh!" out of exasperation.

Berry related that the stop lasted 36 minutes. Some research has found that Black drivers are more likely to have longer stops when compared to White drivers (Ridgeway & Riley, 2004). Berry told me later that he was alarmed that after the officer learned that he was looking for an address, that Berry was not committing any crime, and that he was a former police officer, the officer still asked for consent to search his car. In the end, the officer did not search Berry's car or call for a canine (police dog) even though he threatened to do so. An atmosphere of coercion was very prevalent in participants' stories of being stopped by the police. Participants believed the police used coercion tactics in an attempt to get consent to search their cars. In Berry's case, the officer had no probable cause. He clearly used a pretext for stopping Berry (failing to signal 100 feet before making a turn). The officer used threatening and coercive language after Berry refused the search when he said he would call for a canine unit, which he never did.

Being a former police officer, Berry knew the officer factored race in his decision to stop him. He also knew that the police officer had no probable cause to search his car and that the officer's remark about calling a canine unit was used solely in an attempt to get Berry to consent to a search. Furthermore, Berry knew the stop was pretextual and that the police as a matter of essential traffic enforcement policy do not usually seek out traffic violators who do not use their turn signals 100 feet before making a turn. The irony to the pretext violation in Berry's stop is not that he did not use his turn indicator, but that he did not use it 100 feet before turning. Instead, he stopped at a stop sign in a residential neighborhood and then signaled his turn. Research has shown that African American and Hispanic men are less likely to report that during a traffic stop encounter the police acted properly (Allen & Monk-Turner, 2010). Black males are also less likely to report that the police "had a legitimate reason for the stop" (Lundman & Kaufman, 2003, p. 195). In Berry's case, the officer wanted to stop him.

What is troubling is that according to many participants, the police use this coercion as a matter of routine when dealing with racial minority citizens and trying to get consent to search. Moreover, many participants did not know that they could refuse to let the police search. This is not surprising especially after learning about how police officers phrase their requests, for example, "would you mind if I take a quick look in your car?" and "I will have you back on the road in a few minutes but first would you mind if I search your car?" When the officer stopped Berry, he assuredly did not expect him to be a former police officer and someone who is versed on search and seizure laws, pretextual stops, and racial profiling.

Discussion Questions

1. If you were appointed as a racial profiling task force member with the authority to investigate citizen complaints of racial profiling, what kinds of specific evidence would you have to see to sustain the allegation?
2. Read one of the cases reported in this chapter. What issues, if any, support a case of racial profiling? What issues, if any, do not support a case of racial profiling?
3. Examine the first 10 traffic violations presented in Table 5.2. Do you think the police enforce these 10 violations on a regular basis or do you think they are selectively enforced?
4. In regard to Theme six (Race and Place), do you think that minority citizens are more prone to being stopped in affluent, predominately White neighborhoods? Why or why not?
5. Do you think the "Unifying Experience of Perceived Racial Profiling Experiences" presented in the chapter (Table 5.4) fit the definition of racial profiling? Why or why not?

References

Allen, J., & Monk-Turner, E. (2010). Citizen perceptions of the legitimacy of traffic stops. *Journal of Criminal Justice, 38*, 589–594.

Becker, H.S. (1973). *Outsiders*. New York: Free Press.

Birzer, M.L. (2008). What makes a good police officer: Phenomenological reflections from the African-American community. *Police Practice and Research: An International Journal, 9*(3), 199–212.

Birzer, M.L., & Smith-Mahdi, J. (2006). The phenomenology of discrimination experienced among African-Americans. *Journal of Black Studies, 10*(2), 22–37.

Glover, K.S. (2009). *Racial profiling: Research, racism, and resistance*. Lanham, MD: Rowman and Littlefield Publishers, Inc.

Hacker, A. (2003). *Two nations: Black and White, separate, hostile, unequal*. New York: Scribner.

Lundman, R.J., & Kaufman, R.L. (2003). Driving while Black: Effects of race, ethnicity, and gender on citizen self-reports of traffic stops and police actions. *Criminology, 41*(1), 195–220.

Parker, K.D., Onekwuluje, A.B., & Murty, K.S. (1995). African-Americans' attitudes toward the police: A multivariate analysis. *Journal of Black Studies, 25*(3), 396–409.

Ridgeway, G., & Riley, K.J. (2004). *Assessing racial profiling more credibly: A case study of Oakland*. Santa Monica, CA: Rand.

Skolnick, J.H. (1966). *Justice without a trial: Law enforcement in democratic society*. New York: John Wiley & Sons.

Trusting the Data

6

"Successful field research depends on the investigator's trained ability to look at people, listen to them, think and feel with them, talk with them rather than at them."

Ned Polsky, *Hustlers, Beats, and Others* (1967)

Introduction

The overall purpose of this chapter is to describe the procedures that were followed to check the validity of the data. A secondary purpose is to discuss the concepts of validity and reliability as it is generally used in social science research. Finally, this chapter examines the methods that qualitative researchers employ to ensure the data is valid and trustworthy.

In any qualitative research study, it is important to ensure that the data is valid. This is a challenging task for two reasons: (1) the subjectivity of the research may lead to difficulties in establishing the validity, and (2) because the researcher is an instrumental part of the data, it is difficult to prevent or detect bias introduced by the researcher. However, I should point out that subjectivity on the part of the researcher is not necessarily a bad thing and is an essential part of doing good qualitative research. This will be discussed in detail later in the chapter.

For these very reasons listed, the discussion here will be open and transparent regarding the qualitative racial profiling data and the process that was used to ensure that it was valid. At the onset, it should be noted that many qualitative researchers refer to validity as trustworthiness, while others use terminology such as authenticity, goodness, verisimilitude, credibility, and plausibility to describe the validation processes of qualitative data.

Before describing the process of how the trustworthiness was ensured in the study presented in the book, let us take a brief look at the general concepts of validity and reliability as applied to traditional social science research.

Validity

If a survey, standardized test, or some other instrument measures what it is supposed to measure, then it is valid. Validity is simply the degree to which a test or some other instrument measures what it is supposed to measure. If it does not, it is not a valid measurement and the data cannot be trusted.

There are a few different types of validity with which you should be familiar before initiating research: (1) internal validity, (2) external validity, (3) face validity, (4) content validity, and (5) construct validity. Please keep in mind that these concepts are mostly important in quantitative research, that is, research that makes use of statistical analysis. It is important, however, for qualitative researchers to have a general understanding of the concept of validity and reliability.

Internal Validity

Internal validity is concerned with ensuring that changes in the dependent variable or outcome variable are really the result of the influence of the independent variable. The researcher attempts to rule out the effect of confounding variables. Confounding variables are those variables that were not accounted for during the experiment and may actually be influencing the dependent variable.

External Validity

External validity is concerned with the ability to generalize from a research sample back to the population. For example, assume that a researcher is interested in studying students' perceptions of racial profiling. The researcher learns that there are 20,000 students attending River City University. He obtains a computer-generated list of all 20,000 criminal justice majors and uses a procedure to randomly select 6000 students who will be mailed a survey to complete. Let us say that 4500 students, roughly 75 percent, returned completed surveys to the researcher. Assuming that errors were kept to a minimum during random sampling of the criminal justice students, it is possible to generalize the results back to the 20,000 students. As you may have noted in this example, the key to generalization is sampling. That is, using a probability sampling technique wherein everyone in a population of interest has an equal chance of being selected for the study.

Face Validity

Face validity is a simple concept. It is concerned with whether the survey or measurement appears on its face value to measure what it is intended to measure. If researchers desired to administer a survey to a number of citizens in order to measure if they believe racial profiling exists in our society, the first step would be to develop a number of questions to be included on the survey. In order to check the face validity, the researcher could present the survey to several colleagues and simply ask them if it appears on its face to adequately gauge citizens perceptions centering on the existence of racial profiling in society. One other way to describe face validity is to say that in the judgment of others the survey or instrument appears to measure what it is supposed to measure.

Content Validity

Content validity asks the question, does my research instrument or survey actually measure what it is supposed to measure? Content validity is concerned with the degree to which questions on a survey, test instrument, or some other standardized instrument represent the domain being measured. Content validity therefore simply examines whether the measure or instrument covers the range of meanings included in the concept. If we design a survey that we intend to measure individuals' perceptions regarding the extent of racial profiling by police authorities in their community, one way that we might check the content validity is to have several experts take the survey. These experts would then judge the relevance of the test items to the content the survey is supposed to measure, which in this case is the perception of the extent of racial profiling in the community. If something measures what it is supposed to measure, then it is said to have good content validity.

Construct Validity

Construct validity concerns the degree to which the test or instrument measures the concept it was designed to measure. Note that a construct and concept mean the same thing here. Constructs get their name "because our understandings come from our mental constructions" (Vogt, 2007, p. 120). A construct is a concept that cannot be directly observed or isolated (Bayens & Roberson, 2011). It is a property that is offered to explain some aspect of human behavior. For example, prejudice, racism, and pain are examples of constructs. We cannot easily measure it. Racial profiling could also be considered a construct. It is not an easy concept that we can accurately measure.

Can you think of a way that racial profiling can be precisely measured? I would suspect that if I asked police officers and minority citizens what racial profiling is, there would be much disagreement.

Reliability

Reliability is concerned with accuracy and precision of the test instrument. If a test or standardized instrument yields the same results time after time, it is said to be reliable. In scientific research, reliability is extremely important. Let me provide a simple example of reliability. This morning when I awoke, I climbed out of bed, walked into bathroom, and stepped on the scale. It registered 175 pounds. I repeated weighing myself five more times yielding the same result each time. Thus, we can conclude that the scale was reliable. It consistently yielded the same weight.

Was the scale also valid? Assume that I went to my physician's office one hour later for my scheduled annual checkup. While at my physician's office the nurse measured my body weight on a calibrated scale. My weight registered 185 pounds, 10 pounds heavier than my scale at home. We can conclude that my scale at home is reliable, but that it is not accurate or valid. It is important to keep in mind when conducting research that just because something is reliable does not necessarily mean that it is valid.

Trustworthiness

One of the central concerns in a qualitative study is if the researcher got it right. In other words, can the data be trusted and confirmed? Because qualitative inquiries are vastly different when compared to quantitative research, it has its own unique approach to evaluating trustworthiness (Ambert, Adler, Adler, & Detzner, 2009). Just as quantitative researchers take every precaution to ensure that their data is valid, qualitative researchers also go to great lengths to ensure that their data is trustworthy. Qualitative researchers generally accept the principles of validity and reliability discussed previously, but they use different terminology to describe their applicability and apply them somewhat differently in actual practice (Neuman, 2012). For purposes of the racial profiling research reported in this book, the terms validity and trustworthiness are interchangeable.

There have been many articles and books written that suggest specific approaches to establishing the trustworthiness of qualitative data. For example, Lincoln and Guba (1985) offered the following advice to qualitative researchers. They instructed that in order to obtain valid and credible data, the researcher should commit to a significant amount of time in the field. This was coined prolonged engagement. They also recommended that interpretations, data, and meanings should be shared with the participants. The participants in this sense would be asked to comment if the interpretations and meanings made sense to them. This procedure is referred to as member checks.

It is also a good idea for qualitative researchers to discuss the data, findings, and conclusions with others who will be critical of the data. This is referred to as peer debriefing. There is some debate on the correct course of action for establishing trustworthiness of qualitative data (Marshall & Rossman, 2012).

Warren and Karner (2005, p. 215) presented a comprehensive process for assessing if qualitative data can be trusted. They suggested:

- Evaluating your data in the contexts of your methodological and analytic choices
- Reframing your analysis—testing its "goodness of fit" with the data
- Seeking external verification from respondents, from other sociologists, or by triangulation

Because this racial profiling study used a qualitative phenomenological approach to study minority citizens' perception of racial profiling, it was important to identify a usable procedure that would lend itself to establishing trustworthiness of common themes, meanings, and ultimately the unifying experience among participants. I drew heavily from the work of Creswell (2007) and Creswell and Miller (2000).

Creswell (2007) identified standards to assess the quality of phenomenology. The standards include the following:

- Does the author convey an understanding of the philosophical tenants of phenomenology?
- Does the author have a clear "phenomenon" to study that is articulated in a concise way?
- Does the author use procedures of data analysis in phenomenology, such as the procedures recommended by Moustakas (1994)?
- Does the author convey the overall essence of the experience of the participants? Does this essence include a description of the experience and the context in which it occurred?
- Is the author reflexive throughout the study (pp. 214–215)?

Creswell and Miller (2000) described nine approaches to establish the trustworthiness of qualitative data—triangulation, disconfirming evidence, researcher reflexivity, member checking, prolonged engagement in the field, collaboration, the audit trail, thick, rich description, and peer debriefing. They advocated that qualitative researchers select one or more of these validation approaches. The racial profiling data was subjected to member checks, triangulation, collaboration, and rich, thick description. Trustworthiness was also supported by the overall responsibility of the researcher to analyze the data, identify significant statements, form common themes, and construct an overall experience. In order to establish the trustworthiness of the data reported in this book, five approaches were used, member checks, triangulation, collaboration, rich, thick descriptions, and researcher reflexibility.

Member Checks

With member checking, "the validity procedure shifts from the researcher to participants in the study" (Creswell and Miller, 2000, p. 127). In member checks, the researcher solicits the participants' view of the data in order to verify the study's findings. Member checks were initiated early and often in the racial profiling study. Member checking was ongoing until the study was completed. Here is an overview of the member checks.

Participants were furnished with copies of the themes, significant statements, associated meanings, unifying descriptions, and conclusions of the study. They were then to examine these data and provide feedback. Many participants revealed that they had not really thought about their experience using the same terminology used by the researcher, but that their experiences were accurately described. For example, one participant wrote to me in an email communication verbatim: "Thanks Professor, you really named this right. I started to cry just reading it, as if it was my own reaction. This is absolutely on the point."

Several participants suggested additional themes that should be investigated and provided comments to enhance the accuracy of the study. The majority of their suggestions were incorporated into the analysis. Participants were also furnished with copies of excerpts from interview transcripts and memos that were integrated into this report, and asked to verify their accuracy. In the end, the findings were validated and endorsed by participants.

Triangulation

Triangulation strategies make use of multiple data sources and investigators to provide collaborating evidence. When using triangulation, "researchers search for convergence among multiple or different sources of information to form themes or categories in a study" (Creswell & Miller, 2000, p. 126). You might ask why this process is called triangulation. That is a very good question. Triangulation actually is taken from the principles of surveying. According to Gibbs (2007, p. 94), "in order to get an accurate estimate of the distance of a far-away object, the surveyor constructs a triangle whose base is a measured straight line and then observes the angles between this and the distant object from either side of the base line...the true distance of the object can be calculated." Triangulation, when applied to qualitative research, suggests that the more information one can gain about a phenomenon the more accurate it will be. Information may include interviews, focus groups, written documents, observations, photographs, and the like.

Multiple data sources were used in this study in order to establish convergence of the data. The multiple sources included in-depth interviews, focus groups, written documents, email communication, official complaint documents, photographs of participants' automobiles, and electronic blogs. Once emerging themes begin to flesh out from the data, supporting evidence was sought out from the sources above, including a vast amount of direct personal or electronic communication with many participants throughout the study. Memos that were written throughout the study were also used to corroborate the data.

Collaboration

According to Creswell and Miller (2000), collaboration is the process where participants are involved in the study as co-researchers or in less formal arraignments. Collaboration may involve multiple forms such as participants' input on research questions, assisting with data collection and analysis, and being involved in writing a narrative account. "By actively involving participants in their studies, qualitative inquirers add further credibility to their narrative accounts" (Creswell & Miller, 2000, p. 128).

Throughout this study, constant contact was kept with the majority of the participants. In some cases, this contact was through email and telephone dialogue, and some over cups of coffee. One effective strategy that was used with some participants was to have them write a description of what and how they felt during an incident of racial profiling.

One other collaborative activity was used in focus group sessions. The sessions would begin by asking participants to write a description of racial profiling. Some of these descriptions provided were very detailed with rich contextual information. Others were brief but had significant words or phrases to describe their experiences. After this activity, participants were asked to write down the first thing that they think of when they hear the term racial profiling. Here is a partial list from one focus group with 9 African American participants (5 males and 4 females): Black men, control, slavery, unbelievable, disrespect, injustice, helplessness, and angry.

Rich, Thick Descriptions

Using rich, thick description is the process where participants described their experiences in depth. Thick descriptions provided by the participants illuminated how they experienced and ascribed meaning to racial profiling. It is important to provide as much detailed description as possible (Creswell & Miller, 2000). These descriptions were taken verbatim from the interview and focus group transcripts. They were used to support thematic categories. Because a vast amount of data in this study involved interviews and focus groups, they were relied upon heavily to draw rich, thick descriptions. Again, once themes began to emerge, the transcripts and memos were examined in order to draw out the data that could provide the most contextual information and description about that specific theme. As you read in Chapter 5, many rich and detailed quotes were included in each thematic category in order to provide context. Careful attention was given to be as detailed and precise as possible in the descriptions of participants' experiences with racial profiling.

It should be mentioned that this is not an easy part of qualitative research. Attempting to make decisions about which quotes provide the richest context to a theme is difficult. Often, I turned to the participants and asked them which among several quotes best described a theme. This was effective and I recommend this approach to other qualitative researchers.

Researcher Reflexivity

Creswell and Miller (2000) suggested that researchers self-disclose their assumptions, beliefs, and biases. This is a process called reflexivity. It is difficult for qualitative researchers to claim to be purely objective in their inquiries, and "reflexivity is the recognition that the product of research inevitably reflects some of the background, milieu and predictions of the researcher" (Gibbs, 2007, p. 91).

Being reflexive involved listening to the participant stories of racial profiling and this in turn helped to develop a full understanding of the these experiences. Tunnell (1998, p. 214–215) pointed out, "a sociological verstehen of crime means accepting the subjective viewpoint and understanding actors states of mind while rejecting the notion that science can deliver a complete or ontological reality." This same principle is applicable to qualitative racial profiling research.

Earlier in the chapter, it was noted that sometimes the subjectivity of the research might lead to difficulties in establishing the validity for the researcher. Subjectivity in qualitative research is not necessarily a bad thing if the researcher knows how to effectively deal with it. It is no longer "accepted to be the omniscient, distanced qualitative writer" (Creswell, 2007, p. 178). In this research, reflexivity by the researcher was engaged often about the data and the narratives that the participants shared. Memos were written throughout the research. Each memo also included a section on researcher reflexivity. As part of my reflexivity, I wrote about my thoughts and stances on the issue. The emotion of many of the stories that were collected made it imperative to be reflexive.

What follows is a memo of one interview that was conducted. This was a particularly emotional interview for the participant. It accurately represents my way of engaging in reflexivity. The names have been changed to protect the identity of the participant and her family as has the city and the police agency involved. As you will see, the last section of the memo is titled "Reflective Notes."

Interview Memo

Participant: Tina Strong, B/F, age 42

Setting

The interview took place in Tina's office. The surroundings were for the most part comfortable but on this particular day, it was a little warm in the office. Tina's office is very small. There was minimal ice breaking involved due to the fact that I have had Tina in class as a student in the past. She is a 42-year-old Black female. The interview was candid and laid back.

The Interview

I began the interview by advising Tina of the confidential nature of the study and what the study was about. I explained to her that she could stop participating at any time during the interview. I asked her if she still wished to participate in the research. She agreed to the interview. She told me her story. She told me her experience with what she believes to be racial profiling.

Descriptive Notes

Tina told me that she was racially profiled in the summer of 2003 at about 12:30 a.m. She was with her husband, three friends, and her toddler grandchild (N = 5). Her husband is a B/M, the other three passengers were B/Ms, and her grandchild was described as a bi-racial male (toddler). They were driving a 1996 Cadillac in River City.

Tina told me that they were driving to their home early one summer morning in 2003 at about 12:30 a.m. They noticed a police car following them but did not think much about it. They proceeded to drive a few more blocks and then they were stopped.

As soon as the officer approached their vehicle, Tina's husband, who was driving, asked the officer why they were being pulled over. The officer, described as a White male, asked for her husband's driver's license and registration, and then immediately asked where they were headed. Tina related that her husband handed the officer his driver's license and again asked the officer why they were being stopped. Without giving a reason for the stop, the officer told them to wait a moment and he (the officer) walked back to his patrol car. After a few moments, Tina related to me that the officer again walked back up to their car. Tina noticed by this time two other police cars had pulled up. Tina (who was seated in the passenger's seat) asked the officer why they were being stopped. The officer stated they had a report that their car was stolen. The officer ordered everyone to get out of the vehicle. Tina said that the officer asked her husband to back away from the car because it was procedure. She noticed that five other police cars had now arrived. She guessed about seven police cars in total were at the stop. She was really beginning to wonder what was going on. The officer asked Tina's husband if he could search the car. Tina interjected and told the officer that he cannot search their car. She then asked why the officers needed to search the vehicle. She asked if their car was reported stolen why they needed to search the vehicle. She questioned the officer about who reported it stolen. Tina told the officer, "You know this is our car, you have the registration." According to Tina, the officer became very belligerent. The officer told Tina that she should "shut up" because he was not addressing her. According to Tina, the officer told her that if she did not shut up, he was going to put her in the back of the patrol car. Tina's husband became very upset at hearing this. He demanded to know why they were stopped. Tina's husband became belligerent and told the officer that the only reason he (the officer) stopped them was because they were Black.

After several minutes, suddenly the police officer told them they were free to leave. Tina told me that they were not issued a traffic citation. She said that the officer who had originally stopped them made the following statement at the end of the contact: "I suppose now that you are going to accuse us of racially profiling you."

- - -*The next few paragraphs of the memo text purposively taken out* - - -

Reflective Notes

If the police did in fact have the report of a stolen vehicle, then it may be protocol to handle the situation as described above. As a White male, I can never really know what it is like to walk in the shoes of a minority citizen. I do know of accounts where minorities have to work a bit harder to get their foot in the door. The fact is that it is hard for many minority citizens. Moreover, it is also hard to fully recognize this if you are Caucasian. The officer's reaction (becoming belligerent) as described by Tina probably did not help the situation either. Police officers should try to control their emotions regardless of the situation. This is critical. We don't need hot-headed police officers running around.

It's not against the law to become belligerent toward a police officer or even to question the motive of a stop such as this. What I have learned in this interview is that a seemingly law-abiding family was traveling home early one summer morning and was stopped by the police for what they believe was racial motivation. It would be interesting to know whether the police really had a report of a stolen car. I still have many questions, but as a researcher, a phenomenologist, the research is still evolving with many more questions to answer.

Discussion Questions

1. What is the concept of validity and reliability in social science research?
2. Why is it challenging in qualitative research studies to establish validity?
3. What is the concept of triangulation as used in establishing the trustworthiness of qualitative data?
4. What are the standards to assess the quality of phenomenological data?
5. Do you think it is possible to have a perfect study of racial profiling that is free of research error? Why or why not?

References

Ambert, A.M., Adler, P.A., Adler, P., & Detzner, D.F. (2009). Understanding qualitative research. *Journal of Marriage and Family, 57*(4), 879–893.

Bayens, G.J., & Roberson, C. (2011). *Criminal justice research methods: Theory and practice* (2nd ed.). Boca Raton, FL: CRC Press.

Creswell, J.W. (2007). *Qualitative inquiry and research design: Choosing among five traditions* (2nd ed.). Thousand Oaks: CA: Sage.

Creswell, J.W., & Miller, D.L. (2000). Determining validity in qualitative inquiry. *Theory into Practice, 39*(3), 124–130.

Gibbs, G. (2007). *Analyzing qualitative data.* Thousand Oaks: CA: Sage.

Lincoln, Y.S., & Guba, E. (1985). *Naturalistic inquiry.* Beverly Hills, CA: Sage.

Marshall, C., & Rossman, G.B. (2012). *Designing qualitative research* (5th ed.). Los Angeles, CA: Sage.

Neuman, W.L. (2012). *Basics of social science research: Qualitative and quantitative approaches.* Boston: Pearson.

Tunnell, K.D. (1998). Honesty, secrecy, and deception in the sociology of crime: Confessions and reflections from the backstage, in Ferrell, J., & M.S. Hamm (Eds.), *Ethnography at the edge: Crime, deviance, and field research,* Boston: Northeastern University Press, pp. 206–220.

Vogt, W.P. (2007). *Quantitative research methods for professionals.* Boston: Pearson/ Allyn and Bacon.

Warren, C.A.B., & Karner, T.X. (2005). *Discovering qualitative methods: Field research, interviews, and analysis.* Thousand Oaks, CA: Sage.

Striking Revelations

7

"I saw with my own eyes"

Martin Luther King, Jr., January 1965

Introduction

The research reported in this book suggests there is a unifying structure in the way racial minorities experience and give meaning to racial profiling. The primary goal in this chapter is twofold. First, to present the global conclusions from the study and, second, to discuss some of the more striking revelations fleshed out of the study.

As discussed in Chapter 2, a fair amount of the research on racial profiling has made use of quantitative data that primarily examines police stop data. Many states have enacted legislation mandating that law enforcement authorities collect stop data in some form, while in other states law enforcement authorities have voluntarily begun to collect stop data. Recall, the collection of vehicle stop data by law enforcement generally entails police officers recording specific information regarding the stop. Police may record such information as the driver's race and ethnicity, gender, time and location of the stop, and number of passengers in the vehicle, along with other information such as the reason for the stop, if a traffic citation was issued, if a request to search the vehicle was made, and the results of the search if one was conducted.

Studies that use police stop data in racial profiling analyses are important and indeed have the potential to provide insight into racial disparities. However, they fall short of offering holistic descriptions extracted directly from citizens. Collecting police stop data is also somewhat limited in offering a unifying structure of how racial minority citizens experience what they believe to be racial profiling.

You may have had the opportunity to read anecdotal stories of racial profiling that are reported in the handful of books that have been published. While these stories are important, they only go so far in providing thick and rich description into citizen perceptions of racial profiling. Let me explain. Anecdotal accounts or stories from citizens that have not been subjected to an organized qualitative analysis method in order to flesh out embedded themes fall short. The approach used in this study is *qualitative phenomenology*. Qualitative phenomenology allowed for the identification of the essential meanings of racial minority citizens' experiences with racial profiling.

Racial profiling is a phenomenon that many White citizens will most likely never experience in their lifetimes. Racial profiling may be witnessed by White citizens, but not experienced. Even the basic interaction between the police and citizens living in Black communities is most likely "completely foreign to White citizens" (Barlow & Barlow, 2000, p. 86). What was striking about this research is that for many racial minority citizens, profiling by the police remains prevalent in many parts of their lives. Six dominant themes emerged in this study regarding how racial minorities experience and give meaning to racial profiling. These themes were named as follows: (1) emotional/affective, (2) symbolic vehicle, (3) nature of the violation, (4) officer demeanor, (5) normative experience, and (6) race and place. These themes provide a great deal of insight into how minority citizens experience and give meaning to what they believe to be racial profiling. Experience is important. You cannot take a person's experience away. Experience is a critical part of an individual's existence. How one experiences and gives meaning to racial profiling can provide important insight for researchers and policy makers. This is a critically important but overlooked aspect of racial profiling research. Research should take many forms and a problem should be studied from many different methods and approaches. The hard police stop numbers will never really make total sense until we examine the stories, the experiences, and how people give meaning to their experience with racial profiling.

Global Conclusions

As pointed out previously, there is a general belief among the participants that that they are subjected to racial profiling in many aspects of their lives. Racial profiling is manifested often in the reason given for the stop (what is often perceived to be a minor traffic infraction) along with the type and appearance of the car, and in many cases, the geographical area.

Many racial minority citizens described a sense of ambiguity when they were stopped. Many reported that when they asked the officer why they were being stopped, it was often several minutes before they were told. Their inquiries into why they were being stopped were sometimes met with a barrage of questions by the officer, such as Where are you going? Where have you been? Whose car is this? Do you know this person or that person? Some participants reported that they were asked if they were in a gang or if they had any guns or drugs in their car. Many described the experience of being stopped by the police as cold, calloused, and degrading. As one Hispanic male participant related, "The way he [the police officer] was asking me questions, I mean a lot of questions, and not giving me any time to answer, I really felt like I was guilty of something. It bothered me for days after the stop."

Mark, a Hispanic male, shed additional light on the cold and calloused manner in which he was talked to by a police officer during a stop for his window tint. He stated:

> What really made it hard on me is you are asked all these questions. I'm not used to that. I have never been in trouble in my life and hardly have had any contact with police. He was asking me all of these questions and I don't know what it had to do with my window tint. I really felt bad about this.

What follows are bulleted points of the key findings of this study. After that, the more striking revelations that were fleshed out of the study are discussed in detail.

- What is striking in this study is that the dominant themes are the same regardless of the geographical area in Kansas. It did not matter where in the state of Kansas the racial minority citizens experienced what they believed to be racial profiling; they all had fairly the same contextual experiences.
- The study illuminated stories of perceived racial profiling primarily from Black and Hispanic citizens. There was one Asian male participant. When the data were analyzed paying specific attention to race and ethnicity, there were no contextual differences. The ethnic and racial minority groups represented in this study experienced what they believe to be racial profiling in much the same way. The only notable difference is the case with Black males.
- Black males were much more structural in telling their stories. They appeared to be the most affected in terms of the emotional toll that the experience had on them. While Hispanic participants, as well as Black females share this, it was much more pervasive among Black males.
- There is a belief among racial minority citizens participating in this study that police authorities often use traffic violations as a pretext or excuse to stop them when that is really not the motivating reason. They believe the real reason is their race coupled with constructed stereotypes about racial minorities' criminality, especially as drug dealers. The pretextual traffic violations were described as minor, such as not using a turn signal 100 feet from the intersection when turning, failing to signal when pulling away from a curb, cracked taillight, cracked windshield, burned out tag light, and the like.

There is a belief that these traffic violations are not enforced to the same extent among White drivers.

- Many participants alter their driving routine. Participants avoid areas where there is a greater chance of coming across a police officer. It is alarming that many participants reported they alter their schedules and allow additional travel time to drive around some neighborhoods because of the possibility of being stopped by police.

- Many reported they themselves, or others they know, purposively drive bland looking cars in order to avoid attracting police attention. They avoid driving customized cars with chrome rims, loud stereo systems, tinted windows, and flashy colors for fear of attracting police attention.

- For a great many participants, the emotional toll of being stopped by police for what they believe to be racial profiling is profound and lasts for long periods of time. The emotional toll culminates in a distrust of the police and reinforces previously held suspicions. I present this as a form of posttraumatic stress syndrome later in the chapter.

- Many revealed that when they are stopped for what they believe to be racial profiling they are often talked down to by the police. They described the experience as demeaning, embarrassing, and oftentimes accusatory. Participants related in many cases the police do not give them an immediate reason why they are being stopped, and they (participants) have to ask several times.

- The potential of being stopped by the police has become a normative experience for many racial minority citizens who were interviewed. They described this as routine. The data revealed a normative culture of sorts among racial minority citizens. This normative culture dictates to avoid the police, and if stopped, "don't give them a reason to make the situation worse."

Striking Revelations

The Stop

To racial minority citizens, particularly males, being stopped by the police represents a guessing game full of anxiety. There is an expectation when they are stopped by the police that they will be interrogated about where they were going and where they have been, whose car they are driving, and if they know this person or that person. When they are driving, they report that, because of their race, they are often on high alert of the possibility of being stopped by the police. As this research progressed, it became increasingly clear that there was something very profound to this sense of a heightened alert that was described in various ways. It is similar to a conditioning of sorts that takes place.

The heightened alert turned into increased anxiety at the site of a police car. Many reported that as they drive, as a matter of routine, they monitor their rearview mirror for the site of a police officer. If they see a police officer, they have an expectation that the officer will follow them. They spoke of the entire ordeal as being an anxiety-producing experience. Some related that the police probably mistake their anxiety and the watching and constant looking in their rearview window as suspicious behavior, which in some cases they believed may have contributed to their stop and interrogation by the police.

It is reasonable to conclude that any citizen regardless of race would be anxious upon spotting a police car. Think about the last time you were driving in your automobile and you observed a police car in your rearview mirror. You most likely begin to exhibit perfect traffic habits. However, there is something more to this with racial minority citizens. They seem to describe a heightened sense of anxiety. The anxiety was more intense and in some cases long lasting.

By contrast, for many White Americans the sight of a police officer on the roadway may invoke relief. After all, the police provide protection and security that is the benchmark of a safe society. They are the gatekeepers to a criminal justice system fighting a war on drugs, which has cost billions of dollars. A criminal justice system that, according to Alexander (2012), is fictionalized by television's skewed portrayal of the police, crime, and prosecutors, told from the lens of law enforcement. Alexander argues that television "perpetuates the myth that the primary function of the system is to keep our streets safe and homes secure by rooting out dangerous criminals and punishing them" (p. 59). The underpinning of Alexander's argument is that television's portrayal of the criminal justice system presents a perfect world scenario while failing to illuminate the injustices of a system that has been obsessed with fighting a drug war, which has had a significant impact on racial minorities.

Many spoke of hearing stories from friends and family members of abuse at the hands of police authorities. These stories have become etched in their minds. For others, they themselves have experienced abuse. Indeed, being stopped by the police may invoke a fear and anxiety that, unless you are a racial minority, may be difficult to understand.

Below is a diagram of how participants described the stop. This diagram is a construction of the totality of the interviews that were conducted. Each level builds on and is dependent on the next level.

SYMBOLIC VEHICLE

(Driving a vehicle that police authorities symbolically associate with minority driver (tinted windows, custom wheel rims, make and model of car)

▼

VISUAL MINORITY DRIVER

(Some police officers may be familiar with the minority driver from a previous stop)

▼

AROUSED POLICE SUSPICION

▼

SURVEILLANCE

(Police begin to follow)

▼

PRETEXT FOR STOP

(tinted windows, cracked windshield, burned out or cracked tag light or brake light)

▼

AMBIGUITY SURROUNDING THE STOP

(The police are initially hesitant to tell driver why he or she is being stopped)

▼

INTERROGATION

(Where were you going? Why? Whose car is this? Are you in a gang? Do you sell drugs? Do you have anything illegal in the car? Who are your passengers? Do you know this person or that person?)

▼

REQUEST TO SEARCH CAR

(Many participants consent to the search because they say the police will just make it harder on them if they refuse)

▼

STRONG POLICE PRESENCE (in some cases)

(Participants spoke of multiple police officers arriving at the scene)

▼

HUMILIATION

(Participants reflected on feeling humiliated and embarrassed while standing along the road while the police searched their vehicle)

▼

ISSUED CITATION

(Participants spoke of lengthy detentions of sometimes 20 minutes or greater. The police officer concludes stop by either issuing citation or in many cases not issuing a citation or even a written warning)

You're Not Supposed to Be Driving Here

Recall, one dominant theme emerging in this study was named "Race and Place." The race and place theme has several meanings for racial minorities. First, it was reported they sometimes purposively drive out or their way, in some cases, great distances to avoid neighborhoods such as affluent White neighborhoods where they say they would attract police attention.

As the race and place theme boldly presented itself in the research, I was reminded of Professor Cornel West's book, *Race Matters*. Professor West is an African American and preeminent professor and scholar of religion and philosophy at Princeton University. In his book, he describes an experience of being stopped by the police when driving from New York to teach at Williams College. Professor West described the encounter with police like this:

> I was stopped on fake charges of trafficking cocaine. When I told the police officer I was a professor of religion, he replied, "Yeah, and I'm the flying nun. Let's go, nigger!" I was stopped three times in my first ten days at Princeton for driving too slowly on a residential street with a speed limit of twenty-five miles per hour. (West, 1993, p. XV)

Was Professor West out of place? Here is a story that was collected during the research.

Rodney, a 62-year-old African American male, paints homes for a living. During an interview, he related that he was finishing an exterior paint job on a home located in an "upscale White neighborhood." He was returning from lunch back to the home when he noticed a police car following him. The police officer followed Rodney for several blocks. Rodney said that it was obvious that the officer had him under surveillance. Rodney said he was nervous and if it were not for the paint job, he would have never traveled through this neighborhood. When Rodney pulled into the driveway of the home he was painting, he said the police officer slowed to get a good look. Rodney was convinced that the only reason the officer began to follow him was because he was a Black male driving through a predominately "upscale White neighborhood."

Some participants reported they leave for their destinations a few minutes early in order to allow extra time as they detour around affluent White neighborhoods. Many avoided driving through some high crime areas because they believe it would increase their chance of being stopped by the police. It is important to point out that many participants lived near these high crime areas. They often have to drive through these areas in order to get to their homes or the homes of family and friends.

Many participants believe the police have a proclivity to judge them primarily by the color of their skin. They believe that when police observe them driving in a place the police do not think they ought to be, it is brought on solely because of their race. They argued, if not race, what else can it be? Participants related that they have not broken any laws but the police are alerted to them, for example, when driving through White affluent neighborhoods. They say that the police then stopped them for a minor traffic violation and investigated them.

For participants it amounts to the single factor of race that prompts the police surveillance of them. It is reinforced in the violation for which they are stopped (cracked brake light, cracked windshield, failure to use turn signal 100 feet before making turn, etc.). Of course, in the technical sense, they have violated a traffic code or infraction. However, it is probably one that is not enforced routinely among the motoring public, but rather a traffic code that the police can enforce at their discretion.

Could it be that police officers develop stereotyped images of the symbolic criminalized Black citizen? Many participants believe they do. This may be a result of several factors. These factors include innate bias and prejudices that, in some cases, are developed after years in police service and acted out through racial profiling and other biased policing practices, their day-to-day encounters with racial minorities that lead police to a generalization of sorts that includes even law abiding racial minority citizens as potential criminals. Andrew Hacker (2003) in his book, *Two Nations: Black and White, Separate, Hostile, and Unequal,* made a compelling observation regarding police suspicion of Black men. Hacker wrote:

> Even today, in most parts of the country, black men who stir suspicions cannot count on being accorded a presumption of innocence. ... While the possibility of guilt always exists, might there be an urge to undercut the stature of black men? We certainly know that being prominent provides no protection. Indeed, the opposite may be the case. Witness the trials of Mike Tyson, O.J. Simpson, and Marion Barry, along with what sometimes seems just a few too many indictments of black legislators and judges, as well as the sons of black officials. (Hacker, 2003, pp. 219–220)

This presents a dilemma of sorts for the police who patrol high crime neighborhoods as well as the citizens who work or live close to these neighborhoods. On the one hand, the police may come under great pressure from the community if they scale back policing activities in high crime areas. Police authorities have been criticized in the past for not expending the same amount of police resources in racial minority or inner city neighborhoods when compared to other White areas that experience high levels of crime. On the other hand, many citizens have complained that the police disproportionately stopped and questioned citizens living in these neighborhoods.

Police have also been accused of being heavy handed in their enforcement strategies in inner city neighborhoods that experience high crime. These aggressive police tactics often entail the police making many car stops in hopes of uncovering drug or gang activity with the objective to reduce crime. This law enforcement strategy began in the 1980s with the Drug Enforcement Administration's Operation Pipeline.

Operation Pipeline was an aggressive drug interdiction strategy that many U.S. law enforcement agencies were trained to make use of. In part, Operation Pipeline entailed developing certain drug courier profiles. The strategy also called for police to increase their stops and searches with the objective of "getting a hit," that is, seizing drugs and other fruits of the drug trade (i.e., money, guns, paraphernalia). Drug interdiction strategies such as Operation Pipeline have fallen on primarily poor and racial minority communities. That is, police drug strategies have largely been directed at inner city neighborhoods that largely consist of Black and Hispanic residents (Yates, 1995). Operation Pipeline will be discussed in detail later in this chapter.

The "race and place" theme brings to light several questions. If racial minority citizens do indeed attract police attention while driving through affluent White neighborhoods, why is that? First, could it be that the police who patrol these neighborhoods know who does and does not belong? Persons recognized as not belonging in the neighborhood are then subjected to increased surveillance. Simply not belonging in the neighborhood is problematic and may lead to racial profiling. To say someone does not belong in a neighborhood as a purpose of making a stop is a slippery slope for a police officer. To rationalize that a person does not belong in a neighborhood is a broad statement and can mean many things.

Police officers are suspicious by nature. They are trained to investigate persons, places, or things that seem out of place. So is it possible to control for potential racially biased police practices? In addition, is it possible as a matter of police policy to control the discretion of officers who may act on their biases? Moreover, can police policy control for potential biases in police officer decision making about stopping a person appearing to be out of place without sacrificing legitimate police practices?

Adams (2001) offered three criteria that should be calculated in a police officer's decision to make a temporary field stop and interview:

1. There must be a rational suspicion by the officer that some activity out the ordinary is occurring or has taken place.
2. Some indication must exist to connect the person under suspicion with the unusual activity.
3. There must be some suggestion that the activity is related to crime (p. 335).

According to Adams, "the circumstances must be sufficiently unique to justify your suspicions, and you need to be prepared to explain the circumstances causing you to choose to conduct a field interview" (p. 335).

Racial minority citizens driving through a neighborhood regardless of whether they live or work within the neighborhood, absent other factors relating to an unusual activity or crime, is not grounds for a stop. It is not an illegal activity to drive through a neighborhood where you do not live. If a police officer does indeed stop an individual for the purpose of a field interview based on unusual factors centering on criminal activity, it is important that the officer follow proper legal guidelines and departmental policy.

Jerome Skolnick argued in his classic book *Justice without Trial*, first published in 1966, that because of the dangers associated with police work, police officers develop a symbolic assailant of sorts. Skolnick argued that the police, when developing the symbolic assailant, develop a "perceptual shorthand to identify certain kinds of people as symbolic assailants," which according to Skolnick is based on an individual's gesture, language, and attire that the officer recognizes as a prelude to criminal activity (p. 42).

Could it be that some police officers develop a latent symbolic assailant that includes, among other factors, race? Race used here is referred to as racial minority citizens driving through a White neighborhood. Many racial minorities that were interviewed believe this to be the case. They believed they are perceived as not belonging in certain neighborhoods, which will in turn get them stopped and questioned by the police.

Police officers may also act on their own biases. That is, they see a racial minority driving through a White neighborhood and their personal biases help shape their decision to follow and subject the citizen to increased surveillance. In essence, the bias alone dictates the police response, which is or can be perceived as racial profiling. This is difficult to prove unless the officer freely admits to it.

However, is the line not blurred between police suspicion and stereotyping? Is police suspicion a byproduct of stereotyping? And if this is the case, how do police avoid it? Stereotyping is not only harmful in its own right, but also it does damage by nurturing prejudice and discrimination. Stereotypes include a variety of allegations about groups based on race, ethnicity, gender, and nationality. It is the process of assuming a person or group has one or more characteristics because most members of that group have (or are thought to have) the same characteristics. For example, all Black citizens driving through an affluent White neighborhood are out of place and may be up to something.

Meehan and Ponder (2002) suggested that stops and searches of racial minority citizens have increased significantly due to the shift in economy. They argued that because shopping and leisure venues have steadfastly shifted from urban to suburban locations, this trend "has brought minorities into traditionally white areas, although not, for the most part, to reside there" (p. 404). Barnes (2000) argued that even those Black Americans living in predominately White upscale neighborhoods and driving BMWs are not immune from being stopped by what she describes as "racist policing."

In some cases, race is factored in to a police officer's decision to stop a motorist. For example, a police officer receives a radio report of a burglary that just occurred and the suspects are described as two Black males in their early 20s last seen leaving the area in a blue unknown 1990s model Chevrolet. Suppose that an officer responding to the call happens to spot a blue 1990s model Chevrolet with a Black male driver and passenger in the area. The police officer would be derelict in his or her duties if he or she did not stop the car and investigate further. The officer was dispatched to a burglary and provided with a description of the suspects and what they were driving. Based on the circumstance, race is appropriately considered in the decision to stop the car. On the other hand, a police officer who decides to stop a racial minority in a neighborhood because the neighborhood is inhabited by predominately White citizens has not only committed racial profiling but also has demonstrated extreme bias in carrying out his or her police duties. Race cannot be used as the sole factor in a police officer's decision to make a stop.

It is troubling that racial minority citizens purposively travel out of their way in order to avoid driving through specific neighborhoods because they believe that their chance of being stopped by the police is greatly increased. Citizens have the right regardless of race and ethnicity to drive anywhere within their communities without being deemed as looking or acting suspicious, or that they do not belong in the neighborhood, absent other unusual circumstances.

Is It Socioeconomic Class and Not Race?

While the race and place theme was a disturbing revelation that bore out of this research, policy makers and police leaders asked if racial profiling might be more about social class than race. Here is a little more detail of this exchange.

A few months ago, the author was presenting the findings of this research to a group of public policy leaders and law enforcement officials from the local and state level. They were sincere in their desire to learn more about racial profiling. At the conclusion of the presentation, one of the law enforcement leaders asked if racial profiling might be more about socioeconomic class than it is about race. That is, is it social class that is more of a factor of who is stopped than race? As argued previously in this book, it is naive to dismiss the variable of race in police stops of motorists. Race permeates through the criminal justice system. An examination of the mere numbers of racial minorities currently under the supervision of the U.S. criminal justice system makes this point.

The law enforcement leader went on to speculate that perhaps lower-income White persons believe the police stop and harass them simply because they live in the lower-economic areas of the community. In addition, perhaps many of these predominately White and lower socioeconomic areas have elevated crime rates, which explains why they are being stopped. It appears that the underlying premise of this law enforcement official's argument is that middle- or upper-class racial minorities are less likely to get what is alleged to be profiled by police authorities. That in fact, both racial minorities and lower-class White citizens may perceive they are profiled and stopped by the police and this may be more about their class status, which dictates where they live and many other aspects of their lives. While undeniably social class may indeed play a role in who is stopped by the police, many racial minorities believe class doesn't matter, and it is their race that is the predicting factor.

Consider one more incident where the socioeconomic class issue came up. A few years ago, the author attended a panel session on racial profiling at the Annual Meeting of the American Society of Criminology. The panel session was titled "Author Meets Critic." Several noted authorities were discussing a recently published book on racial profiling. The book made use of some interview data of racial minority citizens regarding racial profiling. Several of the scholars providing a critique of the book argued that many of the stories in the book were from middle-class Black Americans. They argued that research should flesh out the stories from those Black citizens living in ghetto or inner city areas. There was some indication that these experiences of racial profiling may prove to be different for citizens living in ghetto areas.

Without question, up to a certain point, socioeconomic class may indeed be one factor that causes racial minority citizens to come into contact with the police when compared to persons of the well-to-do classes. However, based on the qualitative data reported in this book, race is believed to be the primary factor in being stopped by the police and to a lesser extent social class. Citizens interviewed for this book represented the lower, middle, and upper-middle classes. It is also noteworthy that participants believed both Black and Hispanic males are the most at risk of being stopped by police authorities regardless of their social class. In addition, regardless of socioeconomic class, the participants' experiences with racial profiling were largely the same. That is, the contextual basis of how they experienced the stop, the manner in which the officer communicated with them, the emotions, anxiety, and degradation they described, and the uniform manner of their description of the ambiguity of the stop were strikingly similar.

Some studies have examined the perceptions of racial profiling and socioeconomic class. For example, Weitzer and Tuch (2002) found that middle-class Black citizens were more likely to report they had been racially profiled by the police than lower-class Black citizens. They argued middle-class Blacks perceived that they were racially profiled because they are more susceptible to traffic stops than disadvantaged Blacks (Weitzer and Tuch, 2002, p. 451). They explained that because middle-class Black Americans are more likely to have greater mobility to drive across a larger geographical spectrum, this in turn makes them more likely to be in an area where they are perceived to be out of place.

While social economic class is an important variable in the context of who is stopped by the police, the fact remains that race is also a dominant factor. Again, race is just too ingrained into the criminal justice system to say it is not a factor. Many racial minority citizens interviewed for this book related that it was race or others factors symbolized with race (i.e., cars and customized apparel) that they believed to be a motivating factor for why they were stopped by police authorities.

The Emotional Roller Coaster

Many participants discussed the emotional impact of being stopped for what they believe was solely because of their race. The emotional impact appeared to be exacerbated during the stop. Often, the demeanor of the police officer was called into question. This seemed to have great significance among participants. For many participants, it was clear that the stops resulted in long-term emotional distress. For example, recall the case of Tony discussed in Chapter 5. Tony, a 60-year-old Black male who retired several years ago from professional corporate management, seemed to be emotionally troubled by being stopped by law enforcement authorities for what he believed was racial profiling. During the interview with Tony, he struggled to tell his story. Tony stopped several times during the interview in order to regain his composure. It was clear, after spending a considerable amount of time talking with Tony, that this experience affected him deeply and emotionally.

The participants spoke of the embarrassment of being stopped by the police. In some cases, they were made to stand alongside the road while their cars were being searched by police, resulting in a great deal of humiliation for participants. Participants felt a sense of embarrassment because they wholeheartedly believe that the sole reason for their stop and detention was for driving while Black or Brown. Read how one African American participant explained it:

Imagine for a moment from my point of view, you think that you have done nothing wrong and you are stopped for a turn signal violation, cracked brake light, or some other minor traffic charge. Imagine that the officer's tone during the stop becomes accusatory and interrogative. Maybe he questions how I can afford a car like this, and then the officer says that he can't even afford a car like this. This is how you know it's not about some little brake light or cracked windshield or film cover on your tag. It's about you being a Black man. That's what it's really about.

Another participant equated the emotionally burdened nature of the stop to posttraumatic stress disorder. This participant stated:

Although I have not pursued it, I do believe that my experience places me at some level of risk for PTSD [posttraumatic stress disorder]. I'm contemplating contacting my mental health provider to deal with the aftereffects of this matter.

Posttraumatic stress disorder (PTSD) is an emotional illness that is classified as an anxiety disorder and usually develops because of a frightening, life-threatening, or otherwise highly unsafe experience. Sufferers of PTSD may re-experience the traumatic event or events in some way. They tend to avoid places, people, or other things that remind them of the event, and are exquisitely sensitive to normal life experiences. Is it possible that racial minority citizens who believe they have been racially profiled by the police developed some form of PTSD. This research appears to show that some of the participants do indeed experience PTSD. They may re-experience their past incidents of racial profiling at the mere site of a police officer or police car.

It is common in PTSD for persons to re-experience an event that was traumatic for them. Re-experiencing symptoms may include flashbacks or reliving the trauma repeatedly. Re-experiencing symptoms may cause problems in a person's everyday routine. They can start from the person's own thoughts and feelings. Reminders of the event such as words, objects, or situations can also trigger re-experiencing. After the event, persons typically feel confused and angry. One thing is clear; many participants in this study held on to emotions of being profiled by police authorities, that is, the feelings do not go away.

Symptoms of PTSD
- Intrusive, upsetting memories of the event
- Flashbacks (acting or feeling like the event is happening again)
- Nightmares (either of the event or of other frightening things)
- Feelings of intense distress when reminded of the trauma
- Intense physical reactions to reminders of the event (e.g., pounding heart, rapid breathing, nausea, muscle tension, sweating)

Symptoms of PTSD: Avoidance and Numbing
- Avoiding activities, places, thoughts, or feelings that remind you of the trauma
- Inability to remember important aspects of the trauma
- Loss of interest in activities and life in general
- Feeling detached from others and emotionally numb
- Sense of a limited future (you don't expect to live a normal life span, get married, have a career)

Symptoms of PTSD: Increased Anxiety and Emotional Arousal
- Difficulty falling or staying asleep
- Irritability or outbursts of anger
- Difficulty concentrating
- Hyper vigilance (on constant "red alert")
- Feeling jumpy and easily startled

Interviewing Toni, a 57-year-old Black female, effectively captures the emotional ambivalence of being stopped by the police. The emotional ambivalence in Toni's story was similar to the experiences of a great many racial minorities that were interviewed. Toni was driving home from shopping at a lawn and garden supplier. She had borrowed her daughter's Chevrolet SUV (it had rims) in order to haul some mulch that she purchased. The rear of the SUV was full of cedar mulch. It was slightly sticking out of the cargo bed of the SUV. A police officer stopped her. The police officer asked for her driver's license and proof of registration. Toni asked the officer why she was being stopped. According to Toni, the officer seemed to ignore her question and then asked, "Do you have a receipt for the mulch?" Toni related that she was appalled that the police officer would ask her that type of a question. Toni produced the receipt for the mulch. Toni related that the officer began to count each bag of mulch.

Toni related that this incident was both emotional and embarrassing for her. She said that the police officer was rude and seemed to be very non-caring about the way she felt. She said as the officer was counting the mulch at the back of the SUV, a carload of White male teenagers drove by at a very high rate of speed and yelled "Hey, Nigger."

Toni told the author that the police officer was not at all fazed by the passing teenagers and he continued to count the mulch. After a few minutes, the officer told her she was free to leave. He never explained why Toni was stopped and did not offer much in the way of an explanation as to why he asked if she had a receipt for the mulch. Toni thinks the police officer probably thought that she had stolen the mulch. Toni related that she did not receive any type of warning or citation.

The Symbolic Hooptie

Many racial minorities in this study believe law enforcement authorities hold stereotypes about the types of cars they drive. They also believe some of the cars they drive are criminalized by the police, at least symbolically. This seems to suggest that the police target certain characteristics associated with race such as certain make and model along with the way in which a vehicle has been customized, or the mere appearance of the vehicle. That is, if a racial minority citizen is driving a certain make and model of car, with the right customization, then they are suspected of being involved in selling drugs or in gang activity or other criminal activity. For example, a car that sits low to the ground and sports a flashy customized paint job is referred to as a low rider. Some low riders have their suspension systems modified with a hydraulic suspension so that their ride can change height (up or down) at the flip of a switch. The low rider has become popular among urban youth in the United States. Many racial minorities believe that if you drive a low rider you are certain to attract unwanted police attention.

In some cases, citizens were driving what they referred to as a "hooptie" when they were stopped by police. A hooptie (pronounced hoop-d) is typically a large and quite long 1970s or 1980s model car such as a Buick Electra, Chevrolet Impala, Chrysler New Yorker, Lincoln Town Car, or a Cadillac Coup deVille. The hooptie is often associated with an African American driver because these cars can invariably be seen rolling through inner-city areas of a community.

The hooptie is a car that may appear to be ready for the salvage yard—it is purchased in poor condition. It is purchased cheap and then "hooked up." That is, the hooptie is painted a solid color, customized with large and flashy chrome rims, spinning hubcaps, tinted windows, and a stereo system with gigantic speakers so that the vibrating bass can be heard for several city blocks. Sometimes the wheels are much larger than the stock wheels originally intended for the car, while at other times the wheels are much smaller than what is supposed to be on the car. The hooptie may sport interiors that have been refurbished to include earthy tones, prints and patterns, and colors. The hooptie is definitely catching to the eye. If you see one on the street, you are most certain to give it a second glance. The photograph in Figure 7.1 was given to the author by a participant. The participant told the author that

Figure 7.1 Symbolic hooptie.

it was a photograph of a hooptie. He is an African American male and has been stopped several times while driving the hooptie.

Many racial minorities believe if you are driving a hooptie, it is only a matter of time before you are stopped by the police. In other words, it is not a matter of *whether* you will be stopped by the police; it is a matter of *when* you will be stopped by the police. Sometimes the hooptie, along with other factors, justifies the stop for police. These factors may include driving in a high crime area, driving in an affluent White area, and driving with more than one person in the car (usually African American males).

Luther, a 22-year-old African American male drove a hooptie. Luther's hooptie was a 1986 LTD Crown Victoria. It looked like it could have been a police vehicle at one time. The Crown Victoria fashioned a bright garden hose green paint job and dark tinted windows, which seemed to blend very well with one another. Luther's hooptie sported oversized chrome rims and shiny black tires that appeared much too big for the car and made it seem to be somewhat elevated. The trunk had little room for storage due to the two very large stereo speakers. Luther bragged about how the stereo system would literally shake the car when the volume was "cranked up."

Luther admitted that driving his hooptie has resulted in much unwanted police attention and even police stops and checks on several occasions. These stops usually conclude without a traffic citation being issued. Every time he drives the hooptie it is at the back of his mind, the fear of being stopped by the police, the fear of being detained and peppered with questions. Luther, like many racial minorities, has considered selling the hooptie and buying a "plain looking car" in order to reduce the chances of being stopped by the police. Luther explains:

> I've thought about getting rid of it. Buying a plain looking car like a Focus or something. It's a damned shame I have to worry every time I pull out of my driveway in my ride. I always have to check the rearview mirror. I have to watch my speed, make sure I use my turn signal well in advance of the turn, and check my brake lights to make sure they are working before I drive the hooptie. Sometimes it's just a hassle to go through that. Every single time I drive. It's not just me, I have many friends that go through and have gone through the same thing with their rides. The constant thought of being watched and then stopped by the police. It's just part of our world living in the ghetto.

Luther wondered if White Americans go through the ritual before they pull out of their driveway. He wondered if they consciously have to check their rear view mirrors for police, to be aware of the neighborhoods in which they are driving. Luther surmises that White citizens probably do not have to go through this ritual just to drive to work or to the shopping mall or to a friend's house.

Consider the interview of Rosalie. Rosalie is a 28-year-old Hispanic female. She had earned some college credit hours, she was employed full time, and she had never been in trouble. Rosalie described being stopped by state trooper for what she says was because of how her car looked. When she was stopped, the State Trooper told her she was being stopped for a tinted windshield check. Rosalie described her car as a 2000 Honda Civic with custom chrome rims and tinted windows. After the trooper asked for Rosalie's driver's license, he told her he was going to conduct a safety check on her vehicle. He then asked her if she would mind if he searched the car. Rosalie stated she was a little intimidated and let him search. According to Rosalie, the trooper checked the brakes, headlights, turn signals, tag light, and then searched the interior of car. The trooper issued Rosalie a ticket for the windshield tint, which she says was within the legal tint level. Rosalie believes that the trooper saw the "souped-up" car and that is what motivated him to stop her. The trooper used the tinted windows as a pretext for the stop. Rosalie also believes racial minorities are very likely to be stopped by the police if you have a "souped-up car." Rosalie described a "souped-up car" as one having rims and window tint. She said that the police know Hispanics and African Americans drive souped-up cars. "They associate these cars with something bad, I guess." Rosalie contested the windshield tint ticket and it was dismissed during the court appearance, but she was upset because she still had to pay court costs.

Barnes (2000) argued it is a common experience for Black Americans, especially Black males, driving a nice car to be stopped and searched by the police. It is troubling that many racial minorities believe the police criminalized the type of car they choose to drive such as the low rider and hooptie, or simply a car that has been "hooked up" or "souped-up." Many believe when driving a hooptie or low rider they will be subjected to the police somehow associating this with criminality. Think about it for a moment. Should the type of car that a citizen decides to own and drive relate directly to criminality? If a citizen desires to purchase a 1980s model Ford LTD, paint it, tint the windows, and install spinning chrome rims and large wheels, in what way would this relate to criminality? Perhaps this is more urban style, the desire to be hip and to be noticed by one's friends.

How Can You Afford That Car?

While driving a symbolic hooptie or low rider may be enough to attract unwanted police attention, many believe driving an expensive car such as a Lexus or BMW will also potentially get racial minorities stopped by the police. Recall the case of Angela discussed in Chapter 5. Angela is an African

American female who reported that she had been stopped many times while driving a Jaguar but never received a traffic ticket or warning. She is convinced that she was stopped so many times because of the "nice car" she was driving. This too seemed to be an undercurrent in the research. Many reported that they were stopped for driving a nice car. In one stop the officer actually said, "How can you afford a car like this, I can't even afford a car like this."

Why You Harassin' Me, Man?

This research bore out another pattern. The seemingly minor traffic offenses that racial minority citizens reported was the "cause" of them being stopped. They claimed that minor traffic violations are used to harass racial minority citizens. Many complained that these same traffic infractions are not enforced in the White community. As reported in Chapter 5, of the 92 stop incidents that were studied, 30 were for looking suspicious or having tinted windows. Tinted windows were discussed much by the participants. In the state of Kansas where the interviews took place, the tint on the windows to the right and left of the driver of Kansas-registered vehicles, windows to the right and left behind the driver, and the rear window of the vehicle must allow at least 35 percent of light to pass through when used in conjunction with the manufacturer's tint and glazing materials (35 percent total light transmission value).

In regards to being stopped for looking suspicious, it was perceived that looking suspicious was actually code for a racial minority citizen driving too nice of a car like a BMW, Lexus, or a Cadillac SUV, or for driving a low rider or a hooptie. A corollary belief is that looking suspicious was equated to a racial minority driving through an affluent and predominately White area of the community.

Twenty stops were for a burned out brake light, a cracked taillight, or for what many described as "just being checked out by the police." One could hardly argue that these violations are strong predictors of being involved in a traffic accident or some other traffic hazard. Many thought these violations were just a tool to stop and harass racial minorities. One African American male in his late twenties described the stops for minor traffic infractions as fishing adventures. That is, the police use minor traffic infractions to stop as many cars as they can in an effort to net criminal behavior. If the police stop enough cars, they will assuredly net someone with a suspended or expired driver's license, an old warrant, or some other violation that would lead them to an arrest, threat of an arrest, and the purpose of the stop search of the car.

Many questioned if police stopped White citizens in affluent neighborhoods for these same kinds of traffic violations. They questioned what the result would be and if it would be tolerated. Many believe that there would be an outcry and that this police practice would not be allowed to continue in affluent White neighborhoods. They were quick to point out that, in reality, this type of police traffic enforcement does not happen in affluent White neighborhoods; that is, the police do not stop White citizens in these neighborhoods for minor infractions such as a cracked taillight, making too wide of a turn, failure to use the turn signal so many feet from an intersection before making a turn, and looking suspicious or "just checking you out."

Perhaps this is a pattern made normative when dealing with racial minorities and similar to other practices that many believe are injudicious practices inflicted on racial minorities. For example, Miller (1996, p. 9) pointed out that "the most frenetic law enforcement in the black community had nothing to do with violent crime. When the justice juggernaut is wheeled into the streets, it tends to crush those more easily identified by race and socioeconomic status than by their violent or serious criminal behavior."

While the majority of the participants were unaware of the legal authority of the police to use the pretextual stop, they described and complained about the police practice perfectly. They believed that the police use minor traffic violations to stop them because they are racial minorities. Once stopped the police can pepper them with questions or investigate further. Many did not realize that this police practice was legal. Again, they believe that the police use a pretextual violation to stop them knowing that they are not interested in the minor traffic violation but are using it for a reason to stop and investigate. Continuing on this theme, here is what was constructed as the participants' stories were woven together. Police authorities see a racial minority, especially an African American, driving an expensive car. Why would they be more likely to be suspicious? Could it be that they see the vehicle and then the driver and this prompts them to start following the car, looking for a reason, continual surveillance while developing the pretext for the stop when all along the police are thinking, "What is this Black guy doing driving a car like this? He must be a dope dealer." Would this level of arousal on the part of police authorities be the same if the driver of the expensive car were White?

A letter received by the author from James, a 26-year-old African American male, offers some insight into the symbolism that the police ascribe to racial minorities. James believes the large number of inmates currently in prison perpetuates the stereotypes the police hold regarding racial minorities. Because of this mass incarceration, police fall into a trap believing that all racial minorities commit crimes, which may be related to the symbolism to which they ascribe (e.g., cars, clothing, and urban style). James begins his letter by offering reasons for why he believed racial profiling occurs in American society. Here are some excerpts from the letter.

> I believe racial profiling is an issue that plagues African Americans because we represent a disproportionate number of inmates in our correctional facilities.

Law enforcement uses these numbers to create biases and form stereotypes about African Americans that in turn give them justification for stopping us. Then they do illegal car searches and question individuals. There is a lot of tension among African Americans and law enforcement agencies because of racial profiling. Some law enforcement agencies do not believe racial profiling is a problem and tend to "sweep" reports of wrongdoings under the carpet.

I believe that racial profiling will continue to be a problem in many minority communities, especially in the African American community, until more law enforcement agencies accept that racial profiling is a problem that is occurring more often than it's reported.

Welcome to My World

There was a general agreement among racial minorities who were interviewed that being stopped by the police is a routinized experience for many racial minorities. In a strange sense, the experience has been normalized in their lives. For example, many highlighted the fact that growing up, they were instructed by their family members to avoid the police. The police are to be respected, but always kept at a distance. Many heard horror stories of police brutality and bad cops, and they were instructed to avoid giving the police a reason to question or stop them because the outcome would not be good. This was especially pronounced for African American males. This reality sharply differs between Black and White Americans. These realities are constructed by history, current cases of police brutality (real and perceived), and the current number of racial minorities under the supervision of the criminal justice system.

When interviewed, David, a 44-year-old Hispanic male stated he has been stopped on several occasions by the police because he is Hispanic. He stated he is stopped by the police for what he described as a "routine check." David believes the national media attention on immigration, especially from Mexico, has resulted in all persons of Hispanic ethnicity being stopped for no reason and checked out. David specifically recalled on one occasion asking the police why he was being stopped and the police officer said, "We are just checking you out." He stated the police always ask to search his car and he usually lets them search just to avoid a problem. David stated he has no criminal record, is employed full time, and does not use drugs. He believes they assume because he is Hispanic, he is transporting drugs.

A 58-year-old Hispanic male who was interviewed made reference to the normalcy of being stopped by the police for what he thinks is because of his Hispanic ethnicity. He said, "I've gotten used to being stopped, searched, and harassed." He went on to say that he believes that societal stereotyping about Hispanics being drug smugglers has resulted in the police being more suspicious of them as a race.

Certainly, the war on drugs has nurtured and sustained a symbolic view of the racial minority as both the drug smuggler and dealer. Consider the U.S. Drug Enforcement Administration's (DEA) Operation Pipeline, which was created in 1984. Operation Pipeline was a drug interdiction strategy used by DEA and other law enforcement agencies across the United States. As part of Operation Pipeline, the DEA trained thousands of law enforcement officers in techniques of how to detect illicit drug smugglers. Early in the program, law enforcement authorities were trained that one of many factors to consider in drug interdiction was race and ethnicity. For example, a person traveling from a drug source country would be fair game to stop and question. A drug source country was generally interpreted to mean a South or Latin American country. In other instances, racial minority males were stopped and questioned because of their appearance, for example, wearing gold jewelry, flashy clothes, traveling with a cash one-way airline ticket, and the like. These were considered characteristics of a person involved in the illicit drug trade. Although Operation Pipeline relied in part on training officers to use characteristics to determine potential drug traffickers, the DEA maintains that the program does not advocate such profiling by race or ethnic background. The DEA claims that law enforcement officers are trained to recognize a number of exceptional indicators that would lead them to suspect criminal activity.

I Think of Young Black Males

During one focus group session with a group of African American participants, the author posed the following question: What do you think of when you hear the term racial profiling? After a few seconds of silence, one focus group participant said, "*I think of young Black males.*" Immediately following his comment and in almost unison fashion, the other members of the focus group agreed. They replied with comments such as, "Yes," "You better believe that's right," "That's right," I know that's right," and "Isn't that the truth."

There was something compelling about "*I think of young Black males.*" It came up far too often to be dismissed as a coincidence. The disconfirming evidence that I threw at it did not win out. There is something more to this and it was deeply intertwined in the data. The simple fact is that Black males appear to be much more troubled and emotionally impacted by their experiences of racial profiling. This leads to an important question—why is it that Black males appeared to be more troubled and emotionally affected by their experiences of racial profiling? This proved to be both a perplexing and complex question with no easy answers.

I recently had the opportunity to tour a jail located in a large urban city in the state of Kanas. It is a modern jail that sprawls down about two city blocks. The jail has the capacity to house over 1000 inmates. It is a rarity if this capacity is not met on a daily basis. As I toured the jail there was one thing that disturbingly stood out—the number of Black males that were incarcerated. In every jail pod that I walked through, the number of Black males was startling. It was readily noticeable. To be candid, many of their faces looked haggard as to somehow suggest how their lives had been on the outside. I later learned that just over 40 percent of the jail's population was African American (of these, the largest percentage were Black males). Think about this for a moment. Forty percent of the jail's population were African Americans in a community where African Americans make up about 12 percent of the population. This trend, while alarming, is common in U.S. jails and prisons. Mechoulan (2011, p. 2) predicted that "given current trends, one black child out of three will go to prison at some point in his lifetime." Mechoulan also reports that the rates of imprisonment among Black men are 15 times higher than for Black women.

It is undeniable that Black males are significantly overrepresented in the U.S. criminal justice system. In 1999, Marc Mauer, who is the Director of the Sentencing Project, prepared a report for the U.S. Commission on Civil Rights regarding the crisis of young African American males and the criminal justice system. Mauer reported:

- 49 percent of prison inmates nationally are African American, compared to their 13 percent share of the overall population.
- Nearly one in three (32 percent) Black males in the age group 20 to 29 is under some form of criminal justice supervision on any given day—either in prison or jail, or on probation.
- As of 1995, one in fourteen (7 percent) adult Black males was incarcerated in prison or jail on any given day, representing a doubling of this rate from 1985. The 1995 figure for White males was 1 percent.
- A Black male born in 1991 has a 29 percent chance of spending time in prison at some point in his life. The figure for White males is 4 percent, and for Hispanics, 16 percent (Mauer, 1999).

Recent data continue to reflect these staggering incarceration trends among Black males. The U.S. Department of Justice reported at the end of the year 2010 that Black males had an imprisonment rate of 3074 per 100,000 U.S. Black male residents. This is seven times higher than White non-Hispanic males. Moreover, just over 7 percent of Black males aged 30 to 34 were in state or federal prison (U.S. Department of Justice, 2011). Coley and Barton (2006, p. 27) add perspective to the high incarceration rates of Black men:

When the national unemployment rate rises to 10 percent or more, we characterize the economy as past a recession and in a depression. If at least 10 percent of the U.S. men in this age range were fighting a war, the country would experience serious challenges to its productivity. And if that percentage were hit by a deadly virus, the proportion would be labeled epidemic.

The incarceration rates among Black males are of such disturbing numbers that they cannot be viewed in isolation (Coley & Barton, 2006). Because Black males have significantly higher incarceration rates when compared to other racial or ethnic groups, it is likely they have had more contacts with police authorities in various aspects of their lives. It is likely some of these contacts have been negative. Many of these contacts with police authorities have resulted in them being arrested, ticketed, searched, and in some cases treated harshly. Because of an over-presence of Black males in the U.S. criminal justice system, the police may engage in the stereotyping of the Black male as a symbolic criminal figure. Thus, they are to be watched, stopped, and checked out with regularity. Mauer (1999, p. 5) pointed out that "there is strong evidence regarding the propensity of police to stop black males while driving for alleged traffic violations."

When released from jail or prison and upon returning to their neighborhoods under the supervision of a probation or parole officer, they are still watched and monitored closely. In many jurisdictions, the Department of Corrections sends the names of inmates soon to be released to police authorities in the jurisdiction where the inmate will return. In order to send a message that they are aware of the individual's release, the police may make it a point to drive by their homes, to stop them, or just pay them a visit.

The vast arrest and incarceration of Black men has created a host of problems. The fact is the mass incarceration of Black males will have a negative effect on their lives and the lives of their family and communities. Inner city neighborhoods have been left devastated. Most unfortunate is the state of their children. Children of incarcerated individuals are particularly at risk to a host of problems including but not limited to social stigma, social adjustment, low school test scores, poor performance academically, increased anxiety, aggressiveness, skipping school, and other inappropriate and delinquent behavior (Gable, 1992; James, 1994; Reed & Reed, 1997). Wagner (2008, p. 34) summarized some of the more pressing risks that children of incarcerated parents face:

- They are five to six times more likely than their peers to be incarcerated themselves.
- They are more likely to abuse substances and engage in antisocial behaviors.
- They are likely to drop out of school, run away, and become homeless.
- They suffer from a negative self-image, fear, anxiety, anger, resentment, and sadness.

- They have high levels of truancy, physical aggression, and disruptive behavior.
- They are traumatized by separation, stigmatized by the shame of having a parent in prison.

What I am arguing here is that there are many factors that may indeed result in Black males' experiences of racial profiling being much more structural and emotional. For many, the experiences are coupled with the fact that they themselves have had fathers or other family members who have been swept into the criminal justice system, a system that they perceive to be fundamentally flawed and biased.

Many of the perceptions of the police and the larger criminal justice system as being biased toward them may have been shaped by vicarious experiences. That is, a negative experience that happened to a family member or friend, or the mere perception that it happens because that is what they have learned from others. Put another way, vicarious experiences in what they believe to be as the police unfairly targeting Black males. Peffley and Hurwitz (2010, p. 68) illuminated this point, "regardless of how or whether the problem is defined in terms of courts having harsher sentences to blacks, police stopping and questioning blacks disproportionately, or police caring more about crimes committed against whites than blacks" it is all salient, in part, to why Black men appeared to be somewhat more impacted by their racial profiling experiences by the police.

Discussion Questions

1. How can vicarious experiences of racial minority citizens exacerbate allegations of racial profiling?
2. What is the central problem in the *symbolic vehicle* theme that may give rise to the perception of racial profiling?
3. Describe posttraumatic stress disorder and how the author proposes that some racial minority citizens may develop this after being stopped by the police for what they believe is racial profiling.
4. Do you think the war on drugs has contributed to racial profiling? Why or why not?
5. Imagine that you are a police chief in a middle-sized law enforcement agency that employs about 500 sworn police officers. The mayor has just told you that you are to attend a meeting with a group of minority community leaders because they allege that racial profiling is widespread in the department. The specific complaint is that racial minority citizens are being stopped disproportionately for minor traffic infractions such as failing to use a turn signal 100 feet from

the intersection, cracked windshields, cracked brake lights, tinted windows, and the like. How would you specifically respond to their concerns at the meeting?

References

Adams, T.F. (2001). *Police field operations* (5th ed.). Upper Saddle River, NJ: Prentice Hall.

Alexander, M. (2012). *The new Jim Crow: Mass incarceration in the age of colorblindness*. New York: The New Press.

Barlow, D.E., & Barlow, M.H. (2000). *Police in a multicultural society: An American story*. Prospect Heights, IL: Waveland Press.

Barnes, A.S. (2000). *Everyday racism*. Naperville, IL: Sourcebooks, Inc.

Coley, R.J., & Barton, P.F. (2006). *Locked up and locked out: An educational perspective on the U.S. prison population*. Princeton, NJ: Educational Testing Services.

Gable, S. (1992). Children of incarcerated and criminal parents: Adjustments, behavior, and prognosis. *Bulletin of the American Academy of Psychiatry and the Law, 20*, 30–45.

Hacker, A. (2003). *Two nations: Black and White, separate, hostile, and unequal*. New York: Scribner.

James, B. (1994). *Handbook for treatment of attachment—trauma problems in children*. New York: The Free Press.

Mauer, M. (1999). *The crisis of the young African American male and the criminal justice system*. www.sentencingproject.org.

Mechoulan, S. (2011). The external effects of Black male incarceration on Black females. *Journal of Labor Economics, 29*(1), 1–35.

Meehan, A.J., & Ponder, M.C. (2002). Race and place: The ecology of racial profiling African American motorists. *Justice Quarterly, 19*(3), 399–430.

Miller, J.G. (1996). *Search and destroy: African American males in the criminal justice system*. United Kingdom: Cambridge University Press.

Reed, D.F., & Reed, E.L. (1997). Children and the environment. *Social Justice, 24*(3), 152–169.

Peffley, M., & Hurwitz, J. (2010). *Justice in America: The separate realities of Blacks and Whites*. New York: Cambridge University Press.

Skolnick, J.H. (2011). *Justice without trial: Law enforcement in democratic society*. New Orleans, LA: Quid Pro Books.

United States Department of Justice, Bureau of Justice Statistics (2011). *Prisoners in 2010* (NCJ 236096). Washington, DC: U.S. Department of Justice.

Wagner, J.O. (2008). Children of incarcerated parents. In S. Kerka (Ed.), *What works: Shared vision for youth*. Columbus, OH: Learning Work Connection, pp. 33–37.

Weitzer, R., & Tuch, S.A. (2002). Perceptions of racial profiling: Race, class, and personal experience. *Criminology, 40*(2), 435–456.

West, C. (1993). *Race matters*. New York: Vintage Books.

Yates, D.L. (1995). Prejudice in the criminal justice system. In R.H. Ropers & D.J. Pence (Eds.), *American prejudice: In liberty and justice for some*. New York: Plenum Press, pp. 185–207.

Where Do We Go From Here?

8

"The time is always right to do what is right."

Martin Luther King, Jr.

Introduction

Two important objectives of racial profiling research are: (1) it should offer sufficient information in order to enhance our understanding of it; and (2) it should be practical enough to offer guidance that may lead to new or improved public policy. The purpose of this chapter is to discuss the implications of the data reported in this book. In other words, what does it all mean? In addition, perhaps more importantly, how can it be used to improve fundamental practice or policy? The implications for both the police practice and racial minority citizens are also discussed. This chapter purposively presents the implications in a very practical manner. There is no beating around the bush; the implications evolved directly from the interview data.

Implications for Police Practice

Racial Profiling Training

There were a number of implications from this data centering on training for police officers. The first and perhaps overarching training topic is racial profiling. Racial profiling training should include the purpose and scope of the agency's data collection strategies. Racial profiling training should ensure that both recruit training and in-service training for veteran police officers provide information regarding racial profiling laws in the jurisdiction and data collection mandates (mandatory or voluntary) involving the department. If a police agency is collecting stop data, training should include the proper protocol to record information regarding a stop.

Racial profiling training should be made as hands on as possible. Police officers may benefit from having active role-playing and problem-centered learning exercises. These include scenarios where, for example, racial minority citizens allege the police department engages in racial profiling. Police officers would then work in small learning groups to tailor strategies to address the allegations. Police training authorities should have members of the racial minority community participate in the training sessions. This includes participation in racial profiling training. This can actually result in an understanding from both the police and the citizens. In other words, the police and citizens learn from one another. This may heighten a mutual understanding of why the police do what they do in certain situations.

Cultural Diversity Training

Many participants stated they wish the police had an understanding of their culture. They suggested that the police need training on culture and diversity. The author pointed out in one focus group with African American citizens that the police usually receive training in cultural diversity while in the training academy. The participants replied, "It's not working." According to one participant, "They [police] have to understand that we have our culture too and they don't understand that. Many officers come from a totally different background. They have probably never been in our neighborhoods, until they became officers." Similarly, another African American male said this during a focus group session: "They should learn about our culture if they are going to work in our neighborhood. A white officer should learn about our culture."

It is unknown if multicultural training for the police would result in fewer perceptions among the racial minority citizenry of racial profiling or actual incidents of racial profiling. Likewise, it is unknown if it would make a prejudiced officer less prejudiced. However, diversity training is essential for police officers. It sends a positive message to the community. It has only been in the recent past that police agencies have begun to include diversity training as part of the pre- and post-service training requirements. Training that assists in familiarizing officers with ethnic and cultural groups in their community is important. Training in culture and diversity has a number of potential benefits.

Multicultural training may potentially reduce the number of lawsuits. It may also reduce the possibility of civil disorder. Historically, strategies employed by police in dealing with racial minority issues have differed from other groups. While improvements in those strategies have occurred in the recent past, further improvements are needed. Although these improvements have often focused on African Americans, many cultural diversity issues have similar implications for other racial and ethnic groups. Coderoni (2002) writes:

Cultural diversity training helps police break free from their traditional stance of being "apart from" the community to a more inclusive philosophy of being "a part of" the community. Realizing the difficulty of becoming a part of something that they do not understand causes a desperate need for an intense and ongoing educational process for developing an understanding of cultural differences and how those differences affect policing a free and culturally diverse society. (p. 14)

There are four factors associated with achieving a culturally aware police organization. First, police officers need to understand how their own cultural background molds their values and behavioral patterns. Second, police officers must understand that cultural assimilation is no longer the norm in the United States, and they should learn about the different cultural, ethnic, and racial groups in the neighborhoods they patrol. Third, it is critical that officers understand the effective use of cross-cultural communication. Police officers who have a deeper insight into the beliefs, behaviors, and value orientations of various ethnic groups will rely less often on authority and force to resolve problematic situations. Fourth, and finally, law enforcement officers must develop cross-cultural, analytical, and interpretive communication skills (Weaver, 1992).

It may make police officers' jobs much easier by taking the time to learn about various cultures they will likely encounter. Knowledge and sensitivity to minority concerns, diversity, and historical backgrounds of the various races and groups in a community will enhance and facilitate the crime fighting and peacekeeping functions of the police (Birzer & Tannehill, 2001). For example, consider the case of a police officer called to the home of an Asian American family regarding a miscellaneous complaint. In many Asian American families, the relationship and communicating patterns tend to be hierarchical, with the father as the identified head of the household. While many of the decisions and activities may appear to be decided by the father, many other people may come into the picture. Generally, if there are grandparents, the father would still act as the spokesperson of the family; however, chances are he would consult with the grandparents prior to making a decision (Shusta, Levine, Harris & Wong, 1995).

It is equally important and well justified for the police to have an understanding of those racial and ethnic groups represented in the United States. Because of historical damages, police authorities should make great effort with groups such as African Americans, "for whom contact with law enforcement has long been problematic" (Shusta, Levine, Harris, & Wong, 1995). Consider the following information that may be useful to law enforcement officials when working in predominately African American communities:

- The experiences of slavery and racism as well as cultural differences have shaped African-American culture.
- For many African Americans, particularly those in the lower socio-economic rungs of society, the history of slavery and later discrimination continue to leave their psychological scars.
- There is tremendous diversity among African Americans, which includes individuals at all socioeconomic levels, a number of religions, different regions of the country (rural, urban), and various countries of origin.
- The changing terms African Americans have used to refer to themselves reflect stages of racial and cultural growth, as well as empowerment.
- African Americans react as negatively to stereotypes that they hear about themselves as officers do when they hear such statements as, "Police officers are biased against Blacks" or "All police officers are capable of brutality."
- The predominance of households headed by women, particularly in inner cities, coupled with the myth of women as the head of the household, has created situations where officers have dismissed the importance of the father.
- Young African American males, in particular, and their parents (of all socioeconomic levels) feel a sense of outrage and injustice when officers stop them for no apparent reason.
- The use of African American varieties of English does not represent any pathology of deficiency and is not a combination of random errors, but rather reflects patterns of grammar from some West African languages.
- People in positions of authority have often misunderstood aspects of Black non-verbal communication, including what has been termed the "cool pose."
- Cultural differences in verbal communication can result in complete misinterpretation.
- The existence of excessive force and brutality is still a reality in policing in the United States, even only a minority officer commits these acts. When there is police brutality, everyone suffers, including officers and entire police departments.
- A dynamic exists between some officers and African Americans, particularly in poor urban areas, whereby both the officer and the citizen are on the "alert" for the slightest sign of disrespect (Shusta, Levine, Harris, & Wong, 1995, pp. 188–190).

Police officers should recognize that majority and minority cultures do not always share experiences. Police organizations may benefit from the following strategies:

- Develop training programs that promote awareness of cultural differences.
- Promote positive attitudes toward racial and cultural differences among ethnic groups.
- Recognize common links between different ethnic groups.
- Use alternative channels of communication to maximize understanding between ethnic/cultural groups.
- Identify the concerns and needs of ethnic groups in decision-making processes.
- Challenge stereotypes and assumptions about ethnic groups.
- Include members of all ethnic groups in all after-work organization sponsored events (Hill & Scott, 1992, p. 6).

Because of an increasingly diverse society, it is important that police become "skilled intercultural craftspeople" (DeGeneste & Sullivan, 1997, p. 20). The following elements should be considered in guiding police training and cultural diversity policy:

- Develop and maintain language skills.
- Develop an understanding of cultural issues and cultivate cultural skills.
- Be open and accessible to all groups in the community, offering services in an unbiased manner that respects diversity.
- Foster a sense of trust and rapport with the community; participate in and engage the community.
- Monitor demographic and social trends (particularly those with conflict potential).
- Strive to prevent or mitigate intergroup conflict.
- Demonstrate intercultural respect by example, and embrace diversity in the workplace (DeGeneste & Sullivan, 1997, p 20).

Some of the research reported in this book came from Hispanic participants who lived in largely Hispanic neighborhoods. Hispanic participants repeatedly told the author that there is a perception that the police do not make any effort to understand their culture. A police officer who works in a community that has a large Hispanic population may benefit from learning a few basic things about the Hispanic culture. This may include:

- Understanding relevant Hispanic cultural characteristics, traits, and values.
- Having greater awareness of the officer's attitudes and behaviors, and the impact these have on the Hispanic community that the officer services.
- Recognizing the verbal and nonverbal aspects of communication that may impede working relationships.
- Leaning some basic phrases in Spanish and responding effectively in encounters with Hispanic citizens (Birzer & Roberson, 2008, p. 495).

Fostering Mutual Respect

An important objective in both racial profiling training and cultural diversity training is to provide police officers with information on the issue of mutual respect. In fact, the Department of Justice's Office of Community Oriented Policing Services produced a training curriculum for police officers on mutual respect. They suggest that an important outcome of this training is to increase police officers' awareness of respectful police behavior. By doing so, their ability to work toward better community relationships will be strengthened. They further suggested interim performance objectives of this training should be to:

1. Recognize that we are all influenced by experiences and that treating people with dignity and respect is the foundation of good communication.
2. Recognize that police officers' actions and demeanor shape the image of their agencies and of law enforcement in general.
3. Recognize that good law enforcement practices involve investigating patterns of criminal behavior and the use of race as a reason to stop someone is illegal.
4. Recognize that gaining community support and acceptance requires mutual trust and respect between the citizenry and the police.
5. Recognize that establishing positive community partnerships is an effective use of police authority (U.S. Department of Justice, 2001, p. 6).

Motorist Contacts

Police training should emphasize the importance of acting as a professional during violator contacts. Weitzer and Tuch (2002) make a very important point when they argued that the perceptions that citizens have of police stops might be considered just as important as the actual objective reality of the stop. This is salient in this research. The traffic stop is, in many cases, the only contact a citizen might have with the police. The manner in which the police officer communicates can leave lasting impressions. Many participants perceived that the police are demeaning, hostile, and talk down to them during a stop. Police officers should always act in a professional and courteous manner during a stop of an individual. In some cases, the officer may have to be stern, but being stern is much different than being demeaning and hostile. For example, one participant indicated the officer asked him how he could afford a car like that, and then the officer said to him, "I can't even afford a car like this." This type of statement during a traffic stop is always inappropriate.

In many cases, citizens reported that the police officer "beat around the bush" or was ambiguous about the reason for the stop. It may be beneficial for a police officer upon initial contact with a violator of any race or ethnicity to properly identify himself and then give the reason for the stop. This may result in a more positive outcome for both the police and the citizen. Upon making the stop and initial contact with the citizen, the police officer could follow the following three-line script:

1. Hello, my name is Officer Jones with the Police Department.
2. I am stopping you this afternoon for speeding. I have you clocked on radar traveling 45 in the posted 30 mph zone.
3. Can I please see your driver's license and proof of insurance?

The script is inclusive of (1) the initial identification, (2) the reason for the stop, and (3) request for documents.

Research has shown that racial minority citizens are much more likely to suspect that a police stop was racially motivated if they were treated with hostility, discourtesy, and were not informed of the reason for the stop. Contacts with the police tend to have stronger and longer-lasting effects on the views of racial minorities when compared to whites (Tyler & Hugo, 2002). Racial minority citizens as revealed in this study are more likely than Whites are to leave an encounter with the police upset or angry.

Fridell et al. (2001, pp. 61–62) suggested that an officer who detains a minority citizen can minimize the potential of fear and hostility by following some simple guidelines:

1. Be courteous and professional.
2. Introduce him or herself to the citizen (providing name and agency affiliation), and state the reason for the stop as soon as practical, unless providing this information will compromise officer or public safety. In vehicle stops, the officer shall provide this information before asking the driver for his or her license and registration.
3. Ensure that the detention is no longer than necessary to take appropriate action for the known or suspected offense, and that the citizen understands the purpose of reasonable delays.

4. Answer any questions the citizen may have, including explaining options for traffic citation disposition, if relevant.
5. Provide his or her name and badge number when requested, in writing or on a business card.
6. Apologize and explain if she determines that the reasonable suspicion was unfounded (e.g., after the investigative stop).

Community Coalitions

It may be beneficial for police authorities to establish or enhance their involvement and communication with local racial minority organizations, such as NAACP, Urban League, Boys & Girls Clubs, faith community, Hispanic coalitions, and Asian or Indo-Chinese community centers and coalitions. Coalitions should be formed not only to address issues centering on racial profiling, but also to achieve better police community relations. When the police have good relations with the racial minority community, it is much easier to tailor solutions to underlying causes of friction between the police and the community. It is critical that community input be solicited during this review, including requests for public comment and discussion. Likewise, the police should inform the community of the various options that are available to report racial profiling at the federal, state, and local levels.

Developing coalitions and contacts in organizations such as these will keep management informed about the minority community's issues and concerns centering on not only racial profiling but also other important issues. Many racial minority citizens revealed that often their voices are not included in coalitions and boards, and their voices are sometimes reprinted by persons who are dubbed as leaders in the minority community. They suggested that citizens "from all walks of life" be included in boards and coalitions to ensure their voices are heard and they have input.

Communication

Another striking aspect of this research appeared to be the belief that the law enforcement community avoided communicating with the racial minority community, and when they did, the dialogue was often jaded to the police position. It is the underlying premise of these implications that effective communication between the police and the racial minority community is essential.

Open and regular communication can dispel rumors and resolve potential misunderstandings. The police and the community have to engage in productive dialogue about racial profiling. This can be accomplished through holding regular or semi-regular community forums and town hall meetings. In order to avoid complaining sessions, the community forum or town hall meetings should not be held only when hot button issues have caused the community to get riled up. Other forums of traditional and more progressive dialogue include:

- Sessions with the police chief advisory boards (either one board with members from several minority communities, or several boards, one for each community.
- Chaplain or faith programs involving minority clergy.
- Radio and TV shows with calls.
- Beat meetings that are integral to joint community problem solving.
- Facilitated discussions (with a neutral, third-party moderator), which increase police and resident accountability for following up on agreed upon actions.
- Study circles, which are structured to include three steps: (1) organization of the community; (2) identification of areas of mutual police-citizen concern; and (3) agreement and action taken by both the police and minority groups (Fridell et al., 2001, pp. 105–106).

Citizen Review Panel

Many racial minority citizens believe if a racial profiling complaint is made to the police, little will be done. One participant stated, "The police will cover things like this up." Furthermore, many participants believe it will do little good to file a formal complaint with police authorities.

In order to change this belief among the racial minority citizenry, police management should consider forming a citizen review panel of sorts for working with the police department when investigating a complaint of racial profiling. This could go a long way in sending a positive message to the community that the police department is committed to tackling the issue of racial profiling. Citizens on the panel should ideally represent diversity in terms of race and situation in life. It should not be primarily made up of politicians or other known "community leaders." This was a criticism that often panels and committees are not inclusive of "everyday citizens from the neighborhood." Members should represent the community. Citizens appointed to the review panel would work with assigned police personnel in the investigation of a racial profiling complaint.

Citizen Police Academies

Participants questioned why the police do certain things in certain situations. For example, some questioned why after police had stopped them did the officer, when walking up to their car, quickly grab their trunk lid and lift up. Of course, many police academies train their officers to check the trunk lid as a matter of officer safety (i.e., in the event a person is hiding in the trunk). Citizen police academies serve as a venue to assist citizens in understanding police protocol.

Citizen police academies have increasingly become popular among police departments as a means to foster and improve police community relations (Cohn, 1996). The Citizen Police Academy is a program designed to provide a working knowledge and background of the law enforcement agency and to foster a closer relationship between the agency and the community. It provides an avenue for community involvement and firsthand experience of policing. Interested citizens apply for the Citizen Police Academy and, if accepted, complete a specified amount of time ranging usually from a few weeks to several weeks, one or two evenings a week.

One objective of the Citizen Police Academy is to develop a better relationship between members of the community and law enforcement. Citizens learn about their local law enforcement, ask questions, and gain a more thorough understanding of the inner workings of the police department. The Academy is also a means for participants and police personnel to share information and ideas about the police profession. The Citizen Police Academy may go a long way in improving police–community relations, enhancing cooperation between the police and community, and reducing stereotyping (Whitman, 1993).

Racial Profiling Policy

Regardless of whether a jurisdiction does or does not have legislation mandating that police organizations have a policy addressing racial profiling, they should. A policy is general in nature and represents the department's goals and objectives (Gains, Sutherland, & Angell, 1991). Police agencies across the nation are increasingly adopting policies addressing racial profiling. If there is legislation prohibiting racial profiling within a jurisdiction, policy should be tailored within the scope of the legislation. Having a racial profiling policy conveys to citizens and police officers that racial profiling will not be tolerated. The Police Executive Research Forum strongly recommended that police organizations adopt a policy addressing racial profiling. They proposed a policy that:

- emphasizes arrests, traffic stops, investigative detentions, searches, and property seizures must be based on reasonable suspicion or probable cause;
- restricts officers' ability to use race/ethnicity in establishing reasonable suspicion or probable cause to those situations in which trustworthy, locally relevant information links a person or persons of a specific race/ethnicity to a particular unlawful incident;

- applies the restrictions above to requests for consent searches and even those consensual encounters that do not amount to legal detentions;
- articulates the use of race and ethnicity must be in accordance with the equal protection clause of the Fourteenth Amendment; and
- includes provisions related to officer behavior during encounters that can serve to prevent perceptions of racially biased policing (Fridell et al., 2001, pp. 49–50).

The strength of the above policy is it specifies when it is and is not appropriate to consider race or ethnicity in an officer's decision to stop a citizen. Moreover, the policy provides a comprehensive definition of racially biased policing, and it is strongly embodied within the Fourth Amendment (search and seizure) and the Fourteenth Amendment (equal protection).

Law enforcement authorities are encouraged to make their racial profiling policy a matter of public record. Some law enforcement agencies have placed their racial profiling policy on their website so that it is readily available to the public. The Tarrant County Texas Sheriff's office has done an admirable job of policy development in the area of racial profiling. The sheriff's office website has a link entitled "racial profiling" where members of the public can click and view the racial profiling policy and how citizens can report an incident that they believe to be racial profiling. The sheriff's office website depicts how they define racial profiling. They define it as:

A law enforcement-initiated action based on an individual's race, ethnicity, or national origin rather than on the individual's behavior or on information identifying the individual as having engaged in criminal activity. Racial profiling pertains to persons who are viewed as suspects or potential suspects of criminal behavior. The term is not relevant as it pertains to witnesses, complainants or other citizen contacts. www.tarrantcounty.com/esheriff/cwp/view

Tarrant County, Texas Sheriff's Office Racial Profiling Policy

Retrieved from the Tarrant County Sheriff's Office website: www.tarrant-county.com/esheriff/

WHEREAS, Senate Bill 1074 was recently passed by the Legislature of the State of Texas prohibiting a peace officer from engaging in racial profiling;

WHEREAS, Senate Bill 1074 requires that not later than January 1st, 2002, a law enforcement agency covered by the law must adopt and implement a policy and begin collecting information under the policy;

WHEREAS, the Tarrant County Sheriff and the Constables of Tarrant County are now adopting, before the Tarrant County Commissioners Court, a policy prohibiting racial profiling by their agencies;

NOW, THEREFORE, the Tarrant County Sheriff and the Constables of Tarrant County (hereinafter collectively referred to as "agencies") adopt the following policy:

Section 1.

Racial profiling is defined as any law enforcement-initiated action based on an individual's race, ethnicity, or national origin rather than on the individual's behavior or on information identifying the individual as having engaged in criminal activity.

Section 2.

All peace officers employed by the agencies are strictly prohibited from engaging in racial profiling. All law enforcement-initiated actions, which include all investigative detentions, traffic stops, arrests, searches and seizures of persons and/or property, shall be based on a standard of reasonable suspicion or probable cause as required by law. All peace officers of the agencies must be able to articulate specific facts, circumstances and conclusions, which support probable cause or reasonable suspicion for the investigative detention, traffic stop or arrest.

Section 3.

All peace officers employed by the agencies shall not consider an individual's race, ethnicity, or national origin in establishing either reasonable suspicion, probable cause or as a basis for requesting consent to search the individual or his or her property.

Section 4.

All peace officers employed by the Tarrant County Sheriff's Office must "check out" via radio on every vehicle or subject stop. At the conclusion of each stop, the peace officer will complete either a computerized or written form, capturing all data elements required to be obtained by law. This information will then be uploaded from the MDC to a computer database (if a computerized form) or manually inputted into a computer database (if a written form).

Section 5.

No peace officer employed by the agencies will conduct a search of a person or vehicle after peace officer-initiated contact without completing a written report detailing the search and the facts supporting it. In the event no offense or arrest report is appropriate, a Miscellaneous Incident report will be completed.

Section 6.

If an individual believes that a peace officer employed by any of the agencies has engaged in racial profiling with respect to the individual then the following complaint process shall govern:

  A. Sheriff: If an individual believes that a peace officer employed by the Sheriff's Office has engaged in racial profiling with respect to the individual then the individual must file a written complaint before

the 180th day after the alleged violation with the Tarrant County Sheriff's Department Internal Affairs Division located at 200 Taylor Street, Fort Worth, Texas 76102.
  B. Constable: Refer to Constable Contact Page

Section 7.
The agencies will provide public education relating to the agencies complaint process via the Tarrant County web site located at: www.tarrantcounty.com

Section 8.
Appropriate corrective action will be taken against a peace officer employed by the agencies who, after an investigation, is shown to have engaged in racial profiling in violation of this policy.

Section 9.
The agencies will collect information as required by law relating to traffic stops in which a citation is issued and to arrests resulting from those traffic stops, including information relating to:

  A. The race or ethnicity of the individual detained; and
  B. Whether a search was conducted and, if so, whether the person detained consented to the search.

Section 10.
Each agency will submit to the Tarrant County Commissioners Court an annual report of the information collected pursuant to Section 9 above. Each agency shall first submit information to the Tarrant County Commissioners Court on March 1, each year. The first submission of information shall consist of information compiled by each agency during the period beginning January 1, each year, and ending December 31, each year. The report may not include identifying information about a peace officer who makes a traffic stop or about an individual who is stopped or arrested by a peace officer.

The Garden City, Kansas Police Department, which serves a largely Hispanic community, has also made their position public on their website that racial profiling will not be tolerated by members of the police department and where a citizen can go to file a complaint. They have also made public on their website the official racial profiling policy so that it can be viewed by the public. Their website makes implicit the following statement on racial profiling:

Garden City, Kansas Police Department—Statement on Racial Profiling

Members of the Garden City Police Department are prohibited from engaging in racial or other biased-based policing.
  Racial or other biased-based policing means the unreasonable use of race, ethnicity, national origin, gender or religion by a law enforcement officer in

deciding to initiate an enforcement action. It is not racial or other biased-based policing when race, ethnicity, national origin, gender or religion is used in combination with other identifying factors as part of a specific individual description to initiate an enforcement action.

Any person who believes he or she has been subjected to racial or other biased-based policing may file a complaint with the Garden City Police Department and/or the Kansas Attorney General's Office. Complaints to the Garden City Police Department may be filed in person, by telephone, or by email to the Office of Professional Standards or any on-duty supervisor. All allegations of biased-based policing will be investigated by the Office of Professional Standards and all individuals who file a complaint will receive a written disposition upon completion of the investigation.

All law enforcement officers of the Garden City Police Department are required to attend annual racial or other biased-based policing training.

The Garden City Police Department collects data on all vehicle stops to include: employee identification number, age, gender, ethnicity, religious dress, time and date of stop, location of stop, reason for stop, how information was obtained, action taken, search rationale, type of search, and contraband seized. All data collected will be reviewed by the Garden City Police Department and disseminated to the Police Citizens' Advisory Board and the City of Garden City Commission for their review. Collected data is available to the public during normal business hours (Garden City Police Department, 2012, www.gcpolice.org).

The Pretext Stop

The pretext stop is a significant problem for those alleging racial profiling. Many racial minority citizens were unaware that the police could use a pretext as a reason to stop them even though that was not a motivating reason for the stop. As was discussed in depth in Chapter 3, what is problematic about the pretext stop as authorized in the *Whren v. United States* Supreme Court ruling is that in an environment ripe with racial profiling allegations, the "*Whren* ruling allows police discretion to go relatively unchecked in terms of racial/ethnic biases and discrimination" (Gumbhir, 2007, p. 58). Because of this unbridled discretion, police management should ensure policy is in place to ensure officers do not abuse the pretext stop. Police should continue to use and exercise sound discretion and good judgment when making a pretext stop of a motorist.

The pretext stop will also make it more difficult for police authorities to identify an officer who may be using race as a sole factor to stop citizens, unless of course he or she admits it. Virtually any motorist can be stopped for any reason, and it is recognized that an officer engaging in racial profiling can hide behind the pretext. That is, the officer can say, "I did not stop the car because the driver was Black. I stopped the car because the driver committed a traffic violation." In reality, if a police officer follows a citizen long enough, he or she will observe some type of traffic violation that would legally justify a stop. Because citizens are largely unaware of the legality of the pretext stop, it may be beneficial for the police to educate them during community forums on racial profiling.

It is recommended that police policy require officers to document every stop that is a pretextual category, articulating the reason the vehicle caught the police officer's attention, the infraction that caused the stop, and the events of the stop. This would give first-line supervisors and police management the ability to scrutinize these controversial, but in many cases, legal stops, and would send a signal to officers that they must fill in the blanks of rationale for their actions on these stops. The police agency should issue a written policy requiring or encouraging the use of warnings on pretext stops and other activities that likely have a disproportionate impact on racial minority citizens.

The point to be made is if the police use their unbridled discretion when deciding to use a pretext stop, which is used regularly in high crime areas, often inner city neighborhoods, then the logic goes that it is possible that racial minority and poor citizens who reside in these areas will receive a disproportionate number of traffic tickets for minor types of offenses (failure to use turn signal 100 feet before making a turn, failure to use signal when pulling away from the curb, cracked windshield, and the like).

It is important that policy and training reinforce to police officers that objective and circumstantial evidence during each street stop and encounter will be the standard for review. Thus, police "training curricula must be revamped so that case law and privacy issues are comprehensively addressed through focused police-initiated scenarios and discussions regarding the ethics of policing" (Martinelli & Schafer, 2011, p. 20).

The Consent Search

The Fourth Amendment to the U.S. Constitution requires issuance of a warrant based on probable cause to search an automobile. However, in some cases, police do not need a warrant if there are exigent circumstances. That is, if police have reason to believe a crime is or has been committed they have the authority to search. Examples might include burglars or robbers with a back seat full of merchandise or money, or an automobile filled with marijuana odor even though no drug is visible, or it may very well equate to drug paraphernalia (items that are commonly used to facilitate the use or distribution of illicit substances) visible in plain view on the floor board or front or back seat. With exigent circumstances, a search can be performed any time an officer feels swift action is necessary to prevent imminent danger to life or serious damage or if officers fear important evidence is about to be destroyed.

One other way the police can search a motorist's automobile is simply by getting consent from the driver. Closely related to the pretext stop is the consent search. It is legal for the police to ask a citizen if they can search their automobile. Police often use the pretext stop as a mechanism to stop motorists who are *suspicious*. According to participants, this suspicion could be something as minor as driving an expensive or customized car through a high crime area. Police use a pretext traffic violation as grounds to stop drivers for further investigation with the objective of developing probable cause to search their cars, or to get consent to search from the driver. The motive here is to find incriminating evidence in order to make an arrest.

The national trend for many state law enforcement agencies is to not conduct suspicionless consent searches on traffic stops. For example, New Jersey, Minnesota, Rhode Island, and California State Police/Troopers have discontinued the practice, either by agreement during consent decree or by a ruling of their supreme court. Among the multitude of issues involved with these states was the issue of consent that is free of coercion and undue influence.

Many other states, including the State of Kansas Highway Patrol, have trained their troopers to follow a different protocol. In Kansas and a few others states, the traffic stop has to be ended before the law enforcement officer can ask for consent to search. The motorist has to know it is ended, too. The law enforcement official gives the driver's license back to the motorist and then makes it clear that the motorist is free to leave. After this, law enforcement is free to re-engage in conversation with the motorist in a completely voluntary nature and where, if warranted, a request for a consent to search may be made.

This protocol is recommended as opposed to police requesting search consent while still holding the motorist's driver's license and prior to issuing a traffic citation. This may by its very nature set up an atmosphere of coercion and retaliation. That is, citizens may believe if they do consent, they will not receive the ticket, or if they refuse to grant the consent search then the officer may retaliate and issue them a ticket, or as participants describe, "make the situation worse."

Citizens may feel coerced or pressured into their decision to grant a consent search if the officer is still holding their driver's license and prior to issuing any kind of traffic ticket. If a consent search is requested, police should inform the motorist as a matter of policy that the decision to consent to a search is totally their decision, and completely voluntary. Furthermore, the motorist should be informed he or she is under no legal requirement to consent to a search. This would assuredly reduce the potential for a coercive and retaliatory atmosphere centering on the pretext stop and subsequent request to search.

The Police Warrior Culture

There is a view from racial minority citizens, especially those living in inner city neighborhoods, that the police, as one 20-year-old African American male who was interviewed described it, "roll through our neighborhoods just looking for anything to stop and anything that moves. It's like they are at war with us. They wear black clothes and it's just scary, like we've been taken over." In many respects, the police have moved away from the community-oriented strategies to militaristic strategies as a way to police communities. This is readily evident in the increased weaponry the police are now making use of, such as sophisticated surveillance devices (Wadman, 2009).

The police as warrior was perpetuated largely by the drug war. The drug war has enabled the intermingling of military apparatus and civilian police forces. In 1981, Congress passed the Military Cooperation with Law Enforcement Official Act. Since then the military has become increasingly involved in civilian law enforcement, and has been encouraged to share equipment, training, facilities, and technology with civilian enforcement agencies (Weber, 1999). Similarly, in 1986, President Ronald Reagan officially designated drug trafficking as a "national security" threat. A year later, Congress set up an administrative apparatus, with a toll-free number, to encourage local civilian agencies to take advantage of military assistance, and in 1989, six regional joint task forces in the Department of Defense were created to act as liaisons between police and the military.

A few short years later, Congress ordered the Pentagon to make military surplus hardware available to state and local police for enforcement of drug laws. In 1994, the Department of Defense and the Department of Justice signed an agreement enabling the military to transfer wartime technology to local police departments for peacetime use in American neighborhoods, against American citizens.

The sharing of military resources with civilian agencies has led to an alarming militarization of local law enforcement, and special paramilitary units in departments known as Special Weapons and Tactics (SWAT) teams have proliferated the American landscape. One study by Kraska and Kappeler (1997) found that 90 percent of cities with populations of more than 50,000 had paramilitary units, as did three-quarters of those with populations under 50,000. An increasing number of communities, especially smaller communities, have gained SWAT style paramilitary units (Paul & Birzer, 2008).

The outcome of such militarization is the war it wages on average citizens. An aggressive paramilitary police force has infiltrated many inner city neighborhoods in an attempt to fight the drug war. In some cases, this has perpetuated brutality against the citizenry and created a set of institutional norms that lead to a greater potential for violence by both police and their targets (Paul & Birzer, 2008). Persons targeted as criminals become more violent in their interactions with the police because of the potential for increased harm, while citizens (perhaps seen by the police as criminals in wait) lose trust in the institution designed to protect them.

As an important symbolic step, law enforcement may wish to rethink their military style clothing and gear. Camouflage and black or near-black uniforms should be replaced with a color more consistent and symbolic of democracy, such as ordinary blue, which has been worn for years by the American police. The militarization of the police has created what Kopel (2001, p. 88) argued was the "equivalent of a standing army engaged against the American people." The black law enforcement uniforms tap into associations between the color black and authority, invincibility, and the power to violate laws with impunity (Powers, 1995).

The militarized appearance of the police may be viewed as an act of symbolic violence. Conceived traditionally, violence is any physical act committed against a person or object for the purposes of instilling harm. Paul and Birzer (2004) argued that the removal of traditional police uniforms are symbolic acts used to distance outsiders (e.g., the community) from the practice of policing. Of course, this has had dire consequences for citizens living in inner city neighborhoods.

What has been an apparent building of the military apparatus in American police raises some questions. Can the police just as effectively perform their jobs wearing traditional (blue, in most cases) police uniforms as they have done since the founding of the municipal police forces? How could the police be any more effective wearing military BDUs (battle dress uniform) than they would wearing a traditional uniform that has always been associated with the police? One of the most influential American police reformers, O.W. Wilson, and his colleague R.C. McLaren addressed the issue of the police uniform. They wrote:

> The uniform worn by patrol officers is an important item of equipment because it influences the prestige of its service and the morale of the department. Police uniforms should be distinctive to avoid confusion with those of any other service and to ensure recognition by a stranger (Wilson & McLaren, 1977, p. 547).

Perhaps the militarization of police uniforms functions to maintain an internal legitimacy within the department by enhancing their role as enforcers of public violence, and serves to symbolically construct a hierarchy between the police and the public (Paul & Birzer, 2007). Police authorities should, as a matter of policy, use great discretion when establishing dress code in the wearing of military style BDUs for police duties, especially in areas of the community that have experienced strained relations.

Community Policing

Much of this research pointed to the need for more communication between the police and the racial minority community. Some participants expressed the police need to "understand us better and talk to us and not at us." Can community policing help? The short answer is yes. The fundamental core components of community policing seem to be ideal for solving many of the communication issues and the perception that police are an occupying force aloof from the racial minority community.

The drive for community policing seems to have lost its steam since the September 11, 2001 terrorist attacks in the United States. After the 9-11 attacks, the police seemed to move away from community policing, which was still in infancy, in turn taking on an increasingly paramilitary posture, which defines their warrior image. This has further created a divide between police and communities of color.

Community policing is a strategy based on the concept that the police and citizens working together in creative ways can solve contemporary community problems related to crime, fear of crime, social and physical disorder, and general neighborhood conditions. The strategy is founded on the belief that achieving these goals will require the police to develop new relationships with citizens that include involving them in efforts to improve their neighborhoods while working with them to address problems such as racial profiling and other biased-based policing allegations.

Community policing typically consists of three complementary core elements: (1) community partnerships, (2) problem solving, (3) and organizational transformation. I believe each one of these core elements can address many of the implications discussed previously.

Community partnerships involve the police and the community, the government body, other service agencies, and the criminal justice system working together as a team to solve community problems (Peak & Gleansor, 1999). Partnerships go beyond the standard law enforcement emphasis. Effective partnerships recognize the value of activities that contribute to the orderliness and well-being of a neighborhood. These activities may include helping accident or crime victims, helping resolve domestic and neighborhood conflicts (e.g., family violence, landlord-tenant disputes, or racial harassment), working with residents and local businesses to improve neighborhood conditions, controlling automobile and pedestrian traffic, providing emergency social services and referrals to those at risk, protecting the exercise of constitutional rights (e.g., guaranteeing a person's right to speak, protecting lawful assemblies from disruption), and providing a model of citizenship (helpfulness, respect for others, honesty, and fairness).

Problem solving is an important component of community policing. It is designed to address both large and small problems within a community.

The goal of problem solving is to eliminate the root causes of problems that potentially could become serious police-related problems if not taken care of early. Problem solving is designed to identify and remove the causes of recurring crime and disorder problems that harm communities.

There is a problem-solving model that many police departments use. This problem-solving model may be an effective model for the police and racial minority community to join together to address racial profiling. It could also provide a systematic and organized approach to addressing the issue. The key here is that the police and community work through the problem-solving process together. In brief, this problem-solving model is referred to as SARA (Scan, Analyze, Respond, and Assess). As you read the following text describing the model, think about how this might be used as a guide for the problem of racial profiling.

Scanning identifies a problem through a variety of sources of information, such as calls for service and citizen surveys. Citizens must consider the problem important for this phase to succeed.

Analysis requires the examination of the nature of the problem. Input from police and residents pertaining to the problem is important, as well as the collection of data the department may have about the frequency, location, and other significant characteristics of the problem.

Response fashions one or more preferred solutions to the problem. This step, as well as the preceding analysis step, benefits from creative deliberation, or "thinking outside the box." Input clearly should come from police personnel, but also from residents, experts, and other individuals who can address the problem thoughtfully. The last part of the SARA problem-solving model is assessment.

Assessment evaluates the effectiveness of the expected solution. Agencies must evaluate the solution as objectively as possible because this step speaks to end-products, the key theme in problem-solving initiatives.

SARA Problem-Solving Model
Scanning:
- Identifying recurring problems of concern to the public and the police.
- Identifying the consequences of the problem for the community and the police.
- Prioritizing those problems.
- Developing broad goals.
- Confirming that the problems exist.
- Determining how frequently the problem occurs and how long it has been taking place.
- Selecting problems for closer examination.

Analysis:
- Identifying and understanding the events and conditions that precede and accompany the problem.
- Identifying relevant data to be collected.
- Researching what is known about the problem type.
- Taking inventory of how the problem is currently addressed and the strengths and limitations of the current response.
- Narrowing the scope of the problem as specifically as possible.
- Identifying a variety of resources that may be of assistance in developing a deeper understanding of the problem.
- Developing a working hypothesis about why the problem is occurring.

Response:
- Brainstorming for new interventions.
- Searching for what other communities with similar problems have done.
- Choosing among the alternative interventions.
- Outlining a response plan and identifying responsible parties.
- Stating the specific objectives for the response plan.
- Carrying out the planned activities.

Assessment:
- Determining whether the plan was implemented (a process evaluation).
- Collecting pre- and post-response qualitative and quantitative data.
- Determining whether broad goals and specific objectives were attained.
- Identifying any new strategies needed to augment the original plan.
- Conducting ongoing assessment to ensure continued effectiveness.

Source: Goldstein, H. (1990) *Problem-Oriented Policing.* Philadelphia: Temple University Press.

* * *

Organizational change involves substantial administrative issues beyond the scope of this book and is covered briefly here. For readers who desire additional information on organizational change dynamics, it is recommended that you consult the numerous management and administration textbooks that address this important area.

In general, the concept of organizational change focuses on organization-wide change, as opposed to smaller changes such as adding new officers or modifying a program. Examples of organization-wide change might include a change in mission, restructuring operations, new technologies, mergers, major collaborations, and new programs. A new mission may include being more responsive to the concerns of racial minority communities or racial profiling allegations.

Organizational change requires a clear recognition that forging community policing partnerships and implementing problem-solving activities will necessitate changes in the organizational structure of policing. The police organizational structure is usually in the shape of a pyramid and has many bureaucratic layers that separate the top command and administration from line-level personnel. This is referred to as the line organization or the military type organization. There is some hope that police departments might consider flatter organizations. Flat organizations will have shorter lines of communication between top and bottom levels of the organization (Johnson, 1994). Accordingly, the communications are likely to be faster and have less chances of distortion.

Community policing seems most appropriate for improving communication with racial minority citizens, something that citizens in this research said was lacking. This may improve dialogue on racial profiling. The idea is that community policing strategies will improve the ability of the police and community to come together to discuss problems more frequently (they have more contact with each other), which is believed to improve relations. This is important in areas of the community such as some racial minority neighborhoods where police–community relations are strained and in the midst of racial profiling allegations. Community policing is said to improve police–community relations in the following areas:

- Closer relations with underprivileged and minority groups where the need is greatest for police understanding and involvement.
- More effective and more open communication between the police and the community.
- Increased citizen involvement in crime prevention and solving of social problems as a means of reducing crime.
- Improved understanding between the police and the community, with both gaining recognition of each other's problems.
- Creation of awareness among police–community relations problems, and encouragement of officers to help solve them.
- Direction of all department efforts toward improving relations with the total community, whether these involve crime prevention, public relations, or neighborhood problem solving (Birzer & Roberson, 2007, p. 489)

KEY IMPLICATIONS SUMMARY BOX

- Use the data in this book as a venue to enhance existing or new training programs that focus on cultural sensitivity and racial profiling.
- Reinforce the importance of police officers to inform the motoring public of the reason they are being stopped when initial contact is made.
- Increase ride-along programs specifically for minority communities. This may foster increased understanding between the police and the minority citizenry.
- Use a constellation of police stop data along with qualitative methods such as the one used in this study to shape training curriculum and policy decisions.
- Enhance cultural diversity/sensitivity training focusing specifically on cultural differences.
- Build coalitions and community boards that address racial profiling. It is recommended that board membership should largely be made up of citizens whose voices are typically absent from the policy decision-making process.
- Directly involve members of the minority community in police training regarding racial profiling and cultural differences.

Implications for Citizens

This research suggests that in many cases there appeared to be a lack of understanding of why the police do what they do in certain situations. This lack of understanding further exacerbated negative perceptions of the police and minority citizen experiences with what they perceive to be racial profiling. This section will discuss some of the more practical implications for racial minority citizens. As you will note, many of these apply to citizens regardless of racial or ethnic background.

What to Do When Stopped by the Police

Cooperate, period. If you are traveling along and suddenly you see in your rearview mirror a police car following with emergency lights illuminating and siren whaling, the first thing to do is use your turn indicator to signal and pull over safely on the right side of the roadway. Do not make any sudden or erratic moves. For example, if your driver's license is in the glove box do not reach into the glove box before the police officer makes contact with you. Only do so after you have communicated to the officer that your driver's license is in the glove box. Do not be offended if the officer advises you to remove the wallet slowly from the glove box. Remember, the officer does not know you and has no idea what is in your glove box. The officer's primary concern is safety. He or she could interpret your sudden movement toward the glove box as you reaching for a weapon.

If it is dark, you may want to turn your interior lights on and place your hands visibly on the steering wheel. Remain in your car unless the police officer requests that you get out. Keep in mind that the officer has the right to request that you get out of the car even for something as minor as a traffic infraction. It is also important that you avoid reaching under the car seat or making any sudden motion such as throwing any items around the interior of your car. This may make the officer suspicious of your actions and result in you being ordered to get out of your car. The officer may then try to obtain consent to search your vehicle based on your actions because he or she may think that you are hiding drugs, paraphernalia, or other items.

If the police officer believes that you are carrying a weapon, he or she may conduct a quick pat down search of the exterior of your clothing (i.e., pockets, collar, and waste band). Do not try to run or resist this action or there is a good chance you will be arrested. A quick pat down of your outer clothing by the police is permissible under the *Terry v. Ohio* Supreme Court ruling. The *Terry v. Ohio* (1968) Supreme Court ruling held that the Fourth Amendment's prohibition on unreasonable searches and seizures is not violated when a police officer stops an individual on the street and frisks him without probable cause to arrest, if the police officer has a reasonable suspicion that the person has committed, is committing, or is about to commit a crime, and has a reasonable belief that the person may be armed and dangerous.

After the officer makes contact with you, comply with all requests made of you. If the officer asks for your driver's license and registration, promptly produce these documents. If you do not have them, let the officer know. Avoid engaging in an argument with the officer. An argument could make things worse.

If the officer asks you to get out the car and stand toward the back of the vehicle, do so. If the officer says something rude or offensive, try to remember exactly what was said so that you can contact his or her supervisor once you have the opportunity. It will do no good to argue or contest the stop or traffic citation at the scene. This can be done later in court. In all cases, it is important that you or your passengers in your car do not obstruct the police during the traffic stop. This could result in you or your passengers being arrested.

In most cases, the officer will issue you a traffic citation or a written or verbal warning and release you. After the officer advises that you are free to leave, do so. Do not stick around and argue that you think the ticket or stop was unjust. If you have a complaint, proceed to the local police station and ask to speak to a supervisor. In some cases, you may be referred to the internal affairs or professional standards division to file a complaint.

If you believe that you have been racially profiled, many jurisdictions now have commissions in place that have investigatory powers to make a determination of probable cause that racial profiling has occurred. Consider this case in Kansas. In 2005, an African American man named Aaron Patterson was pulled over by Wichita, Kansas police officers for failing to use his turn signal. Patterson claimed he was stopped solely because of his race and because he was driving an expensive sports utility vehicle. The police officers pulled Patterson out of his car, searched him, and accused him of another charge. He was given a ticket for failing to signal. It was later learned that the stop occurred in a predominantly Black neighborhood after police said Patterson made brief contact with a known drug dealer. The ticket was dismissed during a traffic court hearing later.

Patterson filed a complaint with the Kansas Human Rights Commission. At the time, the commission had the authority to make probable cause findings in cases where racial profiling is alleged. The commission made a probable cause ruling that the police engaged in racial profiling of Patterson. They found that there was no justification for the initial stop and that police had used racial profiling. It was the first ruling issued under a new state law at that time, which provided for outside review of racial profiling allegations. The finding by the commission cleared Patterson to sue the Wichita Police Department in civil court.

Subsequently, Patterson sued the City of Wichita and the case entered the state court system. In granting a pretrial motion for summary judgment, the judge ruled that the actions of the officers were predicated on valid law enforcement activities and were not solely motivated by race. The judge ruled that the police officers had no individual liability and dismissed the lawsuit against them. The court also found no basis for separate liability on the part of the City of Wichita.

Summary of What to Do if Stopped by the Police
- Stay calm. Do not run. Do not argue, resist, or obstruct the police. Even if you are innocent or you believe the police are violating your rights, keep your hands where police can see them.
- Ask if you are free to leave. If the officer says yes, calmly and silently walk away. If you are under arrest, you have a right to know why.
- You have the right to remain silent and cannot be punished for refusing to answer questions. If you wish to remain silent, tell the officer aloud. In some states, you must give your name if asked to identify yourself.

- You do not have to consent to a search of yourself or your belongings, but police may "pat down" your clothing if they suspect a weapon. You should not physically resist, but you have the right to refuse consent for any further search. If you do consent, it can affect you later in court.

If You Are Stopped in Your Car

- Stop the car in a safe place as quickly as possible. Turn off the car, turn on the internal light, open the window part way, and place your hands on the wheel.
- Upon request, show police your driver's license, registration, and proof of insurance.
- If an officer or immigration agent asks to look inside your car, you can refuse to consent to the search. However, if police believe your car contains evidence of a crime, your car can be searched without your consent.
- Both drivers and passengers have the right to remain silent. If you are a passenger, you can ask if you are free to leave. If the officer says yes, sit silently or calmly leave. Even if the officer says no, you have the right to remain silent (American Civil Liberties Union, 2012).

Know Your Rights

Every citizen has rights. Citizens should know what they can and cannot do if stopped by the police while driving an automobile. Many racial minority citizens who were interviewed for this book were unaware, for example, that they could refuse police authorities' request to search. A citizen can refuse to give the police permission to search their vehicle. If asked, and the citizen does not want to allow the search, he or she should simply say, "No, I will not consent to a search."

Citizens may also waive their rights under the U.S. Constitution and give police authorities consent to search their automobiles. In this case, all the police need to establish is that the individual did consent to the search. No probable cause is needed to search in consent cases. It should be noted, the person giving the consent must have the right to consent. For example, if a person is riding as a passenger in a vehicle driven by a friend who is the owner, said person cannot give consent to search for the owner/driver.

While every citizen should weigh the decision to consent to the search of their vehicle, it should be noted if the police conduct a lawful arrest of the driver of a vehicle, they could perform a cursory search of the immediate area where the arrest occurred without consent or a warrant. If for some

WHAT TO DO IF YOU ARE ARRESTED
(SEE ACLU WWW.ACLU.ORG)

- Do not resist arrest, even if you believe the arrest is unfair.
- Say you wish to remain silent and ask for a lawyer immediately. Do not give any explanations or excuses or make any statements. You cannot be forced to answer questions that can incriminate you. The best thing to do, for your own legal protection, is not to say anything.
- If you cannot pay for a lawyer, you have the right to have one appointed to represent you. This will most likely occur at your first court appearance. Again, it is important that you do not say anything, sign anything, or make any decisions without consulting with a lawyer.
- You have the right to make a local phone call. The police cannot listen if you call a lawyer.
- Prepare yourself and your family in case you are arrested. Memorize the phone numbers of your family and your lawyer. Make emergency plans if you have children or take medication.

SPECIAL CONSIDERATIONS FOR NON-CITIZENS
- Ask your lawyer about the effect of a criminal conviction or plea on your immigration status.
- Do not discuss your immigration status with anyone but your lawyer. While you are in jail, an immigration agent may visit you. Do not answer questions or sign anything before talking to a lawyer.
- Read all papers fully. If you do not understand or cannot read the papers, tell the officer you need an interpreter.

reason the arrest is later considered unlawful by the court, any evidence that was discovered during the search will be excluded.

The police can only search a citizen's vehicle if they have probable cause or a warrant or they are given consent to search. Many racial minority participants in the study stated the police make it hard on them if they do not consent to a search. A tactic according to many was that the police would ask them "if they had something to hide." Many racial minorities said they felt bullied and coerced into consenting to the search. Again, it is important to remember if a police officer requests consent to search a citizen's car, the citizen has a right to refuse to grant consent. If a citizen has not been placed under arrest, he or she should politely ask the officer if they are free to leave. In most cases, they will be released unless the police plan to arrest the individual.

The police are legally permitted to visually look through the window of an automobile. If the police spot something in plain view (e.g., lying on the seat or on the floorboard) that they believe to be illegal (i.e., drugs, drug paraphernalia, etc.), they can investigate further and actually enter the car and remove the item. Items in plain view may be seized by the police as long as they are in a place where they may legally be. If a citizen is driving an automobile on a public roadway, he or she generally has less of an expectation of privacy than on private property. Historically, courts have rejected defendants' claims against warrantless searches of automobiles. These types of searches are typically upheld because taking the time to obtain a warrant in light of the eminent mobility nature of a vehicle, would tend to invite claims of unlawful seizure of individuals and would also jeopardize effective seizure of contraband.

Know Reporting Venues

If citizens believe that they have been racially profiled by the police, it is important that they know where to go to file an official complaint. As a start, citizens should call the law enforcement authority in which they have a grievance and speak to someone in supervision or management. The police representative will generally direct the citizen to the appropriate person or division such as the internal affairs unit or, in smaller agencies, directly to the chief of police.

Many local and state jurisdictions have implemented racial profiling boards and commissions that are made up of citizens and police personnel. In some cases, these boards and commissions may have statutory authority to investigate reports of racial profiling. In the state of Kansas, where the data for this book was collected, citizens may file a complaint with the office of the Attorney General. Pursuant to law, the Attorney General's office will review the complaint and can refer appropriate cases to the Kansas Commission on Peace Officers Standards and Training (CPOST), which is the licensing agency for law enforcement officers. CPOST may then do further review, investigate, and take appropriate action based on the complaint (see File a Complaint at http://ag.ks.gov).

Get Involved

Improve relationships between the police and racial minority communities, and engage in dialogue about racial profiling. This requires a lot of work on the part of the community and the police. Citizens should get involved and be willing to engage in productive dialogue with the police, as opposed to just verbalizing concerns. The Police Executive Research Forum recommends the following ways that the police can get involved with the minority community:

- Engage in dialogue about solutions rather than emphasize blame.
- Encourage one another to apply for employment with the police department and support those who do.
- Develop a broad understanding of professional police practices (perhaps through contacts with national and state police organizations) in order to form an objective standard by which to judge police actions.
- Acknowledge police officers who promote police–community relationships with awards or other communication (Fridell et al., 2001, p. 101).

Implications for Research

The overarching purpose of research is to explore, explain, and describe. It involves a systematic and purposeful process by which we gain new insight about a particular phenomenon of interest. The knowledge produced through research is largely the result of the questions the researcher decides to ask, and the specific methods the researcher uses to answer those questions. In criminal justice, many questions come from practice. We observe a phenomenon in criminal justice practice, we think about it, we think about it some more, we wonder about it, and we desire to know more about it and, in many cases, we ponder what can be done to change it. Questions may also flow from the literature related to the phenomenon of interest. They may also come from deduction based on a specific theory.

Therefore, it is fair to say that the objective of criminal justice research is to develop a body of knowledge that will ultimately enhance theory development, or to impact fundamental policy with the laudable goal of improving criminal justice practice. In order to realize this objective, it is first necessary to employ the application of sound research methods. That is, research methods that are valid and reliable, and methods that produce results that can be trusted contribute to answering the research questions that have been framed.

Not everyone will agree on what methods are the best to study criminal justice phenomenon. The method that a researcher employs will most likely be driven by the specific research questions, what makes the most sense to the researcher, and the researcher's worldview.

Some studies of racial profiling focus on making use of sophisticated quantitative designs such as collecting and analyzing police stop data and then comparing the data to some established benchmark. These analyses can identify disproportionate stops of racial and ethnic groups when compared to benchmark data. Other investigations of racial profiling have been framed as legal analyses (Withrow, 2012). In these analyses, scholars examine existing court decisions, and engage in critical discourse regarding various legal remedies that may be presented under the equal protection clause of the Constitution.

Fewer research studies have examined racial profiling through a qualitative lens. Recall from Chapter 4 that qualitative research is primarily research that produces findings not arrived at by using statistical analysis. The data is generally expressed in words, themes, or codes. It involves establishing rich and thick descriptions of a phenomenon. The researcher then begins to formulate questions and theorizes about what the data means. In keeping with the qualitative tradition, the research reported in this book represents data collected from citizens themselves who say they have been racially profiled.

Phenomenology

Andersen (1993, p. 40), among others, raised two important questions: "How can White scholars contribute to our understanding of racial groups? Can dominant groups comprehend the experiences of outsiders and, if so, under what conditions and with which methodological practices?" I do not think the White researcher can, with absolute certainty, understand fully the experiences that racial minorities have had with various phenomena, like racial profiling, but with the right research method, I believe they can come fairly close.

Recall that the specific qualitative approach used to study racial profiling was phenomenology. The goal of phenomenology is to study peoples' experiences with a phenomenon, and how they give meaning to their experiences. Phenomenology typically culminates with the construction of a unifying description of persons' experiences. That is, what their experiences all shared in common.

Phenomenology as used in this racial profiling inquiry demonstrates that data can be gathered directly from individuals, analyzed, and the findings communicated so that the meaning of the experiences of persons is not distorted, reduced, controlled, or isolated. Qualitative phenomenology was beneficial in providing important insight into what it feels like to experience racial profiling. The stories that people told about their experiences with racial profiling were powerful. Thus, experience is something that cannot be taken away. Lived experiences, as I discovered in my hours upon hours of interviewing racial minority citizens, are, as Tator and Henry (2006, p. 117) argued, "more than mere individual communications; they are embedded in a cultural and ideological context, and taken together, they reveal cultural assumptions that transcend the individual."

In phenomenology, citizens' experiences with what they believed to be racial profiling were regarded as a primary source of knowledge that cannot be doubted if the experience was lived. It should be noted that like other research methods, phenomenological methods could not exhaust the investigated phenomenon completely. As Merleau-Ponti (1962, p. 62) pointed out, "the results of phenomenological research are the essence of certainty to be established with reservations. Phenomenology discerns what human beings are all about outside of the boundaries of traditional science."

Phenomenology offers another approach to racial profiling research. It is my hope that the message in this book has been that it is dangerous for the craft of criminal justice research to tread down a hegemonic path of one accepted method in the production of knowledge. The simple point is, in research giving attention to racial profiling, it is important to use a variety of methods in order to more completely understand this troublesome phenomenon. Phenomenology presents another way to study racial profiling.

Other Research Approaches

Of course many different approaches can be used to study racial profiling. Gumbhir (2007) related that mixed methods approaches that make use of both qualitative and quantitative data could be beneficial in racial profiling research. Specifically, he argued that using mixed methods approaches "can help address the weaknesses of individual benchmarking strategies" (p. 226). Gumbhir stated that qualitative strategies addressing racial profiling could be an enormously valuable resource in enhancing our knowledge.

One problem with the research on racial profiling is that it has not produced a significant amount of theoretical explanations. Theory plays an important role in providing patterns for the interpretation of the data, as well as linking one study with another (Hoover & Donovan, 2011). Therefore, it is important for racial profiling research to develop a set of theories to explain the phenomenon. Some scholars have taken on the laudable task of providing a theoretical perspective of racial profiling, largely from existing social science perspectives (Engel, Calnon, & Bernard, 2002; Petrocelli, Piquero, & Smith, 2003).

Others have proposed new and evolving theory. For example, Professor Brian Withrow's (2004) work with the theory of contextual differences offers a unique perspective on the dynamics of police decision making by focusing on the factors that influence a discretionary police–citizen contact. Withrow's work offers much promise in enhancing our understanding of racial profiling centering on police officer decisions to stop an individual. Likewise, the theory could be beneficial in more fully understanding the "race and place" theme discussed in Chapter 8. In short, the theory proposes the following three components:

1. Police officers use the circumstances associated with a distinct epi-
   sode or location to define what is usual, customary, or expected
   within that particular context.
2. Police officers are differentially attentive toward individuals or
   behaviors that appear inconsistent with predetermined conceptual-
   izations of what is usual or expected within a particular context.
3. Once an individual is defined by the police officer as inconsistent
   with what has been previously determined to be usual, customary,
   or expected within a particular context, the police officer may seek a
   pretext to justify an official encounter (Withrow, 2004, pp. 358–359).

Grounded theory may also be useful in the development of a theory of
racial profiling as opposed to verification of a preexisting theory. Grounded
theory is a qualitative research approach that moves beyond description and
generates or discovers a theory (Strauss & Corbin, 1990). The pivotal feature
of grounded theory is that the theory is literally grounded in the data provided by the participants. According to Creswell (2013, p. 85), the defining
features of grounded theory include following:

> The researchers focus on a process or an action that has distinct steps or
> phases that occur over time. Thus, grounded theory study has movement or
> some action that the researcher is attempting to explain. ... The researcher also
> seeks, in the end, to develop a theory of this process or action. ... This explana-
> tion or understanding is a drawing together, in grounded theory, of theoreti-
> cal categories that are arrayed to show how the theory works.

Using grounded theory in racial profiling research would assist in more
comprehensive theory development. Because grounded theory is theory
that has evolved inductively from the data (i.e., from those individuals that
have experienced racial profiling), it has the potential to be more useful
in offering a more holistic understanding of the phenomenon. It may also
prove to be much more beneficial for public policy that addresses racial
profiling.

Participant observations of police officers in the field could also be beneficial in order to understand the dynamics of the pretext stop and the police
officers' decision leading up to it. Participant observation studies entail the
researcher observing police officers in their daily routines. For example, a
researcher may ride with police officers over a short or long period of time,
interacting with them and observing how they respond to certain situations.
Observational research in some cases may represent the only method for
obtaining data and information about racial profiling, especially police officer behavior in the field. Observational data, which is primarily qualitative

KEY EMERGING QUESTIONS BOX

Future qualitative research might consider the following questions:

1. What is the police worldview regarding racial profiling?
2. Do White drivers have the same contextual experiences when stopped by police authorities?
3. What are the perceptions of individual officers as they relate to the initial vehicle observation coupled with the decision to stop, and as they relate to establishing the pretextual basis for the stop? Understanding police decision-making as it pertains to pretextual stops is important to fully understand the dynamics of perceived racial profiling and disparities in police stops.

in nature, enhances our knowledge of the richness of police behavior in the field. As Gumbhir (2007, p. 226) suggested,

> In terms of qualitative research, participant observations and in-depth interviews are needed to obtain a detailed understanding of the work of police officers and administrators, and the interplay between these individuals, police culture, and institutions of law enforcement. Qualitative research should focus on the social construction of the suspicion and its application in the work of officers and administrators, as well as the identification of key elements and processes related to officer decision-making.

The White Male Researcher

The White qualitative researcher studying racialized phenomenon in criminal justice poses unique methodological problems. Interviews of racial minority citizens about their experiences with racial profiling, by White researchers, present challenges that must be negotiated. These challenges are "compounded by the social distance created by class and race relations when interviewers are white and middle class and those that are being interviewed are not" (Andersen, 1993, p. 41). There is also some thought in the literature that interracial interviews, particularly research that explores racial topics, can affect the accuracy of what participants say and how the White researcher will interpret the data (Gunaratnam, 2003; Rhodes, 1994).

In his classic book, *Caste and Class in a Southern Town* (1937), John Dollard contemplated how he would study the personalities and adjustments of African Americans in a segregated city in the south. He fictitiously named the city Southerntown for purposes of his research. Dollard gave much thought to how he would implement fieldwork in Southerntown. Would he be met with hostilities from White citizens for interacting with African Americans? How would he go about collecting life histories on African Americans? He considered the various ways he would go about establishing and maintaining rapport with participants. He questioned where he would interview his participants. Would they be fearful to talk with him? Would they trust him enough, a White researcher from the north, to talk openly and candidly? If they did talk with him, would they give him only selected information, that is, the information that he wanted to hear?

Dollard indeed faced many challenges of doing race research especially in such a blatantly segregated and racist society. It was the 1930s in the American south. The following excerpt from Dollard's book is most telling of the challenges he faced in this research:

> My inner feeling was that of being tolerated by the white people, of living in an ill-defined but ever-present atmosphere of hostility, and of suffering a degree of isolation as a penalty for my research interest in the Negro. With some people my status as a university researcher was an important fact. Many others would talk to me so long as I suppressed completely any dissenting or objective comment on the situation (Dollard, 1937, p. 12).

In doing racial profiling research, I certainly did not face the extent of the problems that Dollard faced, but there were challenges that I experienced as a White male researcher interviewing minority citizens about their experiences with racial profiling. Let me provide a brief discussion of some of these challenges.

Gatekeepers

It took some time to establish gatekeepers. Gatekeepers are those individuals who the researcher develops to assist in reaching potential participants. While gatekeepers may play many roles in a qualitative racial profiling study, an important role is recruiting participants who will provide rich data.

It was challenging to locate good and reliable gatekeepers. I contacted many leaders in the racial minority community with mixed results. These contacts included members in leadership positions of the local NAACP, cleric leaders, and other well-known leaders in the community, especially leaders who had a solid reputation in the community. There were times, after meeting with individuals who were in leadership positions in order to help open doors to address racial profiling in Kansas, that I was left with the impression that these individuals were reluctant to engage themselves in issues associated with racial profiling. They seemed to drag their feet on the issue even after my numerous contacts with them.

I found that it proved more beneficial to meet with community activists and local editors of minority centered publications to advise them of the research. They generally had a grasp on the pulse of the community, and knew how to get the word out. With their assistance, I was surprised at how fast the word spread about the research through the various minority communities across Kansas. Each gatekeeper was provided with the purpose and objective of the study, and the anticipated outcomes. Likewise, gatekeepers were informed of the importance of ensuring the confidentiality of the participants. I would strongly recommend imparting this information to gatekeepers and meeting with them on a regular basis.

Screening

After a few months into the research, there were many phone calls and emails from citizens who wanted to report their racial profiling experiences to me. This became somewhat of a challenge because many citizens thought that I was investigating the police, and that I could take official action Of course, that was not the case.

Often I would receive a telephone call or an electronic note from a citizen. After several minutes of phone screening or back and forth email notes, it would become clear that they had not been racially profiled but simply wanted to discuss or make me aware of a bad experience that they had with a police officer. In some cases, it was simply to chat about an incident they were aware of involving a specific police officer. The phone screenings were an invaluable tool. It saved much valuable time in screening out those individuals who did not have a racial profiling experience but had some other grievance with police authorities. This saved time in the sense that it did not require me to negotiate a meeting time and location and then finding out that they did not have data to offer for study.

It would be difficult to calculate the many hours spent on the phone with countless numbers of citizens, chatting with them about racial profiling and other racialized issues in their communities. Many citizens would call to talk about racial profiling and experiences they had in the past with the police. A large number of these persons did not officially want to go on the record or to meet with me. I listened to their stories but did not include them in the data reported in the book. However, what they told me reinforced many of the same themes that were fleshed out of the data reported in this book. This was reassuring.

Establishing Rapport

Building rapport with participants is important. Interviewing racial minority citizens about racial profiling experiences should be approached with

much patience. Many participants who were interviewed seemed to be somewhat suspicious about the motives of the research. Initially, I sensed that
many were suspicious of me. For some, it took several interviews to break the
ice. When doing interracial research where the researcher is White and participants are racial minorities, it may very well take several 60- to 90-minute
interviews to establish the full trust of participants and to get them to feel
comfortable enough to tell their stories. I always began an interview by relating to participants that as a White male, I will never know what it is like to
experience racial profiling, but I wanted to learn about it from their worldview. Approaching the interview in a conversational style can help ease the
tension and begin to establish a relaxed atmosphere, which is most conduc-
tive to a good interview.

If the interview is too intense, there is a great risk that the participant
will not fully reveal his or her story. As a caveat, if the interview is taking the
form of an intense question-and-answer format and void of conversation, it
is suggested that conversation be introduced. For example, if a participant
seemed to be giving me brief answers to questions I capitalized on changing directions by asking them about where they worked, about where they
went to school, and about their families. I would work this into the interview
slowly and within a few minutes, the interview would suddenly turn to a
conversation rather than a question and answer format. Pertinent questions
about their racial profiling experiences were then worked into the interview.

Rather than just listening and answering questions, sometimes researchers may need to answer some of the same questions about themselves that
they have posed to the participant (Rubin & Rubin, 2005). I often found
myself answering questions such as what anxiety or emotions do I feel when
I see a police officer in the rearview mirror? How do I react when I see a
police officer? Am I on heighted alert and always mindful of their presence?
Am I thinking in the back of my mind that there is a good chance that I may
be stopped? Interview memos that were completed after each interview also
kept me somewhat grounded in the data.

As the research progressed, I developed research relationships with
many participants who would contact me on a regular basis to talk about
the research. This presented a great opportunity to share the emerging
themes with them. I believe this helped my credibility with the participants
as someone who was genuinely interested in their experience with no hidden agenda. Moreover, this further helped in getting the word out about the
study. Creswell (2013) points out the importance in qualitative interviewing
of the interviewer to engage in much reflection about the relationship that
exists between the interviewer and interviewee. Creswell's point here is that
the interview has the potential to set up an unequal power dynamic between
the interviewer and interviewee, which is ruled by the interviewer. I was con-
scientious of this throughout the research and attempted to minimize the

unequal power dynamic by allowing for a back and forth conversational style interview. Allowing the interviewees to establish the flow of the interview is also helpful (see Kvale & Brinkmann, 2009 for an excellent discussion on power asymmetry in qualitative research).

Interview Location

Location, location, location. The location of the interview matters. As much as possible, I allowed the participants to choose the location of the interview. They would be asked: "Where would you like to meet?" Many participants wanted to meet at "neutral" locations such as a restaurant, the lobby or even the bar of the hotel where I happened to be staying, and in some cases they felt comfortable meeting at a gatekeeper's house. Meeting in some locations proved to be problematic because of noise levels, which affected the use of a tape recorder. In these cases, another location was negotiated with the participant. In some cases (if geographical distance was not a problem), a few participants requested to do the interview at the researcher's campus office, but this was a rarity.

Discussion Questions

1. How can a police department make racial profiling training more hands on?
2. What is the fundamental of the citizens' police academies? How can they be used to minimize the perceptions of racial profiling among racial minority citizens?
3. Write a model police policy addressing racial profiling. What should it include? Compare your policy with others in class.
4. What would a policy addressing the pretextual stop include as discussed in this chapter?
5. Discuss a few other research approaches that may be used to study racial profiling.

References

Anderson, M.L. (1993). Studying across difference: Race, class, and gender in qualitative research. In: S.H. Stanfield & R.M. Dennis (Eds.), *Race and ethnicity in research methods*. Newbury, Park, CA: Sage, pp. 39–52.

American Civil Liberties Union (2012). *Know your rights: What to do if stopped by the police, immigration agents or the FBI*. Accessed from: https://www.aclu.org

Birzer, M.L., & Roberson, C. (2007). *Police field operations: Theory meets practice*. Boston: Pearson.

Birzer, M.L., & Roberson, C. (2008). *Police field operations: Theory meets practice.* Boston: Pearson/Allyn and Bacon.

Birzer, M.L., & Tannehill, R.L. (2001). A more effective training approach for contemporary policing. *Police Quarterly, 4*(2), 233–252.

Coderoni, G.R. (2002). The relationship between multicultural training for police and effective law enforcement. *F.B.I. Law Enforcement Bulletin, 71*(11), 16–18.

Cohn, E.G. (1996). The citizen police academy: a recipe for improving police–community relations. *Journal of Criminal Justice, 22*(3), 265–271.

Creswell, J.W. (2013). *Qualitative inquiry and research design: Choosing among five traditions* (3rd ed.). Los Angeles, CA: Sage.

DeGeneste, H.I., & Sullivan, J.P. (1997). *Policing a multicultural community.* Washington, D.C.: The Police Executive Research Forum.

Dollard, J. (1937). *Caste and class in a southern town.* New Haven, CT: Yale University Press.

Engel, R.S., Calnon, J.M., & Bernard, T.J. (2002). Theory and racial profiling: Shortcomings and future directions in research. *Justice Quarterly, 19*(2), 249–273.

Fridell, L., Lunney, R., Diamond, D., Kubu, B., Scott, M., & Laing, C. (2001). *Racially biased policing: A principled response.* Washington, DC: Police Executive Research Forum.

Gaines, L.K., Southerland, M.D., & Angell, J.E. (1991). *Police administration.* New York: McGraw-Hill Publishing.

Garden City Police Department (2012). Statement on racial profiling. Retrieved from www.gcpolice.org/.

Goldstein, H. (1990) *Problem-oriented policing.* Boston: McGraw-Hill.

Gumbhir, V.K. (2007). *But is it racial profiling? Policing, pretext stops, and the color of suspicion.* New York: LLB Scholarly Publishing.

Gunaratnam, Y. (2003). Researching race and ethnicity: Methods, knowledge and power. Thousand Oaks, CA: Sage.

Hill, A.C., & Scott, J. (1992). Ten strategies for managers in a multicultural workforce. *H.R. Focus, 69*(8), 1–6.

Hoover, K., & Donovan, T. (2011). *The elements of social science thinking* (10th ed.). Boston: Wadsworth.

Johnson, R.A. (1994). Police organizational design and structure, *FBI Law Enforcement, 63,* 5–7.

Kopel, D.B. (2001). Militarizing law enforcement: The drug wars deadly fruit. In T. Lynch (Ed.) *After probation: An adult approach to drug policies in the 21st century* (pp. 61–90).

Kraska, P.B., & Kappeler, V.E. (1997). Militarizing the American police: The rise and normalization of paramilitary units. *Social Problems, 44*(1), 1–18.

Kvale, S., & Brinkman, S. (2009). *Interviews: Learning the craft of qualitative research interviewing.* Los Angeles: Sage.

Martinelli, T.J., & Schafer, J.A. (2011). Updating ethics training–policing privacy series: Taking race out of the equation. *The Police Chief, 78*(1), 18–22.

Merleau-Ponty, M, (1962). *Phenomenology of perceptions* (C. Smith, Trans.), London: Routledge.

Paul, J., & Birzer, M.L. (2004). Images of Power: A critical analysis of the militarization of police uniforms and messages of service. *Free Inquiry in Creative Sociology, 32,* 121–128.

Paul, J., & Birzer, M.L. (2008). The militarization of the American police force: A critical assessment. *Critical Issues in Justice and Politics, 1*(1), 15–29.

Peak, K.J.,& Glensor, R.W. (1999). *Community policing and problem solving: Strategies and practices* (2nd ed). Upper Saddle River, NJ: Prentice Hall.

Petrocelli, M., Piquero, A.R., & Smith, M.R. (2003). Conflict theory and racial profiling: An empirical analysis of police traffic stop data. *Journal of Criminal Justice, 31*, 1–11.

Powers, W.F. (1995, May 4). *Dressed to Kill?* Washington Post.

Rhodes, P. (1994). Race of interviewer effects in qualitative research: A brief comment. *Sociology, 28*(2), 547–558.

Rubin, H.J. & Rubin, I.R. (2005). *Qualitative interviewing: The art of hearing data.* Thousand Oaks, CA: Sage.

Shusta, R.M., Levine, D.R., Harris, P.R., & Wong, H.Z. (1995). *Multicultural law enforcement: Strategies for a peace keeping society.* Upper Saddle River, NJ: Pearson.

Strauss A., & Corbin, J. (1990). *Basics of qualitative research: Grounded theory procedures and techniques.* Newbury Park, CA: Sage.

Tator, C., & Henry, F. (2006). *Racial profiling in Canada: Challenging the myth of a few bad apples.* Toronto: University of Toronto Press.

Tyler, T., & Huo, H. (2002). *Trust in the law.* New York: McGraw-Hill.

U.S. Department of Justice (2001). *Mutual respect in policing: Lesson plan.* Washington, DC: Office of Community Oriented Policing Services.

Wadman, R.C. (2009). *Police theory in America: Old traditions and new opportunities.* Springfield, IL: Charles C Thomas Publisher, LTD.

Weaver, G. (1992). Law enforcement in a culturally diverse society. *FBI Law Enforcement Bulletin, 61*(9), 1–7.

Weber, D.C. (1999). *Warrior cops: The ominous growth of para militarism in American police departments.* Washington D.C.: The Cato Institute.

Weitzer, R., & Tuch, S.A. (2002). Perceptions of racial profiling: Race, class, and personal experience. *Criminology, 40*(2) 435–456.

Whitman, S. (1993). Police academies for citizens. *Law and Order, 41*(6), 66–67, 69–71.

Wilson, O.W., & McLaren, R.C. (1977). *Police administration* (4th ed.). New York: McGraw-Hill Publishing.

Withrow, B.L. (2004). Driving while different: A potential theoretical explanation for race based policing. *Criminal Justice Policy Review, 15*(3), 344–364.

Withrow, B.L. (2004). Racial profiling litigation: Current status and emerging controversies. *Journal of Contemporary Criminal Justice, 28*(2), 122–145.

Withrow, B.L., and Dailey, J.D. (2012). Racial profiling litigation: Current status and emerging controversies. *Journal of Contemporary Criminal Justice, 28*(2) 122–145.

Cases Cited

Patterson v. City of Wichita et al., 06-CV-2816 (D. Kan., 2008).
Terry v. Ohio, (1968) 392 U.S.

Index